THE CHILDREN FOR CHRIST

RAISING YOUR CHILDREN IN A CONSECRATED CHRISTIAN HOME

ANDREW MURRAY

EREMITICAL PRESS
SURREY, BRITISH COLUMBIA

The Children for Christ: Raising Your Children
in a Consecrated Christian Home
Andrew Murray (1828–1917)
Originally published as *The Children for Christ: Thoughts for Christian Parents*
on the Consecration of the Home Life

Edited by Gladys Ng
Set in Minion Medium 11/14

This paper is acid free and meets all ANSI standards for archival quality paper.
ISBN 978-1-926777-17-7

Contents

Preface

GOD IS AWAKENING in many hearts the longing to live a truly consecrated life—to be and do all that he would have of us. No sooner has the surrender to such a life taken place, but the desire comes to have all who belong to us partake of the blessing, especially to have our home life—with all its affections, its interactions, its duties—sanctified too. Many a parent finds this a hard, almost a hopeless, task. In the days when their own Christian life was halfhearted and feeble, the spirit of the world was allowed to come in and get possession. With a partner or children who do not entirely sympathize, where the help and hearty response of spiritual fellowship is wanting, the consecrated one finds it difficult to maintain the personal life. How much more to influence the whole circle and lift them up to the more blessed life that has been entered on!

To parents who are in this position—to all parents who long to have their homes truly consecrated by God's presence and service—God's Word has a message of comfort and strength. It is this: that God is willing to be the God of their house and, with his Divine power, to do for it more than they can ask and think. If they will but open their hearts in faith to rest in the promise and the power of God, he will prove himself to be for their house what he has been to themselves. The one thing needful is that they should know and believe what he has undertaken to be and to do as the God of their seed. They will find that the lesson they learned in entering upon a life of entire consecration is just what is needed here again. There all was comprehended in the one word, "surrender"—the surrender of faith and obedience. They surrendered themselves to expect and accept all God had promised and to do all that he commanded. This surrender of faith must take place definitely with regard to the family. As a parent I put myself and my children into God's hands, believing that he will fulfill his promise—yes, that he does at once accept and take charge. I confess the sins by which I have prevented God from working through me as he would for my home. I yield myself to be his humble, holy witness—his loving, obedient servant, and humbly but trustingly I say: "Oh, when will you come unto me? I will walk within my house with a perfect heart."

A parent's faith needs just what the faith of every believer does—to understand, to get an insight into, what God has undertaken to do. "By faith we understand." When faith has seen God planning and undertaking, it is a simple thing for it to rest and trust, to praise and act. I trust that this book may help believing parents to meditate on God's revelation of his purpose with the family, and to see what abundant ground there is for their expecting him to fulfill their desire to have their house holy to the Lord. It is as we get into the mind and plan of God that faith will grow and its power be manifest, both in ourselves and those for whom we are believing.

In a note at the close of this volume on the Church's duty to parents, I have explained the origin and the object of the book. I send it forth with the prayer that it may be blessed to make our glorious God better known, as he would gladly be known and honored, as the God of the families of Israel, and that this knowledge may strengthen many a parent's heart to a larger faith and a more entire consecration of home life to their God.

—Andrew Murray

FIRST DAY

The Family as God Created it

> "God created man in his own image: in the image of God he created him; male and female he created them. And God blessed them; and God said unto them, Be fruitful, and multiply, and replenish the earth."—*Genesis 1:27–28*

GOD'S PURPOSE in the creation of man was to show forth and make visible to the universe his own unseen glory and perfection. Man was not only to have single points of resemblance to God; in all he was and did upon earth, he was to prove that he was indeed created in God's image and after his likeness.

The traits of that likeness were very varied and most wonderful. In the dominion he was to have over the earth, he was to exhibit the power of God as King and Ruler of the universe. In the wondrous mental powers with which he was endowed, fitting him for this work, there was to be seen the image of God as the All-wise. In his moral powers, there was to be some reflection of the light that is inaccessible and full of glory—God's righteousness and holiness were to be revealed.

But then there still remained one trait of the Divine perfection, the very highest, to be set forth. God is love. As Infinite Love, he lives not for himself alone, but finds all his blessing in imparting his own life. In his bosom he has the Son of his love, begotten of the Father from eternity. In the Son he has peopled the universe with living beings, that upon them the fullness of his love might flow out. As the Loving One he is the fountain of life; as the Living One he is the fountain of love. It was that in this, too, man might bear the image of God, that his whole life might be a life of love, and that in loving he might give life to those on whom his love might flow forth, that God created man in his image, male and female. In the home on earth—in the love of husband and wife, of parent and child—were to be reflected the love and the blessedness of the Father's home in heaven, and were to be imaged forth the deepest secrets of the life of Godhead in the fellowship of the Father and the Son by the Holy Spirit.

It is to this last and highest trait of the image of Divine perfection—man's creation, to shadow forth the mystery and to enjoy the blessedness of a life in love—that we want especially to draw attention. In undertaking the study of God's Word for the sake of discovering what it teaches us of the parental relation, we must ascend the true Mount of Sources and follow up the stream of Divine truth to those hills of Paradise whence they all take their rise. We will find the sure foundation of the family constitution, its purpose, its law, and its glory in the teaching of God's word, "God created man in his own image, in the image of God he created him; male and female he created them."

Let us think of it for a moment. In God's love, and the fatherhood which sprang from that love, we have at once the highest glory and the deepest mystery of Godhead. Because God is love, he must needs have some worthy object on whom his love can rest, in whose fellowship his love can find its blessedness. Because he is God, the only and all-perfect One, that Son, must be the only One, the Father's image, and the Heir of all things. Before the world began, from eternity, God was in him the Most Blessed One. In God's Fatherhood of Christ is his perfection and his blessedness.

Man was created after that image of God which was seen in Christ. When man had fallen, Christ came to take us up into fellowship with himself, to give us a share in his Sonship and Heirship, to make us, too, the children of God. In him, and his life given us in regeneration we, too, become the sons of God. God's Fatherhood of believers is the deepest mystery, the highest glory, the perfect blessedness of redemption. The Fatherhood of God is the summing up of the incomprehensible mystery and glory of the Divine Being.

And of this Fatherhood, the father of the family on earth is to be the image and the likeness. In the life he imparts to his child, in the image he sees reflected, in the unity of which he is conscious, in the loving care he exercises, in the obedience and the trust he sees rendered to himself, in the love in which family life finds its happiness, the home and the fatherhood of earth are the image of the heavenly.

What a solemn and what a blessed view this truth gives us of the parental relation! What a sanctifying influence the right apprehension of it would have upon its privileges and its duties! How much better, in the light of this Divine origin and purpose of the family, we can understand and value our relation to our children. And how, on the other hand, all our intercourse with them would strengthen our obedience and our confidence toward the Father in heaven! We should see how the action of the heavenly and the earthly home on each other is reciprocal. Every deeper insight into the Father's love and the Father's home would elevate the intercourse in the home on earth and enlarge our expectations as to the blessing the God who appointed it will certainly bestow upon it. And every experience of what the love and blessing of a home on earth can be would again be a ladder by which to rise up and get nearer the great Father-heart in heaven. "In the beginning God created the heavens and the earth." The two in correspondence with each other—the home in heaven with the Father there being the original of the home on earth and the father there.

How terrible the curse and the power of sin! Fatherhood in the likeness of God, the communication to another being of a life that was to be immortal and ever blessed, and the establishment of a home of love like that in heaven was to have been the high privilege of man, as God created him. But, alas, sin came in and wrought a fearful ruin. The father makes the child partaker of a sinful nature; the father feels himself too sinful to be a blessing to his child; and the home, alas, is too often the path not to heaven, but to hell. But, blessed be God, what sin destroyed, grace restores. And as in these meditations we follow God's revelation in regard to the family, we will find that all the purpose and provision of God's grace point back to the restoration of what at creation was intended—the fatherhood and the motherhood of earth, with its love and its home, its care and its training of the children, the reflection and the fellowship of the home and the love of the Father in heaven.

Let every parent who feels conscious of his own shortcoming, and longs for wisdom and grace to do aright the work entrusted him, look back in faith and hope to the heavenly origin of family life. The God who created it has redeemed it, too, and creates it anew. He watches over it with tender interest, and meets with his own Father-love and blessing every parent who desires to be the minister of his holy purpose. Would you truly be this, begin by making God's thought your thought—the fatherhood and the family on earth the image and the likeness of a heavenly original. Look to God as the Author of your family life; count upon him to give all that is needed to make it what it should be. Let his Father-heart and his Father-love be your study and your stay; as you know and trust it in adoring love, the assurance will grow that he will fit you for making your home, in ever-increasing measure, the bright reflection of his own.

O great and holy Creator of men, you have placed me, too, in the wondrous relation of parent with a child owing its life to me. You would give me, too, the happiness of living a life of love, the Divine joy of loving and being loved. You have placed me, too, in a home to be the image of the home in heaven, where the Father and the Son dwell in everlasting love.

O my God, I humbly confess that I utter these words with shame. How little have the perfect love and joy, the purity and brightness of heaven, been reflected in the home given to my charge! How little I have even understood my calling or truly aimed at the high ideal you have set before me! Father, forgive us, for Jesus' sake!

And hear me when I beseech you to guide my meditations, and to help me in the study of your Holy Word, that I may learn more fully to realize what your purpose is with the fatherhood and the motherhood of this earth, and with what interest and love you look on each home given up to your protection and guidance. Teach me to know you in your infinite Fatherliness, so that the study and the experience of that Divine Original after which the parent's heart was created may fit me to be a true parent to my child. And let a Father's love and blessing rest on our home. Amen.

The Family as Sin Made It

"In the day that God created man, in the likeness of God he made him. And Adam lived a hundred and thirty years, and begat a son in his own likeness, after his image; and called his name Seth."—*Genesis 5: 1, 3*

"Cain rose up against Abel his brother, and slew him."—*Genesis 4: 8*

GOD CREATED MAN in his own likeness; Adam, the fallen, begat sons in his own likeness, after his image. As in the former expression, telling us of man's high origin and destiny, we have the key to the mystery of the incarnation and redemption to eternal glory, so in the latter we have the light that shows us whence sin has such fearful and universal power. It was one of the wonderful traits of God's likeness that man had the power to give life to others. When sin got the mastery, that likeness was not extinguished, but terribly defaced; he still had the power to bring forth, alas, in his own likeness. By one fell blow, sin, in conquering Adam, had conquered the race. If ever the race is again to be delivered from the power of sin, it will doubtless be by this power of man's bringing forth in his own likeness being regained and renewed to be the power for reestablishing God's kingdom. The parental relation has become the strength of sin; when God restores it, it will be the strength of grace.

If we want to realize the full significance of this word, "Adam begat a son in his own likeness, after his image," we have only to study the story of his family at the gates of Paradise. It will teach us lessons of the deepest importance in regard to the family as sin has made it.

Let us mark how the father's sin reappears and ripens in that of the child. "You shall love the Lord your God with all your heart, and your neighbor as yourself." In these two great commandments we have the sum of God's will concerning us. Adam had transgressed the first, and in sinning had cast off the love of God. His firstborn refuses subjection to the second, and becomes the hater and the murderer of his brother. Had Adam continued in the love of God, Cain would have certainly loved his brother. With Adam's sin, his nature had become corrupted; that nature had been imparted to the son in his likeness. The child's sin was the fruit of the father's.

This first picture of family life God gives us in his Word—what a somber light it casts on our homes! How often parents can trace in the sins and evil tempers of their children their own shortcomings and transgressions! How the remembrance that their children have inherited their evil natures from themselves ought to humble them, make them very patient and gentle, as well as very earnest and wise, in dealing with the offenders, and lead them to seek what alone can cure and conquer this evil power—the grace and the life that comes from above! Let parents not be afraid of realizing fully that God visits the sins of the fathers on the children; it will urge and encourage them to believe that he will no less remember the mercy to the fathers, and make the children partakers of that, too.

Let us note further how in that first child's sin we have the root and type of all children's sins. The family had been destined of God to be the image of the bliss of heaven—the mirror of the life of love that reigns there. Sin enters, and the first family, instead of being the emblem and the gate of heaven, becomes the type and the portal of hell. Instead of the love and help and happiness for which God had appointed our social relation, envy and anger and hatred and murder render it a scene of terrible desolation.

The root of all sin is selfishness—separating first from God and then from man. How early in the little ones in the nursery does it manifest itself! How continually does it come up in the intercourse with companions in school or play! How often it rises even against the parent, and refuses the love or obedience that is due! Let believing parents study with care what Holy Scripture reveals of love as the new and great commandment, as the fulfilling of the whole law, as the way to our dwelling in God and God in us, and seek for nothing so earnestly as this: the reign of love in their home. Let them watch over every manifestation of a selfish or unloving spirit, as a seed of the tree that bore such bitter fruit in Cain, and count no care or prayer too great to have it banished. Let them not be content as long as there are no striking outbreaks of the evil; let them fear and root out the seeds which often ripen so terribly in after life. Let nothing less content them than to make it their aim that grace should restore their family life to what God created it to be—a mirror and a foretaste of the love of heaven.

Let us not in this, too, forget the influence of the parent's life, as set before us here: "In his own image, after his likeness." These words refer not only to a blessing lost in Paradise and to a curse that came with sin, but as much to a grace that comes with redemption. Not, it is true, by natural birth in the flesh can a believer beget a child in his likeness, now renewed again after the image of God. But what nature cannot accomplish, the prayer and the life of faith can obtain, in virtue of the promise and the power of God. As we proceed in our inquiries into the teaching of Holy Scripture concerning the family life, we shall find nothing come out more clearly than the blessed truth that to believing parents the promise is given that their child may be begotten again after their likeness, and that God will to this end use them as the instruments of his grace. To the prayer of faith, manifesting itself in the godly training of the child, the blessing has been secured in covenant: "I will be a God to you and to your seed." As faith and prayer claim the promise and the power of God, the influence of the daily intercourse will make itself felt, and there will go forth from the consecrated lives of father and mother a secret but mighty power to mold the lives of the children, either preparing them as vessels of grace, or establishing and perfecting them in it.

And so we come to the blessed but solemn truth: Let parents be what they want their children to be. If they would keep them from the sin of Cain, who did not love his brother, let them beware of the sin of Adam, who did not love the commandment of his God. Let father and mother lead a life marked by love to God and man; this is the atmosphere in which loving children can be trained. Let all the dealings with the children be in holy love. Cross words, sharp reproof, and impatient answers are infectious. Love demands and does not fear self-sacrifice; it needs time and thoughtful attention and patient perseverance to train our children aright. In all our children hear us speak of others, of friends or enemies, of the low, the vulgar, the wicked, let the impression they receive be the love of Christ we seek to show. In all the intercourse of father and mother with each other, let mutual esteem and respect, tender considerateness and willing self-forgetfulness, prove to the children that love is possible and blessed.

Above all, let us remember that it is the love of God that is the secret of a loving home on earth. It is where parents love the Lord their God with all their heart and strength that the human love will be strengthened and sanctified. It is only parents who are willing to live really consecrated lives, entirely given up to God, to whom the promise and the blessing can come fully true. To make our home the nursery and the type and the foretaste of heaven, the ordinary halfhearted religion will not suffice. The love of God shed abroad in the heart and the home and the life by the Holy Spirit—it is this, this alone, will transplant our home from the gates of Paradise Lost, where Adam dwelt with Cain, to within the Paradise Regained, where even amid the weakness of earth the image of the heavenly is seen, and the home on earth is in the likeness of the home above.

Blessed Lord God! We bow before you in deep humility. We desire to feel more deeply the terrible power of sin in ourselves and our children, and the danger to which it exposes our beloved home. We come to confess how far as parents we have come short in that pure and holy love which you meant to be the beauty and the blessedness of family life. In our intercourse with you, and each other, and our children, and fellowmen—O God, forgive us the lack of love! And, oh, let not our children suffer through us, as they grow up in our likeness. Deliver us, we pray you, from the power of selfishness, and shed, oh, shed abroad your love in our hearts by the Holy Spirit.

And, O God, bless our children with the Spirit of love. Give us so to walk before them in love that your Spirit may use our example and our likeness to form them to your Holy Likeness. Give us a deep sense of our holy calling to train their immortal spirits for you and your glory. Inspire us with faith, with patience, with wisdom to train them aright. Oh, that our home on earth might be to them the pathway and the gate to the Father's home in heaven!

Blessed Father! Let us and our children be yours wholly and forever. Amen.

THIRD DAY

The Family as Grace Restores It

> "And the Lord said unto Noah, Come, you and all your house, into the ark: for you have I seen righteous before me in this generation."—*Genesis 7:1*

"BY FAITH Noah prepared an ark for the saving of his house," and was made a witness to future ages that the faith of a believing, righteous parent obtains a blessing not for himself only, but for his children, too. The New Testament teaching, "By faith he saved his house," is in perfect accordance with what is recorded in the Old Testament history: "I have seen you righteous before me: come, you and all your house, into the ark." Even Ham, who, as far as his personal character was concerned, manifestly deserved to perish with the ungodly world, was saved from the flood for his father's sake and by his father's faith. It is the proof that in God's sight the family is regarded as a unity, with the father as head and representative; that parents and children are one; and that in the dispensation of grace, even as in the ministration of condemnation, it is on this principle that God will deal with the families of his people.

We know how it was this fact, of parents and children being one, that had given sin its terrible power in the world. Or was it not in virtue of this that, when Adam had sinned, his whole posterity had been made subject at one blow, as it were, to sin and death? Was not the flood, as well as the fall, a proof of it? We see the children of Seth sunk as deep as the children of Cain because Seth, too, was a son whom Adam had begotten in his likeness, with a sinful nature to be handed to his children too. Was it not this that gave sin such universal empire to thousand generations? The family was sin's greatest stronghold; children inherited the evil from their parents. The unity of parents and children was the strength of sin.

Noah's deliverance from the flood was to be the introduction of a new dispensation—the first great act of God's redeeming grace on behalf of a sinful world. In it God manifested what the great principles of the economy of grace were to be. These were life through death, and faith as the means of deliverance, the one channel through which the blessing comes. And further, it was now to be revealed whether the family was to be one of the means of grace. There was every reason to expect it would be. It had been sin's mightiest ally, the chief instrument through which it had acquired such universal dominion. This principle was now to be rescued from the power of sin, to be adopted into the covenant of grace, to be consecrated and made subservient to the establishment of God's kingdom. How otherwise could the declaration be verified, "Where sin abounded, there did grace much more abound," if sin alone had the power through the parents to secure dominion over the children? Nay, in this very thing we are to have one of the brightest displays of redeeming grace—that the relation of parents and children, which had become the great means for the transmission and establishing the power of sin, was much more to become the vehicle for the extension of the kingdom of God's grace. And though many ages would have to pass before the promised Seed of the woman should be born, yet in anticipation of that holy birth the seed of God's people were to share in the blessing of their parents. It was on the strength of this hope that the children of righteous Noah were blessed with their father.

Let believing parents understand and remember this. The man who is righteous in God's sight is not dealt with only as an individual, but in his relation as parent. When God blesses, he loves to bless abundantly; the blessing must overflow the house of his servant. It is not only for this temporal life and the supply of its many needs that the father must regard himself as the appointed channel through whom the blessings of nature and providence must reach the child, and that he may count upon God's help. The parental relation has a nobler destiny: for the eternal life, too, with its blessings, the believing father is to regard himself as the appointed channel and steward of the grace of God.

When once we understand this blessed truth, and in its fullness of promise by faith accept God's word, "You have I seen righteous before me in this generation," we shall know to value the word that follows:

"Go, you and your whole house, into the ark." The seed of the righteous shall be blessed; the house of his servant God will bless. God gives the assurance that the ark in which the parent is to be saved is meant for his children, too; for his sake, it is for them as much as for him; the ark is to be the house of the family.

And as the blessing is to come for his sake, so through his instrumentality, too. It is not only a promise, but a command: "Go, you and your house, into the ark." It is to him the charge is given to see to it that just as, and when, he enters in, they will, too. God will not deal with the house separate and apart from him; the parent has to bring the children into the ark.

And if the question comes up as to the power of a parent thus to lead his children into the ark as certainly as he himself goes in, the answer is simple and clear: "By faith Noah prepared an ark for the saving of his house." Let us believe that God always gives grace proportioned to the duty he imposes. Let the believing parent live and act and pray, with and for his children, as one to whom the ark and its salvation is indeed the one aim and joy of life, and who is assured that his children are meant of God to be there with him. Let him confidently trust God for the salvation of every child. Let him in that spirit instruct and inspire his children. Let them grow up under the consciousness that to be with the father is to be with one who is in the ark—the blessing cannot be missed. This it is that baptism—the figure of the ark with its resurrection out of the waters of the deluge—seals to us in the blood of Jesus.

Beloved parents! Listen to the blessed tidings of which Noah is God's messenger to you: there is room for your child in the ark; the God who saves you expects you to bring your child with you. Oh, let it no longer be enough to pray and hope that your child may be saved, but accept in faith the assurance that he can be, and act out in obedience the command that you are to bring him in! And to each question as to how, let the answer be taken deeper to heart, "Go, you and your house." Go in and live in the ark; bring up and train your little children there, as one wholly separated from the world and dwelling there; God's blessing will use your training for their salvation. Abide in Christ, and let the child feel that to be near you is to be near Christ; live in the power of the love and the redemption and the life of Christ; your house will be to the child the ark where Christ is known and found. Oh, if you have indeed heard that most blessed word, "I have seen you righteous," let it teach you in the obedience of a joyous faith to fulfill the precept, "Come, you and all your house, into the ark."

"You and all your house"—may the word live in the heart of each believing parent!

O Lord my God! I have heard your message, telling me that since you have accepted me as righteous in your Son, you will have my children saved, too. I have heard your voice of grace, "Come into the ark, you and your house." Blessed be your name for the assurance of the salvation of his children it offers a parent's heart!

Lord, open my eyes to see what your Word sets before me. Let me see in Noah the picture of a believing parent—walking with you, believing your Word, obedient to your command. Let me see in the ark the type of my blessed Lord Jesus, a sure and a safe hiding-place for me and my child. Let me see in the saving of Noah's house the sure pledge of what will be given to every parent who trusts you for his children, and obeys your voice to bring them in.

O my God, give me grace, like your servant Noah, so to walk with you that you may see me righteous before your face, so to believe the promise of your grace, so to obey your command and perform the work entrusted to me, that your blessing may abide on me and my children. And may it all be to the glory of your Holy Name. Amen.

FOURTH DAY

The Child of the Covenant

"And, behold, the word of the Lord came to Abraham, saying, he that shall come forth out of your own bowels shall be your heir. And he believed in the Lord; and he counted it to him for righteousness."—*Genesis 15:4, 6*

"You are the children of the covenant."—*Acts 3:25*

THREE TIMES had God already given to Abraham the promise that he would make of him at great nation, as the sand of the seashore in multitude. When God appeared to him the fourth time, Abraham poured out his complaint before God: "Behold, I go childless. Behold, to me you have given no seed: and, lo, one born in my house is my heir." In answer the word of the Lord came to him, saying, "Lo, this shall not be your heir; but he that comes forth out of your own bowels shall be your heir." And then follow the memorable words, "Abraham believed God, and he counted it to him for righteousness."

The great truth which this narrative sets before us is this: that the longing and asking for, the promise and the gift on God's part, and on our part the reception and the birth of our children, is a matter of faith; a matter in which God takes the deepest interest; in which he holds communion with men; and in which faith must operate and will assuredly be blessed. It is especially as a parent, and in reference to the promise of a child, that Abraham's faith is exercised and found well pleasing to God. In the power of faith the natural longing for a child becomes the channel of most wonderful fellowship with God, and the natural seed becomes the heir of God's promise and the spiritual blessing.

The reason and meaning of all this is easily found. In Noah God had begun to acknowledge the validity of the oneness of parents and children in the dealings of grace.

But it had been of little avail. Immediately after the flood Ham's wickedness burst out, and it was not many years before the whole world had sunk into idolatry. It is ever God's way by degrees and gradually to reveal the ways and the purposes of his grace, and so he resolves to deal differently with Abraham. The children of Noah had been born after the flesh. Before their birth God had not entered into covenant on their behalf. In character they had become independent men before God made them partakers of Noah's blessing. With Abraham he will deal otherwise; his way of dealing in covenant with his servants is to be advanced a distinct stage forward. The child, who was to be taken up into the covenant, was from before his birth to be the object of God's care and the parent's faith. The very birth of the child God takes charge of—to watch over and to sanctify by his word and by faith. Everything connected with Isaac's birth is to be a matter of God's revelation and man's faith. Against nature and against hope, God himself by his promise awakens the faith and expectation of a child. For twenty-five years this faith is tried and purified, until Abraham's whole soul is filled with believing expectancy, that so the child may in truth be the child of faith and prayer, a gift of God received by faith. Before the birth Abraham is circumcised, once again sealed for God in the covenant of circumcision, that so full and clear proof may be given that the birth of the seed of his people is holy in his sight, a matter to him of special interest, the object of his promises and his blessing. In all this God would teach us that it is not only in their individual capacity, but especially as parents, and that from before the first hope of having children, that his saints are taken into covenant with him, are called to exercise Abraham's faith, and to receive their children from his hands. Not only are the children when grown up, but even from the birth, to be partakers of the covenant. Yes, from before the birth, in the very first rising of hope, would God, by the power of his promises given to faith by his Spirit, begin the great work of redeeming love. He would thus reveal to us how that wondrous power with which he had endowed man, of bringing forth and giving life to a child after his own image, and which by sin had become the great strength of Satan's kingdom, was again to be consecrated, and under God's own eye to be rendered subservient to the extension of his kingdom and glory.

Hence it is that the Bible is so full of what cannot otherwise be understood—of Divine promise and interposition, of human activity and expectation connected with the birth of children. Everything concentrates on that one great lesson: the fatherhood and the childhood of this earth has a Divine and heavenly promise, and everything connected with it must with us be a matter of faith, a religious service holy to the Lord and well pleasing in his sight. I must not only believe for myself; if I would fully honor God, my faith must reach forth and embrace my children, grasping the promises of God for them, too. If I would magnify the riches of God's grace, if I would with my whole nature and all my powers be consecrated to God's service, and if I would accomplish the utmost possible within my reach for the advancement of his kingdom, it is especially as parent that I must believe and labor.

And what I see in Abraham—that God thought so long a time needful for the strengthening and ripening of faith before he might receive the promised child—teaches me that this grace is a gift of high value, and cannot be attained but by a close walk with God and wholehearted surrender to his teachings and leadings. The faith which was sufficient to justify Abraham was not sufficient to receive the blessing for his seed; it had to be further strengthened and purified: faith must ever be in proportion to the extent of the promise. And believing parents will experience that there is nothing that so mightily quickens the growth of their faith as the reaching out after this blessing for their children. They will feel in it the mightiest stimulus to a life of entire devotion and unmixed faith, that they may have not only enough for themselves, but to impart to children, in harmony with that law of the kingdom, "According to your faith be it unto you."

But with this solemn lesson Abraham's story gives us the comforting assurance that God will give the grace to attain what we need. With what patience and long-suffering did he lead Abraham and Sarah until they were fitted to accomplish his purposes, and it could be said of them, "Abraham believed that he might become the father of many nations," and, "Through faith Sarah received strength to conceive seed and was delivered of a child." Even now, God, who has undertaken to sanctify his people soul and body and to fill them with his Spirit, will himself train them for the holy calling of believing parents. He will teach us how the birth of our children can become the highest exercise of a faith that gives glory to God and the truest means of advancing our spiritual life and the interests of his kingdom.

With us, too, the promise of God and the power of faith are the wondrous links by which the natural seed becomes the heir of the spiritual blessing, and the parental relationship one of the best schools for the life of faith. It is especially in a believing fatherhood that we can become conformed to the image not only of faithful Abraham, but of the Father in heaven himself.

O our blessed God and Father! What thanks shall we render to you for the wondrous revelation of your will in your servants Abraham and Sarah. The fatherhood and motherhood of earth you took into your covenant charge and keeping; you sanctify and bless, that the seed of your people might indeed be holy to the Lord. Where sin had abounded and manifested its terrible power, you make grace much more to abound; and Abraham's child, the heir of sin and misery, you make the heir of the promise and its blessing. Blessed be your name Gracious God! Open the eyes of your servants to see how, through the birth of your own Isaac, your dear Son Jesus Christ, in our flesh, the birth of our children has indeed been redeemed from the power of sin, and your promise comes to us larger and fuller than ever Abraham could understand. Teach us, teach all Christian parents, to realize that if there is one thing in which you have an interest, in which you give abundant grace, in which you ask and aid faith, it is for a believing fatherhood, for our receiving our children from you and for you. O God, enlighten and sanctify our hearts to realize it: the fruit of our body is to be the heir of your promise. And let our parentage, like Abraham, be what binds us to you in worship and in faith. Amen.

FIFTH DAY

The Promise of the Covenant

"And I will establish my covenant between me and you, and your seed after you, in their generations, for an everlasting covenant, to be a God unto you, and to your seed after you."—*Genesis 17:7*

"The children of the flesh, they are not the children of God, but the children of the promise."—*Romans 9:8*

WE HAVE HERE the first full revelation of the terms of God's covenant, of God's dealing in grace, with Abraham, the father of all who believe; the great foundation promise of what God calls an "everlasting covenant." God had already revealed himself to Abraham as his God, and the God who would give him a child. The thing that is new and remarkable here is the assurance that the covenant now to be established was to be with his seed as much as with himself—"a God unto you, and your seed after you." It is this promise that has invested these words, through all the generations of God's Church, with an imperishable interest. Let us see how entirely the same the promise is for the child as for the parent.

The matter of the promise is the same in each case: "I will establish my covenant"; "I will be a God unto you and to your seed after you." It is God's purpose to stand in the same relation to the child as the father; the believing parent and the unconscious child are to have the same place before him. God longs to take possession of the children before sin gets its mastery; from the birth, yes, from *before* the birth, he would secure them as his own and have the parent's heart and the parent's love sanctified and guided and strengthened by the thought that the child is his. "A God unto you, and to your seed."

The certainty of the promise is the same. It rests on God's free mercy, on his almighty power, his covenant faithfulness. The election of the seed is as free as of the parent himself, or rather, is even more manifestly of free grace alone, for here at all events there is no possibility of either merit or worthiness. God's faithfulness to his purpose is in either case the ground on which the promise rests, and its fulfillment may be expected.

The condition of the promise is in each case the same. In its twofold blessing it is offered to the faith of the parent, and has to he accepted by faith alone. If the promise that comes to a sinner in the gospel, "I will be your God," is not believed, that unbelief makes the promise of no effect. God is true, his promise faithful, his offer of mercy real, but it finds no entrance through unbelief, and the blessing is lost. Not otherwise with the other half, "a God to your seed"—if the parent's faith accepts this for his child, God will see to it that his faith is not disappointed.

The recipient of the promise is the same. It is not as if the first half of the promise is given to the father, the second half to the child. No, but it is the same person to whom the two parts of the promise come. In the one half the individual accepts it for himself, in the other half as a father for his child, but it is one act. The promise is not held in abeyance to wait for the child's faith; but is given to the father's faith in the assurance that the child's faith will follow. With Abraham, as with each believing parent, the same faith accepts the personal and the parental blessing. The blessing is in either case equally sure if faith equally holds it fast.

But here a difficulty arises with many persons. They see that God's promises of mercy to sinners are free and sure, and have found, in believing them, that they have come true; they know that they have been accepted. But it is as if the promise with regard to the children is not equally simple and certain. They cannot well understand how one can so confidently believe for another. They know that the only sure ground for faith is God's Word; but they have not yet been able to realize that the Word of God really means this: that they are definitely to believe that he is the God of their seed. Their impressions are in accordance with views that are ordinarily held, and that may be expressed thus: "God has established a general connection between seed-time and harvest, between faithful parental training and the salvation of the children. In neither case, the seed-time nor the training, is absolute certainty of success secured, or God's sovereignty excluded. It is enough that the promise expresses the tendency and ordinary result of proper training, though not what is to be the issue in every particular case." It is evident that such a general principle, with its possible exceptions, cannot give the rest of faith the parent longs for. Faith needs the assurance that God's purpose and promise are clear and unmistakable; then alone can it venture all upon his faithfulness.

Such was the promise given to Abraham; such is the promise to every believing parent. It is not in the general law of seed-time and harvest that I am to find the parallel for my ground of hope on behalf of my child, but in that other very distinct and definite promise with which God himself has linked it. The first half, "I will be a God unto you," is the Divine pattern and pledge of the second, "a God to your seed." When as a struggling sinner I first sought for mercy, it was not to some general principle that seeking is generally followed by finding that I trusted, but to the very definite Divine assurance, "Everyone that asks receives, and he that seeks finds." I believed the promise; I came and was accepted; I found the promise true: "I will be your God." So the promise is now brought that he is willing to be the God of my seed, too. Wherever God comes with a promise, he expects faith to accept it at once. The promise was not conditional on Isaac's believing: it was intended to be its source and security. And so, as I stand in covenant with God as my God, and see how he offers to be the God of his people's seed, I have the right in faith to claim this promise and to be assured of my child's salvation as firmly as my own, through faith in the God of truth. The analogy between the two halves of the promise is complete. In the first it was the question, Could I trust the love and power and faithfulness of God to accept and renew and keep such a sinner as I am? Faith gave the answer and secured the blessing. And now with the other question, Can I trust the love and the power and faithfulness of God to accept and renew and keep my child? Faith can again give the answer, and this blessing, too, is secured.

And if the thought still come up, as it has come and troubled many, How about election? How can I be sure that my child is one of the elect? The first half of the promise again gives the solution. When I believed to the saving of my own soul, it was not the secret things which belong to the Lord our God that I had to do with, but the things revealed in his Word, his invitation, and promise. I was sure the election and the promise of God never could be at variance with each other. Even so with my child. No believer in God's promise ever had to complain that God's sovereignty had hindered its fulfillment. "They which are the children of the flesh, these are not the children of God, but the children of the promise." Not the fleshly descent from a believer can secure grace for the child, but only this—but this most certainly—that God's free promise, given for the seed of his people, had been claimed and held in faith. The promise is definite: "a God unto you and to your seed." Oh, let us, like Abraham, not stagger at the promise through unbelief, but be strong in faith, giving glory to God, and be confident that what he has spoken he is able and faithful to perform. Let us look upon our children, let us love them and train them as children of the covenant and children of the promise—these are the children of God.

O my God! How shall I sufficiently adore you for the grace you have revealed in the promise of the covenant? As if it was not enough to take such unworthy sinners and make them your children, you offer to provide for their children, too, and make the house of your servants the home of your favor and blessing. You meet them with the sure promise once given to your servant Abraham: "I will be a God unto you and to your seed after you." Blessed be your Holy Name!

And now, Lord, I beseech you, give me grace to take this promise and trust it with my whole heart. I desire to believe that as sure as is the confidence I have that you have accepted me and are my God, so confident may I be that you are the God of my seed. As I yielded myself all sinful to you, and you took me as your own, I give them, all sinful too, to you, and believe you take them as your own. As I accepted your promise for myself, I accept it for them. Give me grace now to look upon them as you look—as children of the promise. May this be what gives me courage and hope for their training on earth and their portion in heaven. They are the children of the covenant, children of the promise. Faithful is he who has promised, who also will do it. Amen.

The Seal of the Covenant

"You shall circumcise the flesh of your foreskin; and it shall be a token of the covenant between me and you. And he that is eight days old shall be circumcised, every man child in your generations."—*Genesis 17:11–12*

"HE RECEIVED the sign of circumcision, a seal of the righteousness of faith." Such was according to the teaching of the Holy Spirit, the meaning of the ordinance of circumcision given to Abraham. And yet there are many who speak of it as if it were only the initiatory rite into the temporal privileges of the Jewish people. As if it could be meant as one thing to him, something deeply spiritual and sacred, and another to his descendants! As if the whole argument of the Epistle to the Romans did not reprove the Jews for looking at it in so carnal a light and degrading it from what it originally was—the holy sacrament of friendship and fellowship with God, the seal of the righteousness of faith, the emblem of the covenant of the Spirit in which God would circumcise the heart, the sure sign of God's faithfulness to him and to his seed. It is only this spiritual aspect of circumcision which justifies the Church in grounding upon it the baptism of the infants of believers. But in this light it is the glorious type of the later ordinance, and its best exposition, when we understand how there was no need in the New Testament for repeating in express words the truth so deeply inwrought into the life of God's people: that their children were as truly in the covenant, and had as sure a right to its sign, as they themselves. May the Holy Spirit lead us to know the mind of our God.

We are taught that circumcision was a seal of the righteousness of faith. A seal is the confirmation of something that has been settled and transacted, the securing of privileges that have already been secured. Abraham had believed; God had counted his faith to him for righteousness and had taken him into a covenant of friendship. Circumcision was to him a Divine seal and assurance of this. But it was also a sign, and that no arbitrary one, but with a spiritual meaning. It was a sign of that purity and holiness which was to be the mark of God's people. The most remarkable feature of the covenant was its passing on the blessing from generation to generation, its taking possession for the service of God's kingdom of the very power of generation. Of this power sin had taken possession; the very first sign of sin with Adam and Eve was that they knew that they were naked and were ashamed. The very fountain of life was defiled and had to be cleansed. And so, when the little child of eight days old had to suffer the taking away of the foreskin of his flesh, it was in token of the defilement there is in our natural birth, a foreshadowing of that Holy One who should be begotten of the Holy Spirit, and of that second birth in him, not of the will of the flesh, but of God, which was to be the blessing of the new covenant. It was a type of the circumcision not made with hands, in the putting off of the body of the flesh, in the circumcision of Christ, being buried with him in baptism. The seal of the righteousness of faith under the Old Testament was the sign of the need of regeneration, a sign for the quickening and instruction of Abraham's faith, and the setting him apart as a father for the service of God.

Circumcision could not be to the infant Isaac essentially different from what it was to Abraham. It was to him, too, a seal of his participation in that spiritual covenant of which God's promise and man's faith were the two marks. All unknowing, he had been taken—with his father, and for his father's faith—into the favor and covenant of God. It was to him, as to Abraham, a seal of faith: faith already existing and accepted. Not his own, but his father's; for Abraham's sake, the blessing came on him. We find this distinctly stated later on (Genesis 26:3, 5): "I will bless you, because that Abraham obeyed my voice, and kept my charge, my commandments, and my statutes, and my laws." And again (verse 24): "I am the God of Abraham your father; fear not, for I am with you, and will bless you, for my servant Abraham's sake." Abraham had not believed for himself alone, but for his child; the faith that was counted for righteousness had entirely reference to God's promise about his child; as a father he had believed and received the child in faith from God; the sign of circumcision in the child was the seal to the child of the father's faith. God dealt with father and child as one; the father believed for himself and his child as one; the child had the same place in the covenant, and the same claim on the seal of the covenant, as the father. And as he grew up, it would be to him a seal not only of the faith his father had, but of God's promise waiting for his faith, too, the remembrancer of the one thing required by God, the one thing counted righteousness by him, the one thing well-pleasing to him, and by which he in turn could pass the blessing on to his seed again.

What circumcision was to Abraham and Isaac, baptism is still to believers and their children. It, too, is a sign, only far clearer and brighter. If circumcision spoke of the shedding of blood and the purifying of the very fountain of life, the water in baptism witnesses of the blood that has been shed and the Spirit that has been given, with their cleansing and renewing. "There are three who bear witness: the Spirit, and the water, and the blood." Of all these blessings it is a sign, and also a seal—a seal from God of the righteousness of faith, that faith in his promise is well-pleasing to him and is counted as righteousness.

And baptism is all this, not only to the believing adult, but to his infant, too. It would indeed be strange if Abraham and every father of his race should, under the Old Testament, have had the privilege of knowing, "My child has the same place in the covenant as I have," and of having this sealed to him by the child's receiving the sign of the covenant, and the Jew, on becoming a Christian, should at once have forfeited the privilege. It need not for a moment surprise us that our Lord, in giving the command to baptize, said nothing of the little ones. So deep had this foundation truth, "My covenant with you and your seed," and therefore the sign of the covenant for the father and the child, too, been laid in the very first establishment of the covenant, and so completely had it become inwrought during two thousand years in the life of God's people that only the very express revocation of the principle could lead us to believe that the New Testament sign of the covenant is for the adult only. No; in this dispensation of larger love and more abounding grace, this beautiful provision of the everlasting covenant shines with new glory, the covenant and the sign of the covenant for parents and children alike.

But then, let us remember, almost more than in the old, in this dispensation of the Spirit, the one condition of blessing, without which the covenant and its sign are of no value, is faith. It is on this that the blessing of infant baptism depends. The parent must meet God as Abraham did, as a believer. It is faith and faith alone that can enter into the covenant, that pleases God, that obtains the reward. He must believe for himself in that Christ who is the surety of the covenant, who is himself the covenant. He must believe for his child. "Your God and the God of your seed"—these are the unchangeable terms of an everlasting covenant. The faith that claims the first may claim the second, too. It has the same warrant—God's Word. It has the same hope—God's faithfulness. It obtains the same blessing of free grace—the salvation of my child as surely as my own. And it has the same sign as its seal—baptism for the infant as well as the adult.

O my God! We thank you for the condescension to our weakness, manifested in giving us, in visible sign, a Divine seal of spiritual and unseen blessings. You know our frame and remember that we are dust. You are the Creator of our bodies, not less the Father of our spirits; you have redeemed them to be the temple of your Holy Spirit. In the body you set the seal of your acceptance of us and your right over us. Lord, teach us to understand this; and let holy baptism, the seal of the New Testament faith and life, be indeed to your people the sign that they are baptized into the death of Christ.

And grant, most gracious God, that where your people cannot yet see eye to eye in the dispensation of this ordinance, it may still be not the symbol of division, but the bond of unity in the Spirit of love.

And teach us, who believe that you yourself have meant this seal of the covenant for our children, too, to recognize its deep spiritual meaning, and to live ourselves as baptized into the death of Christ, and circumcised with a circumcision not made with hands. Teach us in faith to claim the full spiritual blessing for our children, too, and to train them for it. And so fulfill to us, O our God, in full measure the promise of the covenant, "A God unto you, and to your seed." Amen.

Keeping the Covenant

> "I have known Abraham, to the end that he may command his household and his children after him, that they may keep the way of the Lord, to do justice and judgment; to the end that the Lord may bring upon Abraham that which he has spoken of him."—*Genesis 18:19*

FAITH WITHOUT WORKS is dead. Saving faith is an energy, the power of a new life, manifesting itself in conduct and action. In true faith, the soul becomes united to God and seeks to enter into the Divine will, as the surest way of becoming one with himself. As faith grows clearer and stronger, it always sympathizes more fully with God's plans; it understands him better and becomes more conformed to his likeness. This is true not only of individual but also of parental faith. The higher the faith of the parent rises, the more the family will come under its power and be permeated by the spirit of godliness. Parental faith in God's promise will always be known by parental faithfulness to God's will.

Abraham is a remarkable illustration of this. As distinctly as God's Word speaks of his faith, it tells, too, of his faithfulness as a father. In assigning the reason why God's purpose in regard to Sodom should not be kept secret from him, God grounds it upon this part of his character. Not as an eminent believer, not even as the father of the promised seed, but as one called to be the faithful leader of his children and household in the ways of the Lord, God confers on him the high distinction of having his secret counsel revealed to him. Faithfulness in his household gave him access to God's secrets and to God's presence as intercessor for

Sodom. Let us try to understand what this means and why God puts such honor upon parental faithfulness. Let us look to its need, its character, its blessing, its power.

Think what *need* there is of it. Without it, the blessing offered to parental faith is lost, and the purpose of God made void. Were God by direct interposition, or by special agents, to seek the salvation of the little ones, there would be no reason for the part the parent is allowed to take in the covenant. God's object in thus honoring him is distinctly that he, to whose influence the helpless babe is committed, should train it for God. God seeks a people on earth. The family is the great institution for this object, a believing and God-devoted fatherhood one of the mightiest means of grace. God's covenant and the parent's faith are but preliminary steps; it is by the godly upbringing by the parents that the children are led really to enter upon and possess the blessings secured in the covenant. They must learn to know, and choose, and love the God who has given himself to them. The most precious promises on God's part will not avail unless the child is brought up, in the course of patient and loving training, to desire and accept the proffered friendship of the Holy One, to obey him and keep his commandments. God establishes his covenant with parents not only for their comfort, to assure them of what he will do, but also to strengthen them for what they must do, whom he makes his fellow workers in securing the children for him. The sure covenant does not dispense with—the better it is understood, the more it reveals—the indispensable need of parental faithfulness.

What God says of Abraham further gives us an insight into the true *character* of this grace: "I have known Abraham to the end he may command his children and his household after him." The spirit of modern so-called liberty has penetrated even into our family life; and there are parents who, some from a mistaken view of duty, some from want of thought as to their sacred calling, some from love of ease, have no place for such a word as "command," which God here uses, in their family religion. They have seen nothing of the heavenly harmony between authority and love, between obedience and liberty. Parents are more than friends and advisers: they have been clothed by God with a holy authority, to be exercised in leading their children in the way of the Lord. There is an age when the will of the child is to a great extent in their hands, and when the quiet, loving exercise of that authority will have mighty influence. We speak here not so much of commanding in the sense of specific injunctions; we speak of what we see in the heavenly Father; the tenderness of affection combined with an authority not to be despised. It is the silent influence of example and life which also exercises its commanding power, which makes the child often unconsciously bow to the stronger will, and makes it happy in doing so.

The *blessing* of such parental faithfulness is sure and large. God says, "That the Lord may bring upon Abraham that which he has spoken concerning him." It was in the way of a godly education that the blessings of the covenant were to come true. God's faithfulness and man's in the covenant are linked by indissoluble ties. If Abraham was to be blessed, and his seed with him, and all nations again in his seed, it was only thus: he must, as a faithful parent, pass on to others what he knew himself of God. It is only as the children become partakers of the parent's spirit that they can share his blessing. The child is to be identified with the parent, not merely in an imputation in which God looks on it for the parent's sake, but in a similarity of disposition and conduct; so, and not otherwise, would God bring upon Abraham what he had spoken. As it is written, "You see that faith wrought with his works, and by works was faith made perfect, and he was called the friend of God." In a way that passes all comprehension, but that fills us with adoring wonder at the place given to his servants in the fulfilling of his counsel, the faithfulness of God and man, each in his performance of the covenant obligation, are inseparably and eternally interwoven.

The solemn responsibility may well make us tremble. But God's word meets us with Divine comfort. The *power* is provided in the purpose of God. The words of the text are most remarkable: "I have known Abraham, to the end that he may command his children and his home." It was with this very purpose that God had chosen him and revealed himself; God himself was the security that his own purposes should be carried out. It was because God had known, and he truly known God, that he could do it. And so every believing parent has, in the very fact of his being taken into this relation with God, the guarantee that God will give the grace of faithfulness to prepare for the blessing, as well as the reward upon it. In the covenant we have not to trust our God for every other blessing, but look to ourselves for the faithfulness that receives it; no, as for every other, so for this, most of all, we may count upon him: "I have known Abraham, to the end that he may command his household and his children."

It is part of God's covenant that he will first teach man to keep it, and then reward that keeping (Jeremiah 32:40). A covenant-keeping God and a covenant-keeping parent—in these the children must be blessed. "The mercy of the Lord is from everlasting to everlasting upon them that fear him, and his righteousness to children's children, to such as keep his covenant, and to those that remember his precepts to do them."

Believing parent! See here the two sides of a parent's calling. Be very full of faith, be very faithful. Very full of faith: let faith in the living God, in his covenant with you and your seed, in his promises for your children, in his faithfulness, fill your soul. Take God's Word as the only measure of your faith. And then, be very faithful: take God's Word as the only measure of your life, especially in the family. Be a parent such as God would have you be. Let it be your one desire so to live yourself, so to rule your home, so to command your household and your children, that they may walk in the ways of the Lord, that so the Lord may bring upon you that which he has spoken concerning you. You may depend upon it that the blessing will be large and full. In the blessing for your own Christian life, which comes from that self-discipline and exercise of faith which parental faithfulness involve, in the blessing on your home life and your children, in the influence which will come to you on those around you (1 Timothy 3:5–6), in the power given you, like Abraham, to enter into God's secrets, and to plead with him as intercessor for the perishing, God will prove to you that believing, faithful parentage is one of the highest privileges to which man can be admitted. Study Abraham in his fatherhood as chosen of God, faithful to God, blessed of God, and find in him the type, the law, the promise of what your fatherhood may be.

O my God! Have you indeed taken me, too, into this wonderful covenant, in which you are the God of the seed of your saints and make them the ministers of your grace to their children? Open my eyes, I pray you, to see the full glory of this your covenant, that my faith may know all that you have prepared for me to bestow, and may do all you have prepared for me to perform. O my God, may your covenant-keeping faithfulness be the life and the strength of my faith. May this faith make me faithful in keeping the covenant.

And teach me to realize fully what this parental faithfulness is which you ask of me. I would make this the one object of my home life: to train a seed to serve you. By my life, by my words, by my prayers, by gentleness and love, by authority and command, I would lead them in the way of the Lord. O God, be my helper.

Teach me, above all, that as you have appointed this parental training for the fulfillment of your purpose, I may be assured that you have made provision for the grace to enable me to perform. Let my faith see you undertake for me and all I have to do, and an ever-growing faith so be the root of an ever-growing faithfulness. I ask it in the name of your Son. Amen.

EIGHTH DAY

The Child's Surety

"And Judah said unto Israel his father, Send the lad with me; I will be surety for him; of my hand shall you require him."—*Genesis 43:8–9*

THESE ARE THE WORDS of Judah when he sought to persuade his father to send Benjamin with him. And that he realized what his surety-ship for the child meant, and was ready at any sacrifice to fulfill its duties, is evident from his pleadings before Joseph, when he said, "Your servant is become surety for the child with his father," and offered himself as slave in his brother's place. In this he was not only the type of his own descendant, the great Surety of his people, who gave himself in their stead; but also, because the spirit of self-sacrifice passes from the head to the body, of every parent to whom God commits the care of a child amid the dangers of the journey through life. The language and conduct of Judah will teach us some most suggestive lessons as to the little ones who have been entrusted to our charge.

Consider first the meaning of the engagement made. What else is our language, as in baptism we undertake to train a child for God, but this: "Send the child with me; I will be surety for him." In answer to the questions, "How can that little one receive the mark of the covenant, and then be sent forth into a sinful world?" "Would it not be better that it were removed at once from a world of sin to the Father's home? Or else left without that sign of the covenant which has so often been but an empty form?" The answer has been, "Send it with me; I will be surety for it." Most distinctly the question has often again been put to the trembling parents when the little one was threatened with sickness or death, "Shall the child live or die?" and the answer was heard again: "Spare it, leave it, even though it be a world of danger; I will be surety for the child; of my hand shall you require it; send it with me." Solemn thought! Amidst all the dangers down in Egypt, and so many seen perishing, as parent I take charge of the child, and the great God may hold me responsible if I do not bring him back to his father's home in safety. With Judah I have spoken: "If I bring him not unto you, and set him before you, then let me bear the blame forever!"

Consider, too, the duties of such a suretyship, as illustrated in Judah. He was thoroughly in earnest with the engagement he had undertaken. When the governor of Egypt had commanded that Benjamin should be kept as a slave, he at once came forward as a substitute. Not for a moment does he think of his own home and children, of Egyptian slavery and its hardships; everything gives way to the thought, "My father entrusted him to me, and I am surety for the lad." With the most touching earnestness he pleads to be accepted in the youth's stead: "Your servant is become surety for the lad with his father. How shall I go up to my father, and the lad be not with me? Now, therefore, let your servant abide instead of the lad as bondman to my lord, and let the lad go up with his brethren."

Would God that Christian parents realized, as Judah did, what it means that they are surety for their child! Alas, how often, when our children are in danger from the prince of this world, when the temptations of the flesh or the world threaten to make them prisoners and slaves, to hold them back from ever reaching the Father's home—how often are we found careless or unwilling to sacrifice our ease and comfort in seeking to rescue them from their danger! How often the spiritual interests of the child are considered subordinate to worldly prospects or position or profit, and the solemn covenant forgotten in which we undertook to make it our first care that the child should not be lost to the Father in heaven! How feebly we realize that it is only in a life of pure and wholehearted devotion, in which the selfishness and worldly-mindedness of the world are crucified and our life is lived for God, that we can really train children for heaven! And how little we have learned, when danger threatens, and our children appear to be growing up unconverted, to bow at the foot of the throne, until we see that our plea, "I am surety for the child," has touched the heart of the King, and we have his word to set him free. Oh, that the ruling principle of parental life and love might be, "Without the child I will not see my Father's face."

Consider now, too, the encouragement Judah's example gives. It sets before us the abundant reward the faithful surety will reap. In pleading with the ruler of Egypt, Judah thought he had to do with a stranger, a despot, and an enemy. Little did he know that his pleadings were entering the ears of one who was his own and Benjamin's brother. He never dared to hope that it would exercise such a mighty influence, or call forth that wondrous revelation of the ruler falling weeping on Benjamin's neck, with his "I am Joseph." Wonderful picture of the power and the reward of a surety's supplication!

And yet not more wonderful than the parent-surety may expect. Did we but more feel the sinfulness of our children's nature, and the dangers surrounding them, with what fervency we should plead with the great King and Savior of the world for their salvation. It is there, not less than to Judah, that the blessing would come to us. It might be that at the first, as it was with him, we had no conception of the tender relation in which he stands to us and our children as a Brother: as we plead for the child and show ourselves ready to make any sacrifice so he may be saved, we should have our reward in the blessed revelation of what Jesus is to us, as well as in the blessing on the child. The blessing to the pleading surety would be no less rich than to his charge. In Jairus, and the father of the lunatic, and the Syrophenician woman, and in the experience of ten thousand parents, we have proof that while they only thought of obtaining what their children needed, their prayer led to experiences of the power and love of the Savior, to such closer and more intimate fellowship with him, to such personal blessing as they never had found in only praying for themselves. They saw him with whom they were pleading on the throne descend and say, "I am Jesus"; they saw him embrace the beloved one they pleaded for and kiss him; Jesus was never so gloriously revealed as when they were pleading as parents and sureties for their children.

And just as Judah then learned to understand how Joseph was the true surety, who in the path of suffering had won the throne and their deliverance from famine and death, so parents will learn, the more they seek to fulfill their duties as sureties, to know and rejoice in Jesus as their Surety. He has not only undertaken their own personal salvation: he has secured and vouchsafes the grace they need to fulfill their duties; he is the Surety for their suretyship, too, because theirs is grounded in his. The vicarious principle on which redemption rests, and in virtue of which he died, "One for all," runs through the whole of its economy;

most specially does it appear in the family, that image of humanity as a whole. There the father is head, is priest, is king, even as Christ, over his own house; the father is, in limited sense, but most really, surety for the child. And now it is, as he, the surety on earth, under the burden of his charge, draws nigh to the King, and discovers in him the Great Surety, that the revelation will give him new confidence and strength and joy in the work he has undertaken. In the light of the redemption and love and friendship of Jesus, the thought, "I am surety for the child," will gain new brightness, devotion to the training of the children will become more earnest, the readiness to make any sacrifice to save them from the world will be more spontaneous, and the pleading of faith more confident and triumphant. And it will be found now what richest blessings for parents and their family open out in the words, "I am surety for the child."

Blessed Father, most earnestly do we beseech you to open the eyes of the parents of your Church to see and know their holy and most blessed calling. May they understand and realize that you say to them at the birth of each little one entrusted to their care, "At your hands will I require it." May they understand and realize, too, that with each little one they brought and gave to you in baptism, they accepted the solemn charge, and gave the answer, "Of my hand you will require him; I am surety for the child."

O God, show us what the dangers are that surround our children, and how impotent we are. Give us the true surety-spirit, the willingness to sacrifice all rather than be unfaithful to our charge. As we see the power of sin and of the world threatening them, may we plead as for our own life—yes, with the offer of our life—that the children be now saved from sin and Satan. As your eye sees us day by day with our children, may this be the one desire, of our parental love. You find, that they may be wholly yours. May this be our one aim in prayer and education and intercourse.

And, O blessed Lord Jesus, King, Surety, Brother, on the throne, reveal yourself as our Helper and our Joy.

O Lord Jesus, teach us and the parents of your Church that, as you are our Surety, we are the surety of our family. O you who are the faithful Surety, make us faithful, too. Amen.

NINTH DAY

Faith Hiding the Child

"And when she saw that he was a goodly child, she hid him three months."—*Exodus 2:2*

"By faith Moses, when he was born, was hid three months by his parents, because they saw he was a goodly child; and they were not afraid of the king's commandment."—*Hebrews 11:23*

THE STORY OF MOSES will lead us a step further in the study of the way in which the faith of parents will manifest itself in dealing with their children. It was faith that saw the goodliness of the child; it was faith that feared not the king's wrath; it was faith that hid the child and saved its life. In each child born of believing parents, faith sees the same goodliness, meets the same danger, and finds the same path of safety.

It was by faith Moses' parents saw he was a goodly child. The natural love of a parent's heart doubtless made the child a beautiful one in the mother's eye; but faith saw more than nature could. God opened the eyes, and there was the consciousness of something special, of a spiritual beauty, that made their babe doubly precious. And so the eye of faith sees in each little one a Divine goodliness. Is it not a being created in God's image, with the faint light of a Divine glory, of an immortal life, shining from it? Is it not an object of the great redemption—destined to be a partaker of the precious blood and the Holy Spirit of Jesus, to be the object of the joy of angels and God's everlasting love and pleasure? A child, whose worth exceeds that of the whole world? A child, that even in this life can be a brother of Jesus, a servant of God, a blessing for the immortal spirits of fellow men? Surely faith may call the little one unspeakably fair, for it sees it shining as a jewel in the crown of the Lamb—his joy and his glory. We have indeed a surer hope than ever Moses' parents had, and a brighter light in which the heavenly beauty of our little ones is reflected. O Father, open the eyes of all your people that, with each little babe you give them, their faith may see that it is a goodly child.

It is faith that sees, but does not fear the danger. Our children are still exposed to the same danger. Pharaoh had commanded that the children of God's people should all be destroyed. He knew that if the children were cut off, the people would soon die out. There would be no need of the trouble and danger of war; by a slow and silent but sure process, the nation would be cut off. The Prince of this world still pursues the same policy. When parents take a decided stand for God, the world may despise or hate them; it soon learns that it is of little use to attempt to conquer them. But it knows a surer way. The spirit of the world claims possession of the children: if these are won, all are won. And too often, alas, Christian parents give their children a prey to the world. Children are allowed to grow up in comparative ignorance about the blessed Savior, are entrusted to the care of irreligious or worldly teachers, are allowed to associate with those whose spirit and influence is altogether worldly. And in many a Christian home, where at one time, when the children were still young, all was earnest and decided, as they grew up, the tone became changed, and the power of religion was far less to be seen. And the Church, alas, is often too faithless or feeble to warn against it. How little it has realized that in the parental relation, and in baptism, it has a mighty hold on the Church of the future, and given to the instruction and encouragement of parents the prominent place its importance demands. To what a large extent the education of the young has been left to the State, and the secular school, and the spirit of the age, until the youthful heart has lost the simplicity and tenderness of which the Master spoke when he said, "Of such is the kingdom of heaven." Oh, what thousands on thousands of the children of the kingdom are thus drowned in the mighty Nile of this world—the fruitful stream of its pleasures and profits. Would God that the eyes of his people might be opened to the danger which threatens his Church! It is not infidelity or superstition: it is the spirit of worldliness in the homes of our Christian people, sacrificing the children to the ambition or society, to the riches or the friendship of the world, that is the greatest danger of Christ's Church. Were every home once won for Christ, a training-school for his service, we should find in this a secret of spiritual strength not less than all that ordinary preaching can accomplish.

It is faith that still finds the same path of safety. "By faith Moses was hid by his parents." They trusted God on behalf of this goodly child, one of the children of his covenant. "By faith Moses was hid by his parents"—these simple words tell us our duty, what our faith must do. Christian parent! Hide your child. And where? Oh, hide it in that safest refuge—"the shadow of the Almighty," "the secret of God's countenance." Lay your child from its birth daily there in faith, and let your soul be filled with the consciousness that he has indeed taken charge of it. Let the mighty rock of God's strength and the tender covering of his feathers be its ark, while still it is all unconscious of temptation or danger. Let, with the first dawn of reason, the clefts of the rock and the love of Jesus be the place of safety to which you guide its youthful feet. Hide it in the quiet of home life from the excitements of the world without, from the influence of a civilization and culture which is of the earth. In that hiding, where the enemy cannot find, we have one of faith's highest duties. And when the time comes that it must come into contact with the world, oh, you can still entrust it to him who is the Keeper of Israel—let it be a settled thing with your heart that he has accepted your trust, has taken charge, and cannot disappoint your faith. Commit your child boldly to the waters in the ark of the covenant of your God. Fear not the inexorable law which is continually being proclaimed: "The children cannot be kept separate from the world; the children must go with the stream." No, let faith hold it fast that yours are the children of a peculiar people, separated unto God; they must be kept separate for him.

The reward of the faith of Moses' parents will be ours. Not only was Moses saved, he became the savior of his people. Your child, too, will not only be blessed, but also be made a blessing. Each child has not the calling of a Moses. But in his kingdom God needs not only a Moses, but a Moses' mother and a Moses' sister, for the fulfillment of his purposes. Let your faith but, like Moses' mother, do its work: God himself will see to it that our labor is not in vain. The education Moses' mother gave her son during the years of his childhood was such as all the years of his training at Pharaoh's court could not obliterate. His parent's faith bore fruit in his faith, when he, at every cost, chose suffering with the people of God, and was not afraid of the wrath of the king, because he saw him who is invisible. Let faith hide the child in the ark of God's love. Let faith, when God entrusts the child to its care, train the child for God and his people, and when the time comes that it must go into the world, were it even to live at Pharaoh's court, it will be safe in the power of faith and of God's keeping. A child of faith will not only receive a blessing for itself, but be a blessing to those around.

God grant that the Church may indeed become a "Moses' mother," the faithful nurse of the children he entrusts to her care, "hiding" them, and keeping them separate from the world and its influence. He will give a wonderful fulfillment of the promise, wherever he finds the fulfillment of the duty, "Take this child, nurse it for me: I will give you your wages."

Gracious God! With my whole heart I thank you for the teaching of your Word, by which you prepare me to fulfill aright my holy calling as parent. I thank you for the example of Moses' parents, and pray that the grace that taught them in faith to save their child may be given to me, too.

I acknowledge, Lord, that I do not sufficiently realize the value of my children, nor the danger to which they are exposed from the Prince and the Spirit of the world. Lord, teach me fully to recognize the danger and yet never to fear the commandment of the king. Open my eyes to see in the light of heaven that each little one is a goodly child, entrusted to my keeping and training for your work and kingdom. Help me in the humility and watchfulness and boldness of faith to keep them sheltered, to hide them from the power of the world and of sin. May my own life be the life of faith, hid with Christ in God, that my child may know no other dwelling-place.

And grant all this also to all your people, O my God. Let your Church awake to know her place in this world, and her calling to go out to the land to which God has called her. Let, in the training of the children, the mighty power of faith be seen, the difference between them that fear you and them that fear you not. O give us grace to rear our children for you. Amen.

TENTH DAY

A Lamb for a House

"Take every man a lamb, according to their father's houses, a lamb for a house. When he sees the blood, the Lord will pass over the door, and will not suffer the destroyer to enter your houses."—*Exodus 12:3, 23*

IT HAS OFTEN been pointed out that of all the Old Testament sacrifices, there is none that gives a clearer or richer revelation of the person and work of our Lord than the Passover. It has often, however, escaped observation how the whole institution of the Paschal Lamb aimed at deliverance not of the individuals, but of families; it dealt not with the persons, but with the families—the houses of God's people. What else is the meaning of the expression, "A lamb for an house," or (as in verse 21), "Take lambs according to your families," and of the blood sprinkled upon the house? As so it is expressly declared, "When your children shall say unto you, What do you mean by this service? then you shall say, It is the sacrifice of the Lord's Passover, who passed over the houses of the children of Israel, when he smote the Egyptians and delivered our houses." Among the Egyptians it was the firstborn in every house who died, as representing the house, as in Israel it was the firstborn who through the blood was saved from the impending danger and consecrated for God. All teaching how God, in redeeming his people and revealing the principles on which he is to deal with them, lays this down as a fundamental law in the Passover and the blood-sprinkling: I deal with you not as individuals, but as families. As I chose and blessed you, as the seed of your father Abraham, so I still bless every household through the believing father, who sprinkles the blood in obedience to my command. The lamb and its blood are the consecration of the dwellings and the family relations of my people. In the hands of the father, God thus places the destiny and the safety of the whole house.

Christ, our Passover, is slain for us. We love to trace how, in every, even to the most minute particular, the foreshadowings of the Paschal Feast were fulfilled in him. Have we any warrant in God's Word for excepting this so important feature, and allowing the type to hold good in every respect but this? Is, in this one respect, the Old Testament feast to stand higher than the New, and the blood which then was for the saving of the house here to be only for the individual? And not be sprinkled on the houses, too? How the Christian parent might then envy the Jew, who enjoyed the privilege, as he looked at the sprinkled blood, of knowing that he had done it to the saving, not only of himself, but his household, too. And the Christian parent would not have the right thus, in definite and assured faith, to claim the blood for his children? God forbid! Christ, the Lamb of God, is still "a lamb for a house"! His blood may still be sprinkled upon the door, that the destroyer enter not in. In the new covenant, and with the precious blood of Christ, the principle still holds good: it is the believing father's right and duty in faith to appropriate the blood for his whole house. His faith has the Divine warrant, and will be rewarded with the Divine blessing.

Let me endeavor henceforth to live in this faith—fully to realize this privilege. As I think of the precious blood, and seek to walk in the nearness to God which it gives, let me claim its cleansing power for my house as well as myself. Let me be assured that my faith as parent has power and secures a Divine influence. Daily there is the sin of my house, defiling and darkening. Even my sin, pardoned though it be, might justly, in its consequences, be visited on my children. The fullness of the application of the blood will correspond to what faith claims. I have in nature transmitted sin and death—through me, they inherit it. Thank God, as a father, I may also transmit the grace and blessing of redemption.

Not only my own soul, but my house, can daily be kept under the sprinkling and cleansing of the blood. And each time I enter my door, or think of Satan entering it, in the light of heaven I may see it sprinkled with the blood of the Lamb. Parents and children together stand under the cover and protection of the blood: the Lord is our keeper.

Every year in Israel parents had to renew the sprinkling: the blood of the Lamb has been shed once for all. I have now only each day again to renew the consecration of my house to the Lord in the assurance of faith: the blood saves me and my children. In this faith I may confidently expect that the wondrous redemption of the blood will exercise its full and mighty influence, until all our domestic life and its relations are sanctified, our house is wholly the Lord's, and each child is consciously and confessedly one of his redeemed.

To this end, I must notice carefully how God commanded the parents to teach these things to their children (Exodus 12: 26, 13: 14). "The grace of God that brings salvation teaches us." What is secured to the child in redemption must be made his own in free and personal appropriation. And this cannot be without his knowing it. The children were to be taught that they belonged to the redeemed people, that they belonged to the redeeming God. The parent was to act not only as priest—and thus, in a sense, mediator—but also as prophet and teacher. As he had dealt for the child with God in the blood-sprinkling, so he was to deal for God with the child in the instructions he gave him. Let me seek grace and wisdom in the spirit of faith to teach my children what the blood has done for them, to make them know and love the God who accepted them, before ever they knew him!

One thing more is deserving of very special note. The believing Israelite had not only every year to sprinkle the door-posts with blood, and so to testify that it was only in the blood that he and his house could stand before God; he had also to write upon these same blood-sprinkled door-posts the words of God's law (Deuteronomy 6:7–9). In all the going out and coming in of his children, these words were ever to meet their eye, the freedom from Egypt's bondage and Egypt's curse was a freedom to serve God. God wills to be not only trusted but obeyed. It is "unto obedience and the sprinkling of the blood of Christ" that we have been chosen: the door-posts sprinkled with the blood, and inscribed with the words of the law, remind me of the blessed oneness of faith and obedience, liberty and service. I would in the joy of the great redemption train and educate my children to know, and love, and keep the commands of their God. Day by day, in faith and prayer, in teaching and, living, I would seek to set before them in its harmony the blessedness of a faith that freely accepts all that God gives, with a surrender that gives all he claims.

"A lamb for a house." I must pray that God's Holy Spirit reveal in its full power all the truths that cluster round this blessed word. A father redeemed by the blood; his children through him and with him partaking of the sprinkling; the father, God's minister every year anew to sprinkle the house; the father, God's witness and messenger to the children to teach them of this precious blood and of the God it reveals; the blood-sprinkled door-posts inscribed with the words of God's law. Such is God's wondrous provision for getting full possession of his people and making the family the foundation of the kingdom.

Blessed Lord Jesus! The Lamb of God, which takes away the sin of the world, the Son of God, whose blood cleanses from all sin, in humble faith I claim that blood for myself and my children. May my own experience of its ever-cleansing power every day grow fuller and clearer. And may I by your Holy Spirit realize fully my right to claim it for my house.

O most blessed Savior! May the power of your blood work in me so mightily that my faith may in full assurance accept it for each of my children as a present blessing. May we, under the covering of the blood, know ourselves protected from the destroyer.

O most gracious God, whose is this wondrous ordinance of a lamb for a house, I yield myself to you afresh as the minister of your covenant. Use me, my God, to save my children, to train them for you, and you alone. I would have the door-posts not only sprinkled with the blood, but inscribed with the law. I would have your service the one thing they grow up for. As you have chosen us, in sanctification of the Spirit, unto obedience and blood-sprinkling, may faith in the blood and surrender to your will be as the two door-posts between which we daily go in and out. The Lord make it so. Amen.

ELEVENTH DAY

The Father as Priest and Prophet

> "And it shall come to pass, when your children shall say, What do you mean by this service? then you shall say, It is the sacrifice of the Lord's Passover, who passed over the houses of the children of Israel in Egypt, when he smote the Egyptians, and delivered our houses."—*Exodus 12:26–27*

THE PASSOVER sets the believing parent before us in a twofold aspect. First, as dealing with God on behalf of the children, and bringing down the blessing on them; then as dealing with the children for God, and seeking to lead them up to him. In the former capacity, he sprinkled the blood of the lamb upon his house, securing God's protection for the children. In the latter he had to instruct his children, telling them of what God had done, and seeking to lead them to the personal knowledge and acceptance of this God as their God. Those two parts of parental duty are closely and inseparably linked to each other, the first being necessary as the root and origin of the latter. The parent's work as priest fits him for his work as prophet and teacher. The second is indispensable to the full appropriation of the blessing that the former has secured. It was after having sprinkled the blood for himself, and his child, too, that the parent had to instruct him in the meaning of the holy mystery. His interposition with God, his experience of God's blessing on himself and child, were his own training to fit him for the training of his child. As we keep this in view, we shall recognize the beauty of that institution by which God has chosen and appointed the believing parent the instructor of his children, and realize its extreme fitness as the best means of securing a godly seed for the Lord.

Observe—it is the parent, who has himself already experienced the salvation of God, who is appointed to lead the child to know God. The knowledge of God is no mere matter of the understanding; it is to love him, to live in him, to experience the power of his presence and his blessing. It is evident that the man who would teach others to know God must be able to speak by personal experience of him, must prove by the warmth of love and devotion that he loves this God and has his life from him. When God instituted the family as the great instrument of transmitting his fear, he so arranged it as to give it the highest possible efficacy. This consisted in his revealing himself to each head of a family as the God of his salvation. In the other sacrifices in Israel, the priest sprinkled the blood in the holy places, but in the Passover there was this peculiarity that each father sprinkled it on his own house. He thereby performed the act of faith by which the destroyer was kept from his house; and when he went forth from Egypt and undertook the journey to Canaan, he could bear personal witness to God's faithfulness and to the efficacy of the atoning blood of the lamb. He could speak as a living witness from personal experience. As a redeemed one, he could tell of redemption; he could tell of the Redeemer-God. It is even so now still: personal experience of the power of the blood can alone fit a parent for speaking to his children of God. It is the looking back upon the time when personal deliverance from sin was experienced, and the looking up to a God with whom, in the spirit of adoring gratitude, a personal intercourse is maintained, and the looking forward to a home where the longing spirit knows it will inherit a place prepared by the Father. It is this and this alone that fits a parent to speak aright and in power. It is the parent who has himself experienced redemption who can tell his child in truth of the God of Redemption, who can act in accordance with the injunction (Exodus 13: 8): "And you shall show your son in that day, saying, This is done because of that which the Lord did unto me in the day when I came forth out of Egypt."

And as parents in Israel had every year to renew the remembrance of that deliverance, so now it is the parent who lives in the ever-fresh experience of what the powers of redemption are who can, with ever-deepening earnestness and freshness, speak of the mercy and the truth, as well as of the blessed service, of the God of salvation.

But observe, further, this parent has also been constituted and accepted as God's appointed minister in the redemption of the child. It is this that gives an increased fitness for his work as instructor of the child. He can not only speak of a salvation he has experienced—urging and inviting the child to come and taste that to which he is as yet a stranger. No; in sprinkling the blood upon the door of his house, he saved his child, too, from the destroying angel. He was honored to act with God on behalf of the child; what the child could not do, he did for him, and the deed was accepted. The child has initially been made partaker of the blessing of that sprinkling of blood, and has, in growing up, personally to accept what has been secured and sealed to him. And what a mighty vantage ground it gives the believing parent in his labor when he can thus look upon his child in the light of that great transaction between God and himself, of which that child has been the object! With what confidence it inspires his faith! How his energies will be roused! And what a strong motive in pleading with the child himself! He speaks to him as no longer a stranger to the covenant of grace, but as a child of the covenant. He points him to a God who began to deal with him in the feebleness of infancy; he can attest to the reality of an engagement entered into between God and himself, and sealed in the sprinkling of blood. He shows him how God dealt with the houses, with the families of Israel; and if not in the way of argument, yet practically, and in the tone of the language which his faith adopts, he lets him feel that he cannot consent to one of his house refusing to acknowledge the God of the house.

And it gives him no less power in pleading with God on behalf of the child. He reminds the great Jehovah of the blood and the oath of the covenant, and claims for his child the blessings of redemption—that just as he is a child of the redeemed people, he may grow up personally to accept and ratify the covenant. Next to his own personal experience of the blessing of salvation, this consciousness of what, as a believing parent, he has been allowed to do, and of his seed having been received with him into covenant, constitutes the fitness of the believing parent for his being the minister of God's grace to his child.

But there is another thought that brings out still more strikingly the wondrous adaptation of the family constitution for the working out of God's purposes—this, namely, that it is grounded on the natural relation, sanctifying its affections, and adopting them into the service of redemption. It is not any one redeemed man saying to his fellow man, "Come and see what God has wrought for me." Nor is it any one redeemed man saying to some child to whom he sustains a certain official relation, and on whose behalf he has performed an act of atonement, "Come and let me lead you to your God." But it is a father, with his own child. In nature they are one, united by the closest and most wondrous ties. The child has his life from the father. The father looks upon him as part of himself, of his flesh and of his bones; he loves and cherishes him. This love seeks, even in nature, the happiness of the child, and can often make wondrous sacrifices to attain it. And it is this love God lays hold of in the parental covenant and purifies to be the minister and vehicle of his grace. And with a parent's love, there is a parent's influence. The weakness of the child renders him dependent, to a wondrous degree, upon the parent's will. The character of childhood is formed and molded by impressions; unceasing intercourse with the parent can render these impressions deep and permanent. The child's love to the parent rises and meets the parent's love, and the spirit of the parent can thus, in addition to the natural influence of birth, in wondrous measure be breathed into the child. Of all this God's grace seeks to avail itself, and while it is the sole prerogative of the Holy Spirit to renew the soul, and make a child of God, there is nevertheless a need for the means and instrumentalities through which his gracious workings are prepared and applied, are confirmed and established. And of all these instrumentalities, there is none more wondrously devised, or more beautifully adapted to its object, than this of godly parentage. A parent made partaker of God's love and grace himself, accepted and blessed with the promises of the covenant and the Spirit, as covenanting for his child; and then sent forth, in the power of consecrated parental affection, to make all the influences and intercourse of domestic life the auxiliary to the great work of gaining the child for God, this surely is one of the most wondrous exhibitions of God's grace upon earth.

O my God! I come to you again with the earnest prayer for your teaching. You have said, "I will be the God of all the families of Israel." Open my eyes to see clearly, and my heart to feel deeply, what your purpose is in this.

Since sin entered and ruined our nature, you would early take possession of the little ones for yourself. You seek to secure parents with all their love and influence to be your ministers. You enter into covenant with them, giving them the right to claim the Blood of the Covenant for their children, and in that Blood the promise, "A God to you and to your seed." And then you send them, as themselves redeemed, as having claimed and accepted redemption for their children, to use their influence for you, and win and train their children for your love and service.

Lord God, open the eyes of the parents of your Church to their calling, that they may honor you as the God of their families. And, O Lord my God, bless my own house, and give me grace, as one of your redeemed ones, to train my children for their God. May the joy of a personal experience of redemption, and the love of the blessed Redeemer, warm my heart and inspire my words and light up my life, to testify of you, and train them for you alone. Amen.

TWELFTH DAY

Sanctify the Firstborn

"And the Lord said unto Moses, Sanctify unto me all the firstborn. . . . All the firstborn of man among your sons you shall redeem. And it shall be, when your son asks you in time to come, What is this? that you shall say unto him, By strength of hand the Lord brought us out of Egypt; and it came to pass, when Pharaoh would hardly let us go, that the Lord slew all the firstborn of Egypt; therefore I sacrifice unto the Lord all that open the womb, being males; but all the firstborn of my sons I redeem."—*Exodus 13:1, 13–15*

"LET MY PEOPLE GO, that they may serve me"—in these words so often repeated by the Lord in sending Moses to Pharaoh, we see how service is the aim of redemption. God makes his people free from the bondage of Egypt, to translate them into the liberty of his service—the willing, loving, free service of a redeemed people. The deeper God's people enter into the spirit of redemption, the deeper will be the insight into the blessed unity of liberty and service, of liberty and necessity. No true service of God without liberty; no true liberty without service.

We have seen in the Passover what a permanent place the family and the children take in redemption. No less than their parents were they redeemed to serve; all their training was to be a training to the service of God. When Pharaoh said to Moses after the plague, "Go, serve the Lord your God; but who are they that shall go?" the answer was very distinct: "We will go with our young and our old, our sons and our daughters." It was on this point that the negotiations were broken off. The going of the children was what the king would not consent to: "So be the Lord with you, as I will let you go with your little ones: look to it, for evil is before you" (Exodus 9:8–10). And when later on Pharaoh still wanted to keep the property, he felt that this at least must be conceded: "Go, serve the Lord; only let your flocks and herds be stayed; let your little ones also go with you" (Exodus 10:24). It is the future of the nation that is to be secured for God; a people that is really to serve God must, in the first place, see to the little ones.

After the people had left Egypt, the very first command God gave to Moses was in regard to the firstborn, who were to be separated and sanctified for him. In each family the firstborn son was counted the chief and the best; the father looked upon him as Jacob said of Reuben: "You are my firstborn, my might, and the beginning of my strength."

His was the birthright and the place of honor in the family. He was the representative and head of all the children. God looked upon Israel as his firstborn among the nations. Because Egypt oppressed him and would not let him go, God slew his firstborn. And now in commemoration of this, and as a pledge of God's claim on all the children and the whole people, every firstborn belonged to God and was set apart as his peculiar property.

And with what object? For none other but his service. This comes out with great distinctness in the exchange that was made, by which the tribe of Levi was taken instead of the firstborn. "The Levites shall go to do the service of the tent, for they are wholly given unto me from among the children of Israel; instead of all the firstborn of the children of Israel have I taken them to me; for all the firstborn are mine" (Numbers 8:14–19). And in the redemption money, which had to be paid at the birth of each firstborn for his release, the parents had the unceasing reminder that the firstborn belonged to God and his service, and were represented in the Levites.

The principle involved in this is one of the deepest importance. God claims our best children for his own direct and immediate service. The whole people, old and young, were to serve him, but the firstborn, the very best, were to be entirely set apart for the special maintenance of that service, not only by the part they took in the worship, but by instructing the people in the law of their God. Let us try to take in fully the lessons the Christian Church has to learn from this.

In Israel all the firstborn, and as their representatives, all the children of Levi, a twelfth part of the whole nation, were exclusively claimed by God to be continually at his disposal in the service of his house. And in Israel that service consisted solely in the maintenance of what existed; nothing had to be done for the extension of the kingdom or the propagation of the knowledge of God among the heathen. The Christian Church has now not only to see to it that she maintains her hold on what she once has occupied: her calling in her redemption from sin is distinctly and essentially aggressive, to teach all the nations and seek the extension of the kingdom throughout the whole world. And the question is naturally suggested: If Israel had to set apart one-twelfth of its children for the work of God, what portion should the Christian Church devote to the work committed to her? And what portion has she devoted?

Alas, that the answer to the latter question should be so sad! There is hardly a missionary or philanthropic society engaged in teaching and rescuing the ignorant and the lost that has not to complain of lack of laborers. The call is being sounded forth louder every year that the doors to the hundreds of millions of heathen are opened wide, and yet how few, how sadly few, is the number of laborers. And why? Simply because Christian parents do not, as a rule, educate their children under the conviction that they are the Lord's—they do not place them at his disposal, they do not train them to look upon this as their highest privilege, if they are found worthy to bear the name of Christ among the heathen.

Let us just think a moment what would be thought of the loyalty of Englishmen to their Queen if it were found difficult to find men to form her bodyguard or accept appointments in her service! Or what of the enthusiasm of an army where the General could never obtain volunteers for a post of danger and of honor! And Jesus Christ, our King, who came to seek and save the lost, has said that these are his guard of honor, and shall have his richest rewards, who forsake all for his and the gospel's sake. And yet, while in every profession there are complaints of more applicants than openings, the Master has to wait, and his work has to suffer, because his people do not understand that they and their children have been redeemed to serve him who gave himself for them.

And what is the cure of this evil? And what can we do, each in our sphere, to wipe out this terrible reproach? What we can do is this: Let us devote every child to God and his service. Let us cease praying that our children may be saved, while we never think of giving them to serve. Let us cease choosing honorable and lucrative professions for our children, with the truth that they can serve God in any calling, turned into an excuse for declining special service. Let us lay each child upon the altar, specially our firstborn and our best, and seek this one thing: that they may become worthy and fit to be set apart for the service of the King.

And let the Church learn as part of her preaching of redemption to lift aloud her voice and cry, "You are redeemed for service, you and your children." Is not this the reason that so many a parent has prayed for the salvation of his child and been disappointed? The prayer was utterly selfish; it was simply the desire to see the child happy, without any thought of the glory of God or of consecration to his service. When God established his covenant with Abraham and gave him Isaac, it was to have him at his disposal as the channel of blessing to the world. When God rewarded the faith of Moses' parents, it was because he wanted a servant by whom he could save Israel. When God redeemed Israel's firstborn in the night of the Passover, it was to have them for himself. Oh, Christian parent, when God offers to be what he was to Isaac and Moses and Israel's firstborn, to your children, it is because he wants them for his service, his blessed service of love and liberty. Oh, say, has he not a right to claim it, and shall he not have it? He gave his Firstborn, his Only-begotten, for you and your children; can anything be too precious for him? Do not listen to the thought that the demand is hard or the sacrifice great. Know that for yourself, as for your children, it is the path of honor and blessing. And let your example teach the Church that there are those who, just because they love their children most intensely, know nothing better for them than to yield them utterly to the will and the work of their God.

O Lord! You are a great and a glorious God, and your kingdom rules over all. You alone are worthy to be praised; you alone have a right to the love and the worship and the service of all your creatures. And this, too, is their blessedness: in heaven above and on earth below, blessed are your servants who stand around your throne and do your will.

O Lord, we bless you that you ask and accept our children for your service. We acknowledge your claim: let them all be used for your service and glory. But especially would we offer you the first and the best.

O God, teach us to feel deeply that you have need of them. For the building up of your temple, in the struggle of your kingdom with the power of darkness, in the ingathering of your people from the hundreds of millions of heathen, you have need of our children. We give them to you. We will train them for you. We will wait in prayer and faith, and beseech you to inspire them with a holy enthusiasm for the kingdom and its conquests. We beseech you to fill them and us with love to Jesus and love to souls, that they may serve you as your Son did, and give their lives to save men.

O Lord God, you have redeemed us and our children by the blood of the Lamb; let our firstborn, let all our children, be holy unto the Lord. Amen.

THIRTEENTH DAY

The Sabbath and the Children

"The seventh day is a Sabbath unto the Lord your God: in it you shall not do any work, you, nor your son, nor your daughter."—*Exodus 20:10*

AMONG the most precious blessings which a child going out into the world from a godly home can take with him is the habit of reverent observance of the Sabbath. In its separation from evil company, in its leading to God's house, in the calm and thoughtful quiet it sometimes brings over his spirit, it will, even if he is still a stranger to grace, be a safeguard and a help, a schoolmaster to bring to Christ. If he is a Christian, it will be one of his surest aids in the growth and strengthening of the life of faith. It is a part of a parent's duty that needs to be studied in earnest prayer, and for the performance of which much wisdom and grace are needed. The Lord, who has enjoined the duty, will not withhold the grace.

Note in the words of the fourth commandment how specially the children are remembered. It is to parents the command is given; it is in the keeping holy of the day by their children, as well as by themselves, that their obedience is to be manifested. "You, nor your son, nor your daughter, nor your man-servant, nor your maid-servant": it is not so much as a private, nor as a national, but as a *family* ordinance, that the Sabbath was first of all appointed. "You, nor your son, nor your daughter": just as the terms of the covenant, "a God to you and to your seed," the words suggest the two thoughts that it is first the parent, and then the child through the parent, with whom God wishes to deal. The parent must first learn to keep the Sabbath day holy himself, then to train his child to keep it holy too.

The parent's keeping holy the Sabbath precedes the training of the child to do so. Here comes up the principle which lies at the root of all true education: What I am to make my child, I must first be myself. Example is more than precept; being, more than teaching; what I am and do, more than what I tell him to be or do. The question is often asked how we can teach our children to revere and love the Sabbath, and in answer many lessons of great value have been given. But we cannot too earnestly insist on the truth that the first requirement is that the day should be a holy day to the parents themselves. It is as they serve God upon it in the beauty of holiness, as the spirit of holiness breathes on and from them in the services of the Sabbath, as that day is to them a day not only of strict observance, but of joyful worship, of quickened devotion, of real loving fellowship with God, as the Sabbath is a delight, that the first condition will be fulfilled for teaching their children to love it.

Let Christian parents note this. God means the Sabbath to be to your child what it is to you, not in value of your training and habits, but what it is to your own *experience*, as a day you really love and rejoice in. Study to this end its wonderful significance and the riches of blessing connected with it.

Look upon it as the day of rest, of entering into God's own wonderful rest. The rest of God is in a finished work; by faith in that work we enter into that rest, and the great calm, the peace that passes understanding, keeps the heart and mind (Genesis 2:3; Hebrews 4:3–10).

Look upon it as a holy day, the day God has given as a token and pledge that he who is holy makes us holy, too (Exodus 31:13; Ezekiel 20:12). It is in fellowship with God that we are made holy; let his presence, his love, his joy, be the mark as well as the fruit of keeping it holy.

Look upon it as a day of blessing (Genesis 2:3). Of the blessing God laid on the day, sin robbed us. In the resurrection of Christ, the finished work of creation was restored, was finished and perfected in a higher sense. Under the leading of the Holy Spirit, the first day of the week, the day of the Lord Jesus, the Sabbath of the new Life, took the place of the Sabbath of death, when the Lord of the Sabbath was in the tomb. The Sabbath of creation, rendered void by the fall and the law, is now glorified in the Sabbath of redemption. And now all the blessings of the Living Christ, his finished work and resurrection power and eternal rest, and of the Holy Spirit, who descended from Heaven on this new Sabbath, are to be made ours by this day. Oh, let it be to you a day of blessing, in the fellowship of the Father's love, and the Son's grace, through the Holy Spirit, and you have taken the first and the surest step for its being a blessing and a joy to your son and your daughter too.

And now comes the second lesson. It is not enough that the parent keep holy the Sabbath day; the Lord lays it upon him to secure the child's doing so too. As parent he is responsible for it and must make it a matter of distinct effort and prayer. It is not enough that Christian parents seek to keep the day holy: the training of their children to do so is a sacred obligation resting upon them, and requires, just on account of its difficulty, the sacrifice of personal enjoyment, the exercise of thought and wisdom, and the patience of much faith and love.

In seeking to do so, there are two dangers to be avoided. In human nature we find that there are two principles implanted in our hearts to guide us to action—pleasure and duty. The former leads us to seek what is agreeable and for our own interest, and is one of the most powerful motives in all our conduct. When our pleasure, however, is at variance with the interests of others or the will of God, the sense of duty comes in to restrain and regulate the desire for pleasure. The reward of obedience to duty is that in course of time it is no longer a check to pleasure, but becomes itself the highest pleasure. The art of education consists in so bringing pleasure and duty into harmony, that without the sacrifice of either, both may be attained.

In training the child to keep holy the Sabbath day, there is a danger of putting either of these principles too exclusively in the foreground. With our Puritan and Covenanting ancestors, the former principle was urged, and the only sanction sought for keeping the Sabbath was the law. In our days we are in danger of the opposite extreme. To make the Sabbath interesting to the children, to make them happy on it, if possible to make them love it as a day of enjoyment, is so exclusively the object of attention that the thought of obligation is almost lost sight of, and the principle almost unconsciously instilled that the day is to be hallowed and loved only as far as it is made interesting and pleasant. Let parents seek grace from him who, as Divine wisdom says, guides in the midst of the paths of right, to be kept from the right-hand as well as the left-hand error.

Do not hesitate to speak of God's command and of duty. God trained Israel as a child in the life of law for the life of love in Christ. Education consists, in its first stages, more in training to right habits than inculcating principles—these come later. Be not afraid, in connection with the Lord's day, of the element of self-denial and quiet self-control which the thought of obedience to God's will and to your will brings over the child's spirit. They are part of the foundation of noble character. Tranquility of mind and serenity of spirit are invaluable blessings; the quiet of the Sabbath helps to foster them. Holiness is much more than separation; it is a positive fellowship and enjoyment of God. But it begins with separation: the putting away of weekday toys and books and companions, the marking off of the day from other days, even in little things, is, under a wise guidance, a preparation for the truer hallowing of it later on.

This on the one side. On the other, exercise a wise and loving thoughtfulness as to the ways in which the day can be made a happy one. In the picture lessons to the younger ones, in the careful selection of suitable and interesting reading for the elder ones, in the merry singing of psalms and hymns and spiritual songs, making melody to the Lord, in the forethought with which possible transgression is guarded, in the tone of gladsome and loving reverence with which the day is spoken of and spent, in the personal intercourse especially given in Bible study and prayer, the believing parent will find the means of leading the child on to call the Sabbath a delight, the holy of the Lord (Isaiah 58:13), and to inherit the blessing promised to those who do so.

Dear Christian parents, how deeply the thought of how we ought to train our children to love the Sabbath reminds us of our shortcomings and our impotence. But let not this discourage us. We have God, the God of the Sabbath, who gave it to us as a token of the covenant he has with us and our children, to sanctify us. We have himself to teach us and our children to sanctify his day. Let us look to him to give us grace to feel and show that the Lord's day is the happiest of the week. In the divided life of the ordinary worldly Christian, it cannot be so. God's commandments cannot be obeyed without a wholehearted surrender to live for him alone, without a life under the full power of his Holy Spirit. But if God is our chief joy, the desire after his service and love our highest aim, he himself will sanctify our Sabbaths, our hearts, our homes, our children, by his Holy Presence. And the Sabbaths will be but a part of a life holy to the Lord.

* * *

Most Holy God! I thank you for the precious gift of the holy Sabbath day, and the wonderful blessings of which it is the pledge. I thank you above all for its redemption, in the death of Jesus, from the power of sin, and its restoration to us in the power and the joy of his risen life. Oh, grant that each succeeding Sabbath may lead me deeper into your rest, the rest of God in Christ, and so into the fellowship of your holiness and your blessedness. May a daily life that seeks its only joy in Christ, and is wholly yielded to the Spirit, prepare me for keeping the day holy.

Blessed Father, I especially ask for grace to train my children to love and hallow your day. I know it: nothing but the joy of your presence in my own life can fit me for it. Give me this. And then give me the wisdom, as your servant, to bring to them the sense of your Holy Will and your loving-kindness, in claiming the day for yourself, and then giving it to them as your own day, that the fear of grieving you and the joy of pleasing you may each find due place in their hearts. So may the command and the promise, the duty and the pleasure, be one to them, and their delight in your day indeed meet the promised reward, "Then shall you delight yourself in the Lord." Amen.

The Children's Commandment

"Honor your father and your mother; that your days may be long in the land which the Lord your God gives you."—*Exodus 20:12*

"Children, obey your parents in the Lord: for this is right."—*Ephesians 6:1*

"Children, obey your parents in all things: for this is well-pleasing in the Lord."—*Colossians 3:20*

THE FIRST FOUR COMMANDMENTS have reference to God, the last five to our neighbor. In between stands the fifth. It is linked to the first four because to the young child, the parent takes the place of God; from him the child must learn to trust and obey his God. And it is the transition to the last five because the family is the foundation of society, and there the first experience comes of all the greater duties and difficulties of intercourse with men at large. As the training school for all our intercourse with God and man, this commandment lies at the foundation of all Divine and human law, of all our worship of God, and all our intercourse with man.

Of the ten, this one is especially the children's commandment. But just on that account, very specially too, the parents' commandment. A wise ruler makes good subjects; a firm commander, faithful soldiers; it is on the parents' character that the children's fulfillment of this precept will depend. And so it leads us to consider what parents must be if they are to succeed in training their children to honor them.

The sentiment of honor, reverence, is one of the noblest and purest our nature is capable of. The power of perceiving what is worthy of honor, the willingness to acknowledge it, the unselfishness that feels it no degradation, but a pleasure, to render it—all this is itself honorable and ennobling; nothing brings more true honor than giving honor to others. This disposition ought to be cultivated most carefully in the child as an important part of his education. It is one of the chief elements of a noble character and a preparation for rendering to God the honor due to him. If the teaching of Scripture to honor God, to honor all men, to honor the widows, to give honor to whom honor is due, is to be obeyed by our children, they must be prepared for it by learning first to honor their parents. If they are to honor God, it must begin by honoring their parents. If they are, in later life, to do what is so difficult—to honor all men, by recognizing even in the degraded and the lost the worth that belongs to them as created in the image of God—they must be carefully prepared for it in the home school of family life. It is not only to secure a happy home and place the intercourse of parent and child on a right footing, but to fit the child for all his future relations to God and his fellow men, and to lay in him one of the foundation stones of a noble character and a holy life that God has placed this commandment the first of those on the second table. Parents may well study how they can train their children to fulfill it.

The child must honor the parent in obedience. "Obey your parents" is the New Testament version of "Honor your father and your mother." The importance of this word, "obedience," is more than the mind can grasp. God created man, with his wonderful liberty of will, that he might obey him. Obedience to God was to lead to the enjoyment of God. By disobedience sin entered; in obedience, the twofold obedience *of* Christ and *to* Christ (Hebrews 5:8–9), salvation comes. And on the parent the sacred charge is laid of training the child to obey, teaching it to link all the memories of happiness and love in home-life with obedience, working the principle into the very life of mind and heart, not so much by instruction or reasoning as by training and securing the habit of obedience. The child is to be taught to honor the parent. The will of the child, no less than his mind and affections, is given into the parent's hands to mold and guide. It is in yielding his will to the will of the parent that the child acquires that mastery over it and over himself which will afterward be its strength and safety, and make it a fit instrument for doing God's will. Man was created free that he might obey; obedience is the path to liberty.

On this point parents often err; they often say that to develop the will of the child the will must be left free, and the child left to decide for himself. They forget that the will of the child is not free—passion and prejudice, selfishness and ignorance, seek to influence the child in the wrong direction. The superior judgment, the calmer deliberation, the fuller experience of the parent, are to decide for the child whose will has been entrusted to his care.

But are we not in danger of repressing the healthy development of a child's moral powers by thus demanding implicit submission to our will? By no means. The true liberty of the will consists in our being master of it, and so our own masters. Train a child to master his will in giving it up to his parents' command, and he acquires the mastery to use when he is free. Yielding to a parent's control is the path to self-control; and self-control alone is liberty. The child who is taught by a wise parent to honor him and his superior wisdom will acquire, as he gives up his own way, the power over his will, as he never can who is taught to imagine that he need do nothing unless the parent has first convinced him of the propriety of the act and obtained his consent. The New Testament says very distinctly, "Children, obey your parents in the Lord: for this is right." Not because the child approves or agrees, but because the command is given by a parent: this is the true reason for its being obeyed. In obedience, the parent is to be honored.

In all his disposition and conduct, too, the child is to be trained to honor the parent. Familiarity breeds contempt; in language and carriage and conduct, parents often tolerate an easygoing familiarity, which, however it may be miscalled by the name of love or kindness, destroys those sentiments of respect and reverence in which true love has its strength and its real happiness. Manners are of more importance than many think; the neglect of good manners not only reveals a want in the disposition of those sentiments of respect and courtesy to which life and intercourse owe so much, but it reacts on the heart and fosters the selfishness and indifference that cares little for others' feelings. Locke has said that next to religion and virtue, manners are the most important thing in education, more so, he thinks, than learning. Let parents remember that in taking trouble to train their children to show them due honor and respect, even in apparently insignificant things, they are forming habits and breathing principles into them which will afterwards repay all their labor. "Him that honors me, I will honor" is God's law, which has its reflection in the life of earth, too. None have received higher honor on earth than those who have learned to honor all men, to honor the poor and needy.

And now, it is the parent who is to cultivate and develop this sentiment in the child. The young child is guided not by reflection or argument, but by feeling and affection. He cannot yet realize and honor the unseen God. He cannot yet honor all men, the wretched and unworthy, for the ideal, the unseen worth of their creation in God's image. The child can only honor what he sees to be "worthy of honor." And this is the parent's high calling: always so to speak and act, so to live in the child's presence, that honor may be spontaneously and unconsciously rendered. This can only be where, in quiet self-recollection and self-control, the parent lives as in God's fear and presence, and walks worthy of this calling, as one who has been placed in the home, at the head of a family, to be not only its prophet and priest, but king, too. Yes, a king receives honor; let the parent as a king reign and rule in love and the fear of God, his honor will be given him.

Above all, let parents remember that honor really comes from God. Let them honor him in the eyes of their children, and he will honor them there, too. Let them beware of this sin, honoring their child more than God; it is the sure way to grief for parents and children together. But from parents, who in everything seek to honor God, children will learn to honor God and them together; the parent who teaches his child to obey the fifth commandment has guided his feet into the way of all God's commandments. A child's first virtue is the honoring and obeying his parents.

O my God! I come again to you with the prayer to open my eyes and give me fully to realize the place of the family in the purposes of your grace, and the parent's holy calling to train his child for all that you would have him be. I ask of you especially to reveal to me in your own light the full import of the fifth commandment, that I may teach my child to fulfill it according to your will. Fill my own soul, I pray you, with such honor and reverence of your holy majesty that both I and my child may learn what honor is. Teach me to claim honor of my child with the holy aim of leading him to honor you, above all. May honoring his parents and honoring his God work in him the spirit of humility, which will gladly render to all their due. And may, above all, I be kept from the terrible sin of ever honoring my child more than God.

O Lord, I look to you, for grace to secure the keeping of this, the children's commandment, in my home. Oh, grant that I may always live in it worthy of all honor. And may the holy power of training young souls to keep your commandments, to honor and serve you, be the fruit of your own Spirit's work in me. I ask it, my God, in Jesus' name. Amen.

FIFTEENTH DAY

Parental Instruction

"This is the commandment which the Lord your God commanded to teach you, that you might fear the Lord your God, to keep all his commandments, which I command you, you, and your son, and your son's son, all the days of your life. You shall love the Lord your God with all your heart. And these words, which I command you this day, shall be in your heart. And you shall teach them diligently unto your children, and shall talk of them when you sit in your house, and when you walk by the way, and when you lie down, and when you rise up."—*Deuteronomy 6:1, 2, 5–7*

"YOU, and your son, and your son's son"—with these words in the second verse, Moses gave expression to the thought that God's purpose in giving his commandments to his people was not limited to the individual or to a single generation, but had in view the people, through its whole existence. This purpose of God's has therefore to be the law of individual duty: each one who received the commandments of God was to strive not only to keep them himself, but to hold himself responsible for their maintenance among his children. "These are the commandments which the Lord commanded to teach you, that you might fear the Lord your God, to keep his commandments, you, and your son, and your son's son," In the following verses (5, 7) this idea is brought forward more prominently and enlarged upon. In verses 20 and 21 the duty is afresh inculcated of expounding to the children the ground of that wondrous relation in which God's people stood to him, and by virtue of which they had been favored with the Divine Law, even the mercy and faithfulness of God that had redeemed them from the land of Egypt. All concentrating in the one important and blessed truth that the fear and faith of God must be seen in family religion, as domestic piety. The grand means for maintaining and extending the fear of God among his people are the faithful performance of parental duty, in harmony with his purpose that his service and blessing should descend from son to son. The special aspect in which God's will is here set before us is parental instruction, and we are taught in the words we meditate on how hearty, how diligent, how unceasing this ought to be.

Parental instruction must be from the heart. We all know how little influence commands or instructions exercise when given by a listless or uninterested teacher. It is only the heart that gains the heart, the loving warmth of interest and affection that can waken corresponding emotions in the bosom of the student. God would secure all the influence of parental love to gain access for his words and will to the youthful and susceptible hearts of the children of his people. He therefore says, "You shall love the Lord your God with all your heart, and these words shall be in your heart: and you shall teach them to your children." How easy and how blessed the work, so often sighed over, if not neglected, to those who listen to God's guidance. As is your duty and your blessedness, love the Lord your God with all your heart. If you love him, love his words, too; let them live in your heart, let them have a place in your affections. And, with the heart filled with God's love and God's words, how easy to have them in your mouth, too, and to teach them to your children. Let holy love to God and his words mingle with all your fond and tender love to your little ones, and it will be a sweet and happy work to win the beloved on earth to the Father beloved in heaven. As often as the work of instructing the children upon earth threatens to become a burden or a weariness, you may be sure it is a token of something wrong within: the love to God in heaven, or the delight in his Word, has been fading. As often as you seek for fresh vigor to perform your work hopefully and joyfully, you have but to turn to the words that reveal the secret of a godly education, and you will experience that as for your children, so for yourself, there is an unspeakable blessing in the wisdom that has so inseparably connected the heart's secret love with the mouth's spoken words: "You shall love the Lord your God with all your heart. And these words shall be in your heart. And you shall teach them to your children." Oh, that we might remember that this is the Divinely appointed ministry and means for the salvation of our children—parental love elevated and strengthened by the love of God, guided and inspired by his own Holy Word.

The parental instruction must likewise be diligent and earnest: "You shall diligently teach them unto your children," or, as it reads in the original, "You shall sharpen them unto your children." The word is used of the sharpening of weapons, as arrows and spears, to make them penetrate deep. It must be no cold declaration of his will that we communicate, no mere intellectual knowledge. It profits little that the dart be cast or the arrow shot from the bow unless they have been sharpened—to pierce the heart of the enemy. And so the godly parent must use diligence to consider how he can best find access to the heart for the words that he speaks. He does this by carefully considering how he can best gain both the child's understanding and affections: by seeking to avail himself of the best opportunities for securing his interest; by studying the art of speaking in the spirit of love, and not without the preparation of prayer. He does it by striving to make his whole life an attractive example of what he has taught, because there is nothing that does so drive home the word of instruction that has touched the heart as the confirmation of a consistent and holy life. Above all, he seeks to do it by waiting for that Holy Spirit who alone can make the word sharp as a two-edged sword, but with whose aid he may experience how true it is: "The words of the wise are as nails fastened by the masters of assemblies, which only are given from one shepherd." God's promise is sure: from earnest, painstaking, and prayerful effort, the blessing of the Spirit will not be withheld.

And to this end the parental instruction must be persevering and continuous. "You shall teach them diligently to your children, and you shall talk of them, when you sit in your house, and when you walk by the way, and when you lie down, and when you rise up." The entrance of Divine truth into the mind and heart, the formation of habit and the training of character—these are not attained by sudden and isolated efforts, but by regular and unceasing repetition. This is the law of all growth in nature, and of this law God seeks to make use in the kingdom of grace, in dependence upon and subservient to the power of the Holy Spirit. This is the principle that is so beautifully applied by Moses to parental duty. The instruction he had enjoined was not to be by means of set times and stated formal lectures; the whole life, with all its duties, has to be interwoven with the lessons of God's presence and God's service. With a heart full of God's love and God's word, the ordinary avocations of daily life were to be no hindrance, but helps to lead the youthful hearts heavenward. The children were to feel that it was no matter that could be done for the day, in the moments of morning or evening prayer; the continued and spontaneous outburstings of the heart in the language of the lips was to prove that it was a life and a joy, that God's presence and love were a reality and a delight. Sitting in the home, or walking by the way—now in quiet rest, then in the labors and duties of the way—now with the Bible of God's grace, and then with the books of God's glory in nature—home retirement and wayside intercourse were equally to afford opportunity and material for recognizing the goodness and rejoicing in the service of the ever-present One. Lying down and rising up—from early morning and its freshness to evening weariness and its repose—the whole of the day and the whole of life was to be the occasion of an uninterrupted fellowship with the Holy One, and of the pointing of the little ones to the unseen and ever near Father in heaven. And lest the objection should be made that all the speaking would but weary and estrange—an objection often made with terrible truth against mere speaking in religion, while heart and life deny it; an objection that is as often, alas, the excuse for a heart that knows no fervent love—lest this objection should be made, we point once more to what is the source and center and secret of all: "You shall love the Lord with all your heart. And the words shall be in your heart. And you shall teach them diligently to your children, and shall talk of them when you sit in your house, and when you walk by the way, when you lie down, and when you rise up." Such a wholehearted love and such a loving piety! Ah, how would it receive wisdom from on high, and be guided by Divine love to know when and how to speak: how it would influence children's hearts with the flame of its own zeal, and find a willing and a loving ear when others could only weary! And how surely it would.

SIXTEENTH DAY

The Consecrated Home

"As for me and my house, we will serve the Lord."—*Joshua 24:15*

IN GOD'S DEALINGS with Noah and Abraham, with Israel in the Passover and at Mount Sinai, we have repeatedly noticed the deep meaning of the united mention of father and children in his commands and promises. "You and your house," "you and your seed," "you and your children," "you and your son." Such is ever the language of the Covenant God. In the words of Joshua we have the response from earth, "As for me and my house." The principle of the Divine dealing is accepted; the parent boldly vouches for his family as well as himself; the covenant engagement of the Father in heaven is met by the covenant obligation of the father on earth. Joshua is to us here the very model of a godly parent, and in him we can see what parental religion ought to be.

Let it be a personal religion. "As for me and my house"—he began with himself. We cannot too strongly press the truth that for a godly education, the first and the most essential requisite is personal consecration. It is good to reflect on our responsibility, to study our duties and the best way of fulfilling them, to speak with our children, and to pray much for them, but all these may be called accessories. The first thing on the part of the parent is a life devoted to God and his service. It is this that creates the spiritual atmosphere the children are to breathe. It is this that gives our performance of duty and our dealings with our children their spiritual influence. It is this that gives our praying and our working its value with God. "As for me"—there must be no hesitation or halfheartedness in the consciousness or the confession of devotion to God's service. As often as the prayer for God's blessing on the children comes up, it must be in the spirit of David: "You, Lord God, know your servant. Therefore now let it please you to bless the house of your servant." With God and men, in the home and out of it, as well as in the hearts of parents themselves, it must be a settled thing: "As for me, I will serve the Lord."

But let yours be as distinctly a family religion. Take your stand for all who belong to you: "As for me and my house, we will serve the Lord." There are pious parents who do not understand that this is their duty and their privilege. They know not what God has put in their power. They imagine they honor God by thinking that the religion of their children is dependent on God's will, apart from their instrumentality. They are so occupied, either with the engagements of their calling in this life, or it may even be with religious work, that they cannot find the time for speaking out and acting out the grand decision, "As for me and my house, we will serve the Lord." Or perhaps the father leaves the religion of the children to the care of the mother, and the mother thinks that the father as head is more responsible; they hesitate or neglect to come to a clear and definite understanding, and the religious education of the children does not take the prominent place it ought to in the intercourse of parents with each other. Let each believing parent take Joshua's words, first in the depth of his own soul, then in fellowship with partner and children. The more we speak it out in prayer and conversation—our house is and must be holy to the Lord, our children must be trained first of all for God and his service—the more mightily will the power of the principle assert itself and help us so to guide the house that it, too, serves the Lord.

The words of Joshua teach us more. Let yours, like his, be a practical religion: "We will serve the Lord." There are many parents with whom the whole of religion consists in salvation, not in service. They pray most earnestly that all their children may be saved; they comfort themselves, if they see them spend their lives in the service of the world, that they will yet be brought in before they die. No wonder that their education for this life has been a failure: they never understood the truth, and never trained their children under its guiding influence, that salvation is subservient to service—that to train for God's service secures the fullest salvation. Did we not hear God say of Abraham, "I have known him, to the end he may command his children and household after him, that they may keep the way of the Lord; to the end that the Lord may bring upon Abraham that which he has spoken of him?" Do we not remember in connection with Israel's deliverance from Egypt the words of God, "Let My people go, that they may serve me," and of Pharaoh, "Go, serve the Lord; let your little ones also go with you." Has not the Holy Spirit spoken, "How much more shall the blood of Christ purge your conscience to serve the living God"? All redemption is for service. God does not will that he should be worshiped without being served. The glory of heaven will be that "his servants shall serve him." Let our lives and our homes be consecrated to serving God; let obedience to his will, the carrying out of his commands, the doing his work, devotion to the interests of his kingdom, give family life its nobility.

And then let yours be a confessed religion. It was in presence of tens of thousands of the children of Israel, with the first symptoms of the falling away that came after his death already beginning to show themselves, that Joshua witnessed this good confession, "Choose you this day whom you will serve; as for me and my house, we will serve the Lord." His was not to be the religion of the nation or the religion of neighbors: all might reject God, and he be left alone; still the Lord Jehovah would be his God. As with Abraham leaving his father's house, and Israel leaving Egypt, his too was to be a religion of decision and confession; a coming out and being separate—one of a peculiar people unto the Lord. This is the religion we want in our family life, where not the example or authority of pious people, not inclination or pleasure, but God's own holy and blessed will, revealed in the leading of the Holy Spirit, is sought after as the law of the house. Oh, how often one hears it said: "It can be no harm to dance or to play cards; there are so many religious people, there are such earnest ministers, in whose houses it is done." How often parents, where early married life was marked by decision and earnestness, have afterward become conscious of declension and coldness, because they gave in to the desire to gratify their children or their friends. Oh, let us believe that though at first sight it may appear hard to be peculiar, yet, if we trust God for his guidance and yield ourselves to his personal friendship and love to walk with him, the blessing of separation will be unspeakable to ourselves and our children, too.

If this page is read by a father or a mother, or by father and mother together, who are conscious that their own and their house's service of God has not been as marked and clear as God and they would have it, let me venture a word of advice. Speak with each other of it. Say it out what you have often felt, but each has kept to himself, that it is your united desire to live as entirely for God as grace can enable you to do. If your children are old enough, gather them, too, and ask if they will not join in the holy covenant, "We will serve the Lord." Let that covenant from time to time be renewed in a distinct act of consecration, that the conviction may be confirmed: "We do want to be a holy family, a house where God does dwell and is well pleased. Ours must be a home wholly consecrated to God." And do not be afraid that strength will not be given to keep the vow. It is not we who have to do the work, and then bring it to God. It is *with* the Father in heaven, calling and helping and tenderly working both to will and to do in us, that we have to work. We may count upon him as the inspirer, to accept and confirm, and himself carry out the purpose of our heart, "As for me and my house, we will serve the Lord."

O Lord my God! I thank you for what I have seen this day, your servant Joshua, the leader of your people Israel into Canaan, in his faithfulness to you as father in his own home. I humbly ask you to give me grace to say as distinctly and as publicly as he did, "As for me and my house, we will serve the Lord."

Lord, may mine be a personal religion. O my Father, let your love to me, and my love to you, be its inspiration and its joy. May my children see that it is with my whole heart I serve you, that it has become a delight and my very nature.

And may mine be a family religion, exercising its influence on my home, gaining and training all to walk with me. Lord, remove every inconsistency and all weakness that might hinder anyone from being wholly yours. May mine be a truly consecrated home.

May mine, too, be a practical religion, serving you day and night. Let the knowing and the doing of God's will, the working for his kingdom, the seeking his glory, be the one desire of our hearts.

May thus our home be a blessing to others in encouraging them to take a stand for you. Lord God, let your Spirit work mightily in the homes of your people, that everywhere this confession may be heard ringing out: "As for me and my house, we will serve the Lord." Amen.

SEVENTEENTH DAY

Consecrated Parents

> "And Manoah said, Now let your words come to pass: how shall we order the child? And what shall we do unto him?"—*Judges 13:12*

AN ANGEL of the Lord had appeared to Manoah's wife, to predict the birth of a child, who should be a Nazarite unto God from his birth, and a deliverer of God's people. The first feeling of Manoah on receiving the tidings from his wife was that to train such a God-given child for God's service, God-given grace would be needed; he therefore entreated the Lord and said, "O my Lord, let the man of God which you did send come again to us, and teach us what we shall do unto the child that shall be born." And when in answer to his prayer the angel came again, his one petition was: "How shall we order the child? And what shall we do unto him?" Let us consider the prayer, the answer, and the attendant blessings.

1. Mark the deep sense of responsibility and unfitness for the holy work of training a child as a Nazarite unto God. The angel had already given Manoah's wife the needful instruction, but Manoah is so deeply impressed with the holiness of their calling as parents of this child that he must needs ask for the angel to come again and teach them. What a contrast to the thoughtless self-confidence with which, in these Gospel days, many Christian parents undertake the training of their children. How little effort is made to realize the importance and solemnity of the work! How little real prayer for the preparation of the Spirit to fit them for it! How little true surrender to a life for God as the only fitness for

training a child for God! What would be thought on earth of a man offering to manage a bank or to navigate an ocean steamer who had no training to fit him for either? And what must be said of the presumption that feels no fear in taking charge of an immortal spirit of such priceless value and undertakes to guide it through the temptations and dangers of life? Would God that all Christian parents might learn from Manoah to feel and confess their ignorance, and, like him, to set themselves at once to seek and obtain the needed grace.

We note, further, how Manoah's sense of need at once found expression in prayer. He believed in God as the living God, as the Hearer of prayer. He believed that where God gave a charge or a work, he would give the grace to do it right; that where God gave a child to be trained for his service, he would give the wisdom needed to do so aright. Instead of the sense of unfitness and feebleness depressing him, or the sense of his obligation setting him to work in his own strength, he simply prayed. Prayer to him was the solution of difficulties, the supply of need, the source of wisdom and strength. Let Christian parents learn from him. Each child is a gift of God as truly as Manoah's, and has as much as his to be trained for God and his service. Like him, we may count most confidently on the Father, who has entrusted the child to us, to give the grace to train. Let us only pray—pray believingly, pray without ceasing—at each step of our work. We may depend upon it, God hears prayer, and no prayer more surely than of a parent seeking wisdom to train his child.

There is one thing more we must specially observe in regard to Manoah's prayer: it was after his wife had told him of the injunctions the angel had given that he thus asked for guidance. He longed to hear them himself, to have full certainty and perfect clearness. As parents, we have in God's Word plain and full directions as to the training of our children; our own experience or that of others may have supplied us with much of great value to aid us in our task. All this does not diminish, it only increases the need of prayer. With each child, and each of its separate needs, we always need renewed wisdom direct from above; daily renewed prayer is the secret of training our children for God.

2. And now the answer. Let us learn the lesson Manoah's story teaches here: God loves to answer a parent's cry. The angel had nothing new to communicate above what he had previously said to the woman, and yet God sent him because he would not leave his child, who seeks to know his will fully, in the dark. The fact of the angel having come once

was what had encouraged Manoah to hope he might come a second time. Just they who have already had communications with God, and have had Divine teaching about their children, will be those who desire more and pray for it most earnestly.

The answer to Manoah's prayer contained no new revelation; it simply pointed back to the instruction previously given: "Of all that I said unto the woman, let her beware; all that I commanded her, let her observe." In answer to our prayer, it may be that no new truth will be revealed, perhaps even no new thought impressed. But the answer to the prayer may be something better. As the Holy Spirit leads us back to what the Lord has already spoken, to study more carefully and adopt more unreservedly the principles laid down in Holy Scripture for the training of our children, we shall realize as never before how our children are the Lord's and must be kept holy for him; how parents are God's ministers, in whose holy life the children are to be blessed.

It is this last thought that comes out with special clearness. What were the commandments that had been given and were now renewed? The angel had only spoken of the life of the mother before the birth of the child: the Nazarite child must have a Nazarite mother. The giving up of the fruit of the vine, the sacrifice of the stimulus and excitement and enjoyment of the world and the flesh, the not eating any unclean thing, separation to special purity and holiness—this was God's secret of parental duty. Education consists not so much in anything we do or say, but most of all in what we are; and that not only when our children are of an age to see and judge, but long before, even before their birth. In that holy time of mystery, when mother and child are still one, and influences from a mother's spirit pass into the child, God says, "Of all that I said unto the woman, let her beware; all that I commanded her, let her observe." It is a life of moderation and self-denial that does not ask how far and deep it may go into the world to enjoy all that is not absolutely forbidden, but that willingly gives up whatever is not helpful to entire consecration and fellowship with God; it is a life of purity and obedience that is the preparation for a mother's and a father's work. God's answer to the prayer, "How shall we order the child?" is, "As you live, you train: live a Nazarite, holy to the Lord, and your child will be a Nazarite unto God, a deliverer of his people Israel."

3. The blessing that attended Manoah's prayer was something more than the answer. There was the blessed revelation of God himself, and the

wonderful knitting together of the hearts of the parents. Before he left them, the angel of the Lord so revealed himself that Manoah felt, "We have seen God." When he asked the angel's name, he might not know it; his name was WONDERFUL. And the angel did wondrously. And this is still the name of the parent's God, WONDERFUL. It is as with Manoah we pray, and wait for, and accept his Divine teaching, and then ask him to wait that we may bring him an offering, that our eyes will be opened to see wondrous things, and to fall down and worship him. Wonderful in his love, wonderful in his ways, wonderful in his work, wonderful in what he does for us as parents, and wonderful in what he does through us for our children; oh, let us worship the Lord, the parent's God, whose name is WONDERFUL! And let our prayer, like Manoah's, end in praise and worship, in faith and truth.

And how rich was the blessing this revelation brought to the praying couple. What a picture the chapter gives us of the way in which father and mother are lovingly to help each other in all that concerns their children. Manoah's wife gets the message from the angel; immediately she tells her husband. He prays at once for more light and fuller teaching. The angel comes again to her; she runs to tell Manoah, who follows her. He hears again what his wife had been told. When the sacrifice was offered, and the angel did wondrously, Manoah and his wife looked on together, and together fell on their faces to the ground. And when Manoah was afraid, and spoke, "We shall surely die because we have seen God," she comforted him and strengthened his faith.

Blessed fellowship of love and faith, of prayer and worship between husband and wife, to which the coming and the training of a child can lead! Oh, it is not only parents who are to be a blessing to their children; no, but children to their parents, too. As they talk together of God's promises and his commands, as each tells the other what has been revealed to him, as they unite in seeking to know and carry out God's will, as they now pray in presence of each other, and then fall down in worship before him whose name is WONDERFUL, as they unburden their fears, and encourage each other to trust and hope, they experience that the home school is as much for training parents themselves as their children, and that there is nothing that opens the fountains of Divine love and of each other's love more than the prayerful desire to know how to order the children God has given them for his service and glory.

* * *

Blessed Lord! As those whom you have joined together to train children for your holy service, we bow in united worship before you. Make us by your Holy Spirit to be so of one heart and mind, that all you reveal to the one may at once be witnessed to the other. Grant that in our conversations and our prayers, in our weakness and fear, in our faith and our worship, we may feel what blessing and help there is in your having sent us two and two to each little flock of children to be tended.

Lord God, we come to you now for wisdom for each child you have given us. Of each one we would say, "What shall be the ordering of the child, and what shall we do unto him?" Open our eyes to see the treasures of wisdom in your Holy Word, in promise and instruction for parents and children. Especially reveal yourself to us, we beseech you, as the God of the covenant and the promise, the parent's God, whose name is WONDERFUL. Teach us in holy fear and reverence, in childlike trust and joy, in purity of life and separation from the world, to walk before you, and so to train children that are Nazarites, holy to the Lord, prepared to fight for the kingdom and to be the deliverers of the oppressed. Amen.

EIGHTEENTH DAY

A Consecrated Child

> "For this child I prayed; and the Lord has given me my petition which I asked of him: therefore I also have granted him to the Lord; as long as he lives, he is granted to the Lord."—*1 Samuel 1:27–28*

THE INTERCOURSE between the believing parent and the Lord in reference to his child has been set before us under different aspects. In Samuel's story we have a new and very beautiful expression of the relation. Hannah has received a child from the Lord in answer to her prayer; the love and joy of her heart can find no better way of expressing themselves than in her giving her child to the Lord again, to be the Lord's as long as he lives. In very deed, just the thought that comes up into the heart of many a Christian mother as she looks on her firstborn little one—a thought that has only to be considered carefully to open up to us some of the most precious lessons of parental faith and duty. Whether we think of God, of our child, of ourselves, there is every reason to say, "As long as he lives, he is given to the Lord."

Or does not, so the mother speaks, the child belong to God? Was it not to bear his own image, as his servant, for his own glory, that he created man, that my child, too, has been born? God looks upon him as his; he has only been lent and entrusted to me to train. It is indeed not mine but the Lord's. And because I am naturally so inclined to forget this, to love and treat the child as if it were altogether mine, I count it such a precious privilege, in a distinct act of surrender, to give it to the Lord for all the days of its life.

And God has not only a right to the child, but he needs him. The work he has to do upon earth is so great, and he has so arranged for each his work, that he would not miss one single one of his people's children. I have so often heard or read of a mother joyfully sacrificing an only son, or all her sons, for her king or country; and shall I not count it an honor to give to my King the child which is his, and which he has lent me, with the privilege of loving and training and enjoying it? Do I not love him, and have I not often asked what I can render to him for his love to me? And shall I not delight to give what is my most precious possession upon earth to be his? Yes, to him who gave his Son for me, to him alone, all I am and have belongs; my child, too, I have given to the Lord as long as he shall live.

But it's not only for God's sake; for my child's sake, too, I give it to the Lord. The more I love it, the more heartily I give it away to God. Nowhere can it be safe or happy but with him. I do indeed love my precious little one, and yet how little I can do for it! I know it is born in sin, and has inherited from me an evil nature, which no care or love of mine can overcome. If I give it to God, I know that he accepts of it and takes it for his own, to make it his own. He will make it one with his beloved Son, cleansing it in the precious blood, and, in a second birth by his Spirit, giving it a new and holy nature. He, the great God, will adopt my child as his, and make it his here, taking it up to his own home through eternity. He will use me as his minister, giving me all the wisdom I need to train my child worthily as his. Oh, do not ask me why I give my child to God! It is because I love it. Who would not give their child to such a God, for such blessings?

And for my own sake, too, I give it to the Lord, for—and this is so wonderful—the child I give to God becomes doubly my own. In the consciousness of the wonderful partnership between God and me, I feel that the child I give to God, and he then holds for me and yet gives back, I can love with an intenser and a holier love. I then possess it without the fear of sinning in loving it as my own, without the fear of ever losing it. Even if death were to come and take it from me here, I would know that it was still mine in the Father's home, only taken from me for a time to serve in the King's own palace. God gave it me; I gave it back to him. God gave it once again to me; and once again I gave it back to him; giving my child has become the link of a most blessed friendship and intercourse between God and me.

And if he leaves it with me on earth, having given it to him and knowing that it is his gives the confidence that all the grace and wisdom I need for training it will be given. I need have no care; my child is now the Lord's: will he not provide for all his child's needs? If the parent would know to love and enjoy and train his child aright, let him give the child to God.

Such are some of the blessed grounds on which a parent gives his child to God. Let us now consider how this consecration of the child is to be maintained and carried out in education.

Let the parent use it as a plea with God in prayer. The grace promised for training a child, though most certain, is not given at once, but just as the grace for our own personal life, day by day. In the education of our children, difficulties will often arise, in which it is as if God's help does not come. Then is the time for prayer and faith. The power of sin may manifest itself in the child; in his natural character there may at times be more to waken fear than hope. Our own ignorance or unfaithfulness or feebleness may often make us fear that, though God is faithful, we may be the cause of our child's not growing up the Lord's. At such times, as at all times, God must be our refuge. Let us then maintain our consecration of the child, and plead it: we gave it to the Lord; we abide by it; we refuse to take it back because either we or the child are guilty; we plead for grace for the child that has been given by us and accepted by God. The more we do this, it will become in our souls a settled thing, definitely and finally settled, that what we gave God took, that it is his now, and that we can leave it with him. Such faith will give rest and bring a sure blessing.

Let us use it as a plea with our child, too. Let him, even if we do not often say so in words, feel that it is implied in all our intercourse with him that he has been given away to God. Let him know that this is the reason we cannot give way to his will or to allow sin in him—we have a charge from God to keep him for God. Let him mark, in our holy gentleness and firmness, that this is not a profession, but a principle that really animates us. Let him realize it so that it gradually becomes a motive with himself; he has been given to God and accepted by him; how should he disobey or grieve God? Let not our words, but the whole spirit of our life and prayer and education, make the child feel, I am the Lord's.

Let us use it as a plea with ourselves, a motive to the faithful discharge of our duties. The pressing avocations of life, the spirit of the world all around us, the little help we receive from the Church in regard to the consecration of our children and a really consecrated education, makes even godly parents grow unwatchful or negligent. And a really consecrated education needs a high tone of devotion in daily life, and that without ceasing. Let us from time to time look at our children in the light of this great transaction with God—I have given my child to the Lord—to stir ourselves to diligence, to faith, and to prayer. Let us very specially act under the influence of this motive as we think of the profession we educate our child for. God needs servants for his temple; let us ask him what the place is he has for each child in his kingdom. If such a spirit animated each parent who has given his child to God, surely a far larger number of young Christians would grow up to work for God. If all the children professedly consecrated to God were really brought up as such, if we had consecrated parents as Hannah, and a consecrated education as Samuel's, we should have no lack of men to stand up and take their place in the service of God's temple. May God by his Holy Spirit teach us the full meaning and power of the words we use: "I have given my child to be the Lord's as long as he lives."

O Lord my God! Hear, I pray you, a mother's prayer, as I come to you with the child you have given me. O my God, I have heard that you allow the mother to give her child back again to you, and that, having accepted and sealed it for your own, you entrust it to her again. O my Father, it is now yours—and mine! My soul bows in the dust at the thought of this inexpressible privilege, this joint ownership in my child between God and me. I look to you for the grace to enable me to keep this treasure, to be given back to you with usury.

Teach me, I pray you, to love it with a holy love, and to train it for the service of your temple. Teach me to speak to it of you and your love, so that its heart may early be won for you. May my whole life be to it an inspiration, inviting and helping to what is pure and lovely, to what is holy and well pleasing to you. And, of your great goodness, cause my child early to hear the voice that called Samuel, and in childlike simplicity and reverence to answer, "Speak, Lord, your servant hears."

O Lord, you will not despise a mother's prayer. You accept my surrender. By your blessing we shall be a consecrated mother and a consecrated child. Amen.

NINETEENTH DAY

Parental Weakness

> "You honor your sons above me; them that honor me I will honor, and they that despise me shall be lightly esteemed."—*1 Samuel 2:29–30*
>
> "I will judge his house for ever, for the iniquity which he knows; because his sons made themselves vile, and he restrained them not."—*1 Samuel 3:19*

SOME MEN are born to rule; it costs them no trouble, it is their very nature; they often do it unconsciously. Others there are to whom it never comes naturally; they either shrink from it, or, even if they attempt it, they utterly fail. They appear to be wanting in the gifts that fit them for the work; it is always a struggle and an effort. In ordinary life men can choose, or are chosen for, the situations they have to fill as rulers or commanders. In family life we see a strange and very solemn spectacle: every parent has to rule, whether he is fit for it or not. Nor does the fact of his unfitness take away his responsibility; the terrible consequences of his failure to rule are still visited upon himself and his children. The picture of feeble old Eli, faithful to God's cause and ready to die for the ark of God, but unfaithful to his duty as parent and unable to restrain his sons, suggests to us the very needful inquiry as to the causes, the consequences, and the cure of parental weakness.

1. We have spoken of natural incapacity for ruling as one cause. But this is never so absolute that determined effort could not to some extent remedy it, much less that the grace of God could not change it. We must therefore look for other causes. And of these the chief is the want of self-

discipline. A Christian may not ask what is easy or natural, what he likes or what appears possible. His one question must be, "What is duty? What has God commanded?" There is wonderful strengthening, even for the weakest character, in giving itself up to the Divine "ought" and "must" of God's will. The fear of grieving the Father, the desire of pleasing him, the assurance of his strength to aid our weakness—such thoughts awaken and fortify the energies of the soul. The will wakes up, and nothing is so invigorating as the hearty effort to obey. It is because the Christian parent too little realizes, and is too little taught by the Church, that ruling his home well is a simple matter of duty, a command that must be obeyed, that so many children are ruined by parental weakness. Not to restrain the child is to dishonor God by honoring the child more than God, because the duty God has imposed is made to give way to the child's will.

Closely connected with this is the good-natured weakness, misnamed kindness, which cannot bear ever to reprove, to thwart, or to punish a child. It is nothing but a form of sloth: it cannot take the trouble to rule and guide its feelings by God's Word; it refuses the pain which punishing causes the parent. Alas, it does not know that it chooses the greater pain of seeing the child grow up unrestrained. No grace of the Christian life is obtained without sacrifice; this very high grace of influencing and forming other souls for God needs special self-sacrifice. Like every difficult work, it needs purpose, attention, and perseverance.

But the chief cause of parental weakness will be found deeper still—the want of a life of true devotion to God himself. God is the great Ruler and Educator; the powers that be—the parents' powers, too—are ordained of God; he who does not live under command to God in his own life does not have the secret of authority and command over others. It is the fear of God that is the beginning of wisdom, of wisdom for the work of ruling, too; it is the failure in personal godliness that is the root of parental failure.

2. And now the consequences of such parental weakness. There is one element in the law of consequences under which we live that makes it specially solemn and terrible. It is this: that ordinarily they are not experienced until it is too late to redress them. Our actions are seeds; no one who looks at the little seed could ever imagine what a great tree, what noble or what bitter fruit, could come from it. Consequences, as seen in those around us, somehow hardly affect us; self-interest flatters itself with the pleasing hope that, in our case at least, the results will

not be so disastrous. Let me plead with parents, when conscience or experience tells them that they too have been guilty of consulting the will of their children more than the honor of God, to look at the picture of Eli and his home under God's judgment. Let them ponder carefully what God says. Let them remember that throughout the universe there is no well-being but in harmony with the law of our being. In earth and heaven, in nature and grace, in the individual, the family, and the Church, obedience to the law under which God constituted a creature is the only possible path to happiness. To disobey that law is to court misery. And if the parents, destined of God to bear in the home the likeness of his own Fatherly rule, from ignorance or sloth give way to weakness, they must expect the natural results. It may not always become manifest in the same degree or with equal speed, but in the loss of power to their child's character, in the loss of peace and happiness, in many cases in the loss of the soul forever, they must reap what they sow. God appointed parental rule in the family as the symbol of his own authority, in which parents and children alike are to honor him; to dishonor him is to lose his favor and blessing.

3. The cure of such weakness. In speaking of the causes, we have already indicated some of the remedies. The first one is this: the determined purpose, by God's grace, to do God's will. My duty is never measured by what I feel it within my power to do, but by what God's grace makes possible for me. And I never can know fully how much grace can enable me to do until I begin. It is only little by little that the evil habit will be conquered. But to him that has, more shall be given. Let the weak parent accept it as a God-imposed duty: he must rule his children. Let him remember that not to rule and restrain his children means that both parent and child dishonor God by not doing his will. Let him yield himself to the God of grace, with the purpose to do his will, however impossible it appear; the surrender will be accepted, and the grace not withheld. Step by step, amidst many a failure, the honest effort to do God's will cannot remain without its reward.

Next to this, let the parent who has failed study some of the simplest laws in the art of ruling. It is often owing to the entire ignorance and neglect of these that failure comes. Ruling, like any other art we are ignorant of, must be learned. Some of these rules, as often given, are as follows: Do not give too many commands at once; begin if need be with only one. If you secure obedience to one, your own and the child's consciousness of your power to rule is established. Do not command what you cannot enforce, or what the child has not the power to obey. Begin and prove your authority when it is easy for you to secure obedience and the child to render it; in all learning we proceed from the easy to the less easy. Let the command be given in quiet, deliberate tones, with full self-control; hasty, ill-regulated injunctions lead to disobedience. Self-rule is the secret of all rule; as you honor the law yourself in self-command, others learn to honor it, too.

Above all, let the Christian parent who would rule well remember God. He is God's minister, doing God's work. God loves the children, and wants them trained for himself. He is your covenant-God; depend upon him to be your help and strength. It is God who, through you, will rule your home. Yield yourself to him. Pray not only for help, but believe most certainly it is given. Believe not only, but act in the assurance that it is given, and is beginning, little by little, to work in you. Say to your Father that you desire to do your duty at any risk, and to honor him with your children. And, depend upon it, in the spirit of a quiet, restful assurance, that here, too, God's strength will work in your weakness.

O my God! With fear and trembling would I bow before you, the righteous God, who will not give your honor to another, nor suffer sin, even in your servants, to go unpunished. Impress deeply upon my heart, O Lord, the solemn lessons you teach your Church by the terrible sight of your judgment on the house of Eli your servant.

Not to rule and restrain our children—to give them their own way—is to honor them more than you. Before we think it, weakness becomes wickedness, in ourselves and our children too. You have made every parent after your image, a king in his home, that he may rule his home well and command his children in the way in the Lord. On his exercise of authority, and their rendering of obedience, you have made your blessing dependent.

O God, have mercy upon us. Let the thought of your command to rule our home, of your judgment on disobedience, of your promised grace to those who give themselves to obey, of your blessing on a home ordered in your fear, stir us with our whole heart to fulfill our holy calling in your fear. And let us, above all, believe that as we and our children in this fulfill your will, we are in the path of true blessing for this life and the life to come. Amen.

TWENTIETH DAY

The Father as Intercessor

"And it was so, when the days of their feasting were gone about, that Job sent and sanctified them, and rose up early in the morning, and offered burnt-offerings according to the number of them all: for Job said, It may be that my sons have sinned and renounced God in their hearts. Thus did Job continually."—*Job 1:5*

WHAT A BEAUTIFUL PICTURE of a man in whose heart the fear of God lives! He fears lest his children sin against God or forsake him in their heart. He is so deeply conscious of the sin of their nature that, even when he does not know of positive transgression, the very thought of their having been in circumstances of temptation makes him afraid. He so fully realizes his position and privilege as father that he sends for them to sanctify them, and takes upon himself the continual offering of the needed sacrifice. Job is here another example, among Bible saints, of a servant of God in whom faith in God takes up the whole home in its intercession, and whose fear of God extends to the sin of the children too. God could hardly have said of him, "There is none like my servant Job in the earth, a perfect and an upright man, one that fears God, and eschews evil," if this element of true piety had been wanting. The book might have been complete without it, as far as the record of Job's patience and faith is concerned, but we should have missed the so much-needed lesson: a man's entire consecration to God implies the consecration of the home life, too. Let us study the lesson his example teaches.

1. A deep sense of the sinfulness and the sins of his children is

one of the marks of a godly parent. It is to conquer and free from sin that God entered into the parental covenant with Abraham. It was on account of sin, and to deliver from its cause, that the blood of the lamb was sprinkled in the Passover. It was to lead from sin to the service of God that parents were constituted the instructors of their children. In all God's dealings with us in redemption and grace, in his revelation in Christ and his Cross, he has one object: to save us from sin and make us partakers of his holiness. And if the parent is to be God's fellow worker, if the authority God delegates to him is to be used aright, and the blessing promised to him is to come true, it can only be if God finds the parent in harmony with himself, hating sin with a perfect hatred, and seeking, above everything, to keep or cast it out of his home.

And have we not all to confess how superficial our views of sin are? And how easily we often are satisfied, while, under the appearance of what is good and loving, sin may be lurking, or our children be growing up renouncing God in their hearts! And how sadly wanting we are in that deep sense of the grief and dishonor to God which our children's sin is, and which ought to be the motive that urges us most strongly to plead for its forgiveness and strive for its putting away! Let parents ask God to give them a right sense of what sin is in their children, in its curse, its dishonor to God, its power. And let us ask him to work in us a very deep and very clear conviction that his great object in taking us into covenant as his ministers to the children is that sin may be cast out of them. This is the one thing that he aims at, that the power of Christ's victory over sin may be seen in them, that we and they and our home may be holy to the Lord.

2. Very special watchfulness, where there is special temptation, will be the natural fruit of such fear of sin. Job knew that at a time of feasting there would be special danger, and as often as the days of feasting were past, he sent for his sons and sanctified them. What an impression these children must have received of the fear of sin in their God-fearing father, and how it would waken in them the need of watchfulness and the fear of forgetting God! Every thoughtful parent knows how there are times and places when the temptations of sin come more speedily, and more easily surprise even the well-disposed child. Such are the times, both before and after a child goes into the company and the circumstances where he may be tempted, that a praying father and mother should do what Job did when he sent for his sons and sanctified them. A Christian

man, only lately converted, has told of the indelible impression made by his mother taking him into her room, just as he was in full glee to start on his first long journey from home, and praying with him that he might be kept from sin.

Let us ask God to make us very watchful and very wise in availing ourselves of opportunities. There are times when conscience in a child is especially sensitive, and a word fitly spoken will sink deep into the heart. There are times when conscience has been slighted, and when a word or prayer will help to waken it up and restore its authority. A parent who is in sympathy with God's purpose as to destroying sin, and who holds himself at God's disposal, will be guided from on high as to when and how to speak, to awaken and strengthen in the child the consciousness of sin and its danger.

3. A godly parent has power with God to intercede. Job not only sent for his children to speak; he sanctified them, through the burnt-offerings he offered. The parent who has in baptism accepted the sign of the sprinkling of he blood for his child, who has sprinkled the blood on the door-posts of his home, has a right to plead that blood with God. His faith obtains pardon for the child. And he has a right to intercede for the grace that can save and sanctify. We have, through the whole course of God's dealings with parents, from Noah downward, seen that God gives the parent the right and the power to appear and act in behalf of the child, and that such representative action is accepted. To lay hold of this clearly is the very essence of parental faith; to act upon it, the secret of parental power and blessing. The whole family constitution is based upon this; all the other influence a parent is to exert depends much on his being clear on this point: I am the steward of God's grace to the child; I represent the child with God and am heard on his behalf. This makes him confident in saying, I represent God with my child; I have God's help to give me influence and power. I have overcome the power of my child's sin in pleading with God for him; I am sure of conquering it in pleading with my child.

Dear parents! Let us plead very earnestly that God may by his Spirit enlighten our hearts to know this, our calling as parents, to intercede and prevail for our children. We want the Holy Spirit so to shine upon God's purposes with us that in our family life, and the intercourse with our children, the first thing shall be not the happiness of parental love and intercourse, not the care for the providing all the good gifts they daily need; not the thought of their education for a life of prosperity and usefulness, but the yielding ourselves to God's redeeming love, to be every day the ministers of its grace and blessing. Let us live to secure God's purpose—the deliverance from sin; let us act in the assurance that he will use us. And our family life, even though there may be still the remains of sin in the home, shall evermore be lighted up with God's own presence and with the joy of the heavenly home, of which it is the nursery and the image.

Gracious God! I humbly ask you to print deep in my heart the lessons your holy Word was given to teach. May Job, who has taught your saints so much of patience in the hour of trial, and of your wondrous grace in delivering from it, be to all parents a lesson and a model of the God-fearing parent.

Teach us, we pray you, how this marks the fear of God in its full power and extent, when it trembles at the sins of the children and intercedes for them as its own. Oh, teach us, Lord, to fear sin as the one thing your soul hates, and to make it our one care that the children do not sin.

Teach us to realize our God-given position as intercessors, and to plead the blood for them as definitely and as believingly as for ourselves. May we know in faith that we are heard.

And teach us so in prayer to bring them with us, so to speak and pray at the right time and way, that from us they may learn both the fear of God and the confidence of faith. O God, if we are indeed your children, may this element distinctly mark our piety and our faith, that they embrace and influence our homes as much as ourselves, that they stamp home and family life: wholly the Lord's. Amen.

TWENTY-FIRST DAY

The True Good

"Come, you children, hearken unto me;
I will teach you the fear of the Lord.
What man is he that desires life,
And loves many days, that he may see good?
Keep your tongue from evil,
And your lips from speaking guile.
Depart from evil, and do good;
Seek peace, and pursue it."
—*Psalm 34:11–14*

THERE IS A SCIENCE called Ethics, which seeks to discover the laws which should regulate human conduct, and so to teach the art of living aright. In the pursuit of its object, the science seeks to find out what is the moving principle which urges men to act as they do, or, in other words, what the aim is they propose to themselves. In the discussions on this point, the word that comes up universally is THE GOOD. Men propose to themselves some good or other as the reward of their efforts.

The students of Ethics are divided into two great schools according to the meaning they attach to the word "good." With some, it expresses the good of well-being, the possession or enjoyment of what is desirable. They maintain that happiness, our own or that of the human race, the fear of pain and the desire of pleasure, is and ought to be the motive of conduct.

Another school takes higher ground. It maintains that, though the desire of happiness is innate and legitimate, it may not be man's first or ultimate aim. Happiness will be the accompaniment and the reward of something higher. The good not of well-being, but of well-doing, is the only true good. The ideas of right and wrong are deeper and holier than those of pleasure and pain. To teach men to do good is their ideal.

In the words of our psalm, children are invited to come and learn what the secret of a happy life is. The call appeals to the desire for happiness: "Who is he that would see good?" The teacher promises to show the path to the enjoyment of true well-being. That path is: "Depart from evil, and do good." God has so ordered our nature that well-being will follow well-doing: to do good is the sure way to see good.

But our inspired teacher goes further. He not only tells of our seeing good and doing good, but would teach us the secret of *being* good. This human science cannot teach. It may speak of the value of uprightness and purity in the inner motive to make conduct really good; it cannot show us what the true, the only pure and purifying motive is. The Psalmist tells us, "Come, you children, hearken unto me; I will teach you the fear of the Lord." The fear of the Lord—this is the beginning of all wisdom and goodness. It is doing what we do unto the Lord, for his sake and as obedience to him; it is our personal relation to God that makes conduct really good. To fear God—this is being good; then follows doing good; then seeing good.

Christian parents have in this call, "Come, you children, hearken unto me," words prepared for them by the Holy Spirit to use with their children. They are God's ministers to teach the children the fear of the Lord, the path to the true, the highest good. Let us try and take the lessons home to ourselves that we have to give them.

To begin with the lowest, "seeing good": "What man is he that desires life, and loves many days, that he may see good?" Let parents not be afraid of promising their children that it shall be well with them if they do, indeed, fear God. With a Creator of infinite goodness and wisdom it cannot be otherwise: doing right and pleasing him must bring blessing and happiness. The desire for happiness may not be the only or the first motive for a man's conduct. Experience has proved that those who make it their first object fail; while they who gave it a second place, subordinate to duty, find it. It is so in religion very specially. God commands us to be happy; he promises us joy; but always in connection with our being in the right relation to himself and his will. So the previous verse had said (verse 10), "They that seek the Lord shall not want any good thing." The promises that God will do us good are many. "I will surely do you good," he said to Jacob. To Israel he spoke: "Do right and good, that it may be well with you." The principle expressed in the prayer, "Be good to them that do good," tells that the favor and friendship of God, his peace and presence, his guidance and help, will come to those who do his will. Such obedience and doing good will bring a blessing even for this life, too.

Let our children learn it early, that if they would see good, it will be found with God. Let them learn it of us not as a doctrine, but as a personal testimony; let us show them that the service of God makes us happy, and that the good which God bestows is our one desire and our highest joy.

The next step is doing good. Let us seek in the hearts of our little ones to link inseparably well-doing and well-being. "Blessed is the man that fears the Lord." The Christianity of our day has so learned to seek only safety in religion, but pleasure and happiness in the world, that it will need a very clear testimony to fill our children with the thought that to do God's will and serve is in itself blessedness, is enjoyment. No trouble ought to be great if we can teach them these lessons.

And now comes the teaching as to what doing good is: "Keep your tongue from evil, and your lips from speaking guile. Depart from evil, and do good; seek peace, and pursue it." Sins of the tongue, sins of disobedience, sins of temper: these are the three principal temptations children are exposed to, and against which parents have to guard them.

"Keep your tongue from evil, and your lips from speaking guile." Let the Christian parent strive after a deep conviction of the power of the tongue. It reveals what is in the heart; it sets it further on fire, by encouraging the utterance of the evil there. It is the medium of intercourse and influence on others. It is the index of the presence or the want of that integrity or uprightness which is the very foundation of true character. Parents! Study above everything to make your children true—first true in words, and then true in heart and deed. A child's truthfulness and integrity may be the beginning of his walking in the truth of God. "I have no greater joy than to hear that my children walk in the truth"—let this be your aim even with the little children.

"Depart from evil, and do good." To a young child the first evil is that which his parent forbids. The parent is to him as a conscience, as a God. Train your little ones to flee from evil, to depart, to come away from everything naughty and forbidden. And to do good: keep it occupied, if possible, in what is good, as being allowed by you and pleasing to you.

Stir and strengthen its young will, train it to do good—not to think and wish and feel good, but to *do* it. It is the will, and what it does, that makes the man.

"Seek peace, and pursue it." To quarrel is a sin that comes so easily with children. Let us train ours to respect the rights of others, to bear and to forgive when ours are affected, or to seek redress only from the parent. "Blessed are the peace-makers, for they shall be called the children of God"—this is one of the words to which the education of the nursery and the home must lead them.

But we have still the highest good to speak of: we must not only seek good, and do good, but *be* good. Only a good tree can bring forth good fruit. And what is it to be good? What is the disposition that makes the good man or the good child? "I will teach you the fear of the Lord." There is none good, and no good, but God; if we seek and find him, we find all good. It is in the fear of the Lord that good conduct has its spring, that virtue has its worth. "In singleness of heart, fearing God: whatever you do, do it heartily, as unto the Lord"; it is the personal relation to God carried out into all our conduct that constitutes the fear of the Lord. It is not the fear of a slave, but of a child, twin sister to hope and love: "The Lord takes pleasure in them that fear him, in those that hope in his mercy."

And how can the fear of the Lord be taught? Dear Christian parents! You know the answer: only by yourselves walking in the fear of the Lord all the day. Seek to train your children to understand the connection between seeing good, or always being blessed and happy; and doing good, or a life in which we always choose what is right; and being good, or having a heart filled with the fear and love of God. Train them to it by living it. Let them see you walk in the fear of the Lord all the day, his holy presence resting on you and brought with you into daily life. Let them see in your conduct that religion is a holy sentiment and emotion, a power in the heart which moves the will in everything to do what is good. And let the light of your eyes and the brightness of your face be the exposition and the confirmation of God's truth, "Blessed is the man that fears the Lord."

O my God! I ask for grace to take to heart, and wisely to apply in dealing with my children, the lessons of your Word.

May my whole intercourse with them be full of the joyful assurance that the fear of the Lord is the path to the enjoyment of all good, and that your service is happiness. Let this be so real that all thought of there being pleasure in the world or sin may pass away.

Help me to teach them the fear of the Lord by instruction and example and the spirit of my life. May thoughtfulness and truthfulness and lovingness mark the conversation of my home, and the life of all be holy to the Lord. Day by day I would show them, through your grace, how departing from every—even little—evil, and doing good, with a following after peace and holiness, is what your fear teaches.

Give me grace, above all, to teach them that the fear of the Lord itself is the true good, the principle of all good. May we walk as children in the full light of your countenance, only fearful of offending you, or not rendering your Holy Majesty the reverence due to you. And let ours be the true Christian life of your disciples of old, who, walking in the fear of the Lord and in the comfort of the Holy Spirit, were multiplied.

O my God, I beseech you, make me a parent such as you would have me, and let on me and my home your blessing rest. Amen.

TWENTY-SECOND DAY

Training

"Train up a child in the way he should go; and even when he is old, he will not depart from it."—*Proverbs 22:6*

THIS PROMISE is the scripture expression of the principle on which all education rests: that a child's training can decide what his later life is to be. Without this faith, there could be no thought of anything like education; when this faith is elevated to a trust in God and his promises, it grows into the assurance that a parent's labor will not be in vain in the Lord.

Education has been variously defined as fully developing a child's faculties; fitting him to fulfill his destiny; and developing in him all the perfection of which he is capable. Such definitions have their value for every parent who would thoroughly understand his work, and yet their application is dependent upon the further statement of what his faculties and his destiny really are and wherein his highest perfection would consist. It is only when the real aim of education is first clearly and firmly grasped that its work can be successful. Just as, in our text, everything will depend on a correct view of what is "the way in which he should go," only then can the training do its work in the assurance of the Divine fulfillment of the promise.

There have been so many failures in religious training that a spirit of doubt has grown up as to whether a principle like this can be regarded as holding universally good. With such doubt, we undermine God's covenant. Let us rather believe that the failure was owing to man's fault: "Let God be true, and every man a liar." Either the parent did not make "the way in which he should go" his one aim in the child's training, or the training in that way was not what God's Word had ordered it to be. Let us see what the Word teaches us on each of these points.

As to "the way in which he should go," we need be in no doubt. The names Scripture gives to this way make clear what it is. "The way of the Lord," God calls it, when he speaks of Abraham training his children; and we often read of "walking in his ways," "the way of his footsteps," "the way of his commandments." It is called "the way of wisdom," "the way of righteousness," "the way of holiness," "the way of peace," "the way of life." It is "the new and living way" opened by Christ for all who will walk in his footsteps; it is Christ himself, the living Way, of whom Scripture says, "Walk in him."

There are many religious parents who are most anxious to see their children saved, but who do not choose this way for them; they do not decide on it distinctly as the one only way in which they are to walk. They think it too much to expect that they should walk in it from their youth, and so they do not train them to go in it. They are not prepared to regard the walking in this way as always the first thing. It is not their first aim to train wholehearted, devoted Christians. There are worldly interests that must not be sacrificed. They are not always ready themselves to walk in that way only and wholly—"the narrow way"; they have chosen it, but not exclusively and finally. They have their own thoughts as to the way they and the child may go. No wonder that with a great deal of apparent religion their education fails; a mistake here is often fatal. There may be no doubt or hesitancy. The way of the Lord must be heartily accepted as alone "the way in which he should go."

"In the way in which he should go, train up a child." "Train" is a word of deep importance for every teacher and parent to understand. It is not telling, not teaching, not commanding, but something higher than all these: that without which the teaching and commanding is often more harm than good. It is not only telling a child what to do, but showing him how to do it and seeing that it is done, taking care that the advice or the command we give is put into practice and adopted as a habit.

What is needed for such training we can understand easily if we look at the way in which a young horse is trained. How it is made to yield its will to its master's, until at last it is in perfect sympathy with him, and yields to his slightest wish! How carefully it is directed and accustomed to do the right thing until it becomes a habit, a second nature! How its own wild native tendencies, when needful, are checked and restrained! How it is encouraged and helped to the full exercise of its powers in subjection to this rule, and everything done to make it bold and spirited! With what thoughtful care I have seen a coachman watch his young horses, and sit ready, at any difficulty, to help them with voice and hand, lest they should lose their confidence or be overcome by some difficulty they had to surmount! And I have thought, Would that parents bestowed somewhat of this care on training children in the way they should go!

Training may now thus be defined: accustoming the child to do easily and willingly what is commanded. Doing, doing habitually, doing from choice—this is what we aim at.

Doing. The parent who wishes to train not only tells or commands, but sees that the thing is done. To this end he seeks to engage the interest and affection of the child on the side of duty generally, as well as of the duty specially to be performed. Knowing how naturally thoughtless and fickle a child's nature is, he urges or encourages, until the thing which involves self-denial or difficulty is performed. He is careful not to give too many commands, or to give them hastily; he begins with commands to which submission is most easily secured, so that the thought of obedience may not too much be linked with the thought of what is displeasing or impossible. But the great thing is, whether he appeals to the motive of authority or of love, of duty or of pleasure, that he watches the child through the struggle until the consent of the will has become deed and action.

Doing habitually is, we said, an element of training. Success in education depends more on forming habits than inculcating rules. What the child has done once or twice he must learn to do over and over again, until it becomes familiar and natural; it must feel strange to him not to do it. If the educator is content with the first acts of obedience, sloth, forgetfulness, reluctance to effort, the evil of his nature, and self-will may soon come in and break the power of the incipient habit. The parent silently watches and, when there is danger of a retrograde step, interposes to help and confirm the habit until its mastery is secure. Going on from a first and a second command, in which obedience has been secured, the principle is extended until the child comes to feel it quite natural that in all things he should do the parent's will. And so the habit is formed of obedience, which becomes the root of other habits.

Doing from choice. This is something higher—the true aim of education. You may have good, obedient children, in whom there never has been much resistance to a parent's training, who render habitual and willing obedience, and yet, when left to themselves in later life, depart from the way in which they were trained to go. The training was defective; parents were content with habits without principles. The training of the young horse is not complete until he delights, full of joy and spirit, to do his work. It is the training of the will that is the aim of education. Beginning with obedience, the parent has to lead the child on to liberty; the apparent opposites have to be reconciled in practice; really to choose and will for himself what his parent wills, to find his happiness not only in the obedience to the parent's command, but in the approval of the thing commanded—this is what the child must be formed to. And here is indeed the highest art, the real difficulty of training a child in the way he should go.

But just here the promise of Divine grace comes in. No mind has yet apprehended the wondrous interplay of God's working and our working in the matter of our salvation—and as little in the salvation of our children. But we need not to understand it to be sure of it or to count on God's faithfulness. Where the believing parent seeks not only to form the habits of obedience, but in prayer and faith to mold and guide and strengthen the will of the child in the way of the Lord, he may count upon the workings of God's Holy Spirit to do what God alone can do. In covenant with God, as his fellow worker and minister, he does not shrink back from this highest and holiest of tasks, the training of that mighty power, a will made after the image of God's will, and now under the power of sin. He reckons on a Divine wisdom to guide him; he counts on a Divine strength to work with him and for him; he trusts in a Divine faithfulness to make the word true and sure in all its fullness: "Train up a child in the way he should go; when he is old, he will not depart from it."[1]

Holy Lord God! With fear and trembling I bow before you in view of the work to which you have called me. O my God, I feel deeply that I lack wisdom; I come to you, who give liberally and do not upbraid. Your Word has said it shall be given.

Lord, give me the spirit of wisdom, that I may understand aright the wondrous nature of that immortal spirit that has been put into my charge,

1. See Note A, at the close of this volume, on training.

with its power of mind and emotion and will. Give me wisdom, that I may know the way in which the child should go, even the way of your footsteps, and let me so walk in it that he may learn from me that, as there is no other way well pleasing to you, so there is no other way that can give us true pleasure. And give me wisdom, that I may know how to guide and influence the will, that it may give itself first to my will, and then to yours, to choose only and always your way. Lord, give me wisdom to train my child in the way he should go, even the way of the Lord.

And, O my God, strengthen my faith to hold fast the blessed assurance that a godly training in your fear, and under the rule of your spirit, cannot fail. Your promise is sure, your power is infinite; you will bless the seed of your servants. Amen.

TWENTY-THIRD DAY

The Child Choosing the Good

"Before the child shall know to refuse the evil, and choose the good."—*Isaiah 7:15*

OF ALL the wondrous powers with which God has endowed man, his will—the power of determining what he does, and so what he is—is the most wonderful. This is indeed the deepest trait of the Divine image, because even as God was what he is, of himself and not of another, so he gave man to a very large extent the power of deciding and making himself. The mind, with all its wondrous capacities; the soul, with all its wealth of feeling; man's moral and religious nature: all these have been given that he might be able to exercise aright that royal prerogative of the liberty he has from God to will himself, and so to fashion his own being and destiny for eternity.

And it is to the parent that the solemn task is entrusted of teaching the child how to use this will aright. This delicate instrument, on which in later life the wellbeing or woe, not only of the child but of others, is to depend, is put into the hands of the parents to keep, to direct, to strengthen, and to train the child unconsciously to hold and to exercise to the glory of the God who gave it. One would imagine that parents would shrink from the task with trembling, or, if they heard how the wisdom was to be obtained to execute it aright, would count no sacrifice too great to secure it. To those who seek the wisdom from God in faith, and in his fear seek to understand and fulfill their task, success is possible and is even promised.

The problem is one of great delicacy: to combine the greatest degree and the fullest exercise of personal liberty with perfect obedience. God's Word has more than once taught that obedience is the child's first virtue—and that in yielding it, his will is to be exercised. He is to obey, not because he understands or approves, but because the parent commands. In this he is to become the master of his own will, which he voluntarily submits it to a higher authority. Obedience from this principle will thus secure a double good: while guiding the will into right habits, it strengthens the command the child has over it. When first this has been attained, a safe foundation has been laid for the further exercise of the child's free will in the deliberate choice of what appears to him best. It is this that the parent must regard as his highest and most blessed work. "Before the child knows to refuse the evil and choose the good," in this first stage of childhood, simple obedience is the law. As he grows out of it, it is still a parent's influence that must train the young will to exercise the power on which in later life everything depends; he must now be trained himself to refuse the evil and choose the good.

And how is this to be done? The choice of the will depends upon the impulse and motives which prompt it to action. These impulses and motives again depend upon the objects presented to the mind, and the degree of attention with which they are regarded. In our fallen nature, the soul, dwelling in the flesh and surrounded by the world, is far more alive to the visible and the temporal than the unseen and the real: it is deceived by what appears pleasing or beautiful; the influence of what is present and near outweighs that of the distant, though of infinitely greater worth. It is the work of the parent to present to the child the true motives of action, and thus aid it in refusing the evil and choosing the good. The beauty of virtue, the nobility and happiness of self-denial, the pleasure that duty brings, the fear and the favor of God—not in these words, but clothed in forms suited to a child's apprehension, the parent holds up to his view objects that awaken emotions by which the will is guided gladly to choose the good. Amid the thoughtlessness of childhood, that lives in the seen and the present, the parent acts as a conscience to the child, calling it to be true to its higher instincts and convictions, and leads to the true pleasure with which duty rewards even the young. But the training of the child aims specially at teaching it to refuse the evil and choose the good when there is no parent near to help. In conscience every man possesses a guardian and helper of inestimable value in the path of right. A wise training can do much to establish the authority of this inner rule, and to lead the child to look upon the indwelling guest not as a spy or a reproachful enemy, but as the truest friend and best companion. Let the authority of the parent and of conscience be linked together, so that even in the parent's absence the weight of his influence may be felt. If the success of all true education consists in aiding the pupil to teach himself, the aim and success of moral training must specially consist in forming the habit of ruling himself and always listening to the inward monitor. Cultivate in the child the power of self-control, of recollection, of quiet thoughtfulness, so that he may always wait to listen for the gentle inner whisper that tells him to refuse the evil and choose the good.

Conscience, however, can only tell to do the right; what the right *is*, it cannot always teach. The mind may be wrong in its views of good and evil, and faithfulness to conscience may even lead to choose the evil and refuse the good. The inner light shines upon the path of what we think duty: it is only the light from above that shows what that duty really is. "Your Word is a lamp unto my feet, and a light unto my path." One of the most precious influences of a godly education is not so much the knowledge of what the Bible contains, as the consent of the heart to take God's Word as the standard of good and evil, and the desire to let it decide in every choice. The authority of the parent, of conscience, of God's Word: here is a threefold cord that cannot be broken, binding the child to the throne and the will of God, there to know to refuse the evil and choose the good.

We need hardly repeat again how such an education is not to take the place of Divine grace, but to be its servant; both in preparing the way for God's Spirit, by forming a strong and intelligent will to be afterward used in God's service, and in following up the work of grace, by guiding it in the path where all God's perfect will is to be accepted as the rule of conduct. Such a training—that the child may know to refuse the evil and choose the good—is of unspeakable value. When once the eyes of the parent are opened to the meaning of the words, he will see how in every step of life, in every action, there are two motives contending for mastery, and the choosing between the evil and the good is the solemn life-work being carried on all the day. He will recognize the responsibility entrusted to him of awakening, guiding, and strengthening that young will, on which such infinite issues depend, and feel that if he can do this one thing well, he has done his highest work. To know to refuse the evil and choose the good will be to choose Christ and holiness and eternal life.

Dear parents, God's highest gift to man in creation was his will, that he might choose the will of his God. Your highest work is to take charge of that will in your child, and be God's minister in leading it back to his service. Pray earnestly for light on this holy trust committed to you. Study carefully the wondrous character of this remains of the Divine image. See in it the power to which the gospel comes to make it free to choose God and his service, Christ and his love. Realize your own incompetency aright to influence a will in which the powers of light and darkness are wrestling for supremacy. And cast yourself on the covenant for the leading of the Holy Spirit in your work, for the renewal of the Holy Spirit in your child, that it may be your and his joy to see his will given up to choose the good, to choose God.

O Lord, my God! How holy is the work you have committed to a parent. Open my eyes, I pray you, to see its responsibility. May the traces of the Divine image to be seen in the child's power of willing, and so in making himself, stand out clear to me. May the tremendous issues for time and eternity depending upon the right use of his will be ever before me. May I feel aright the danger from the corruption of sin within and temptation from without. May I realize the wonderful power entrusted to me by your giving the child's will into my power. And may a due sense of my own impotence, and your Almighty Power working in me, combine to keep me humble and yet hopeful, conscious of my weakness, but confident in you. O God, teach me to form and train the will of my child to refuse the evil and choose the good.

Lord, make me very gentle and patient under a sense of my own willfulness. And very watchful, because of the sleepless vigilance of the enemy, and the hourly danger of my child. Ever faithful to fulfill my commission well. And very full of trust, because you are my Help and my Father.

O my God, do it for Jesus' sake. Amen.

TWENTY-FOURTH DAY

God's Spirit in Our Children

> "I will pour my Spirit upon your seed, and my blessing on your offspring. One shall say, I am the Lord's; and another shall subscribe with his hand unto the Lord."—*Isaiah 44:3, 5*

EVEN AS in the prophecy of the outpouring of the Holy Spirit, quoted by Joel on the day of Pentecost, express mention is made of the sons and daughters, so here too the blessing of an outpoured Spirit is made to the seed and offspring of God's people. The root principle of the covenant, promising grace to the fathers for the children, to the children for the fathers' sake and through the fathers, is to be the mark of the dispensation of the Spirit, too. The promise is accompanied by the very distinct statement of what would be the fruit of the Spirit's corning on the offspring. Not resting content with a religion inherited from the fathers, the children would openly profess their personal faith in the words "I am the Lord's." Through the power of the Holy Spirit, the religion of parental training would become the religion of a personal profession. Let us seek to grasp the two thoughts—the personal acknowledgment of the Lord as the fruit of the Spirit's work, and the sure promise of the Spirit to do that work.

Among all earnest parents there is the desire that, as their children grow up, they may be found coming forward to make personal confession of the faith in which they have been educated. If we enter fully into the mind of God, it will be one of the great aims of parental training to raise our children for such a profession. And yet there are many Christian parents who would hesitate to admit this. To some the dangers attending a distinctly religious education, of cultivating a formal and traditional faith, appears so great that they leave their children to themselves; they would never think of asking them whether they can say, "I am the Lord's," or encouraging them to do so. They do not believe in the conversion of children: they are so impressible, and so much the creatures of their surroundings, that such a profession is not to be counted on, and ought rather to be avoided. Others are themselves, though living in the fear of God, still so much in the dark on what they consider the intricate question of assurance of faith, that if they themselves have no liberty to say, "I am the Lord's," it is no wonder they never think of helping their children to say it. It is, as they think, only the advanced believer who dare speak thus; in them it would be presumption and pride. With others still, though they admit in theory the duty of making such a confession, and the possibility of a child making it, too, yet the heart is so cold and worldly that the warm, loving confession of Jesus as their Lord is never heard from their lips. Family worship and religious profession testify to anything but the living, loving attachment to a personal Savior. Their children would never learn from them to say, "I am the Lord's."

And yet we see it here promised so distinctly that the Spirit's working, a living spiritual religion, will manifest itself thus. The experience of these last years has proved to many, who formerly were in doubt, that a distinct profession of Jesus as a Savior is as sure a fruit of the Spirit's presence among the children as among older people, and that it can be quite as trustworthy, too. A little reflection will convince us that nothing can be more natural than that this should be the fruit of God's blessing on the labors of believing parents. Do we not tell them from their youth that God is Love, and that he gave Jesus to be a Savior? Do we not tell them that they belong to God, not only in right of creation and redemption, but in virtue of our having given them to him in baptism, and his having accepted them? And why should it appear strange if the child believes what we say and speaks it out: "I am the Lord's"? We tell them that Jesus receives sinners who confess their sins and give themselves to him to be cleansed. This truly is what we ought to hope for as the fruit of our instruction: that when he feels his sins, the child goes and confesses them to the blessed children's Friend, and believes that he does not cast him out, but accepts and pardons. Oh, let us be very careful of casting suspicion on the childlike, "I am the Lord's"! We teach the children what it means to speak thus: that it implies a giving ourselves to be his property, to do his will, and to acknowledge him as Lord and Master. And if their young hearts are touched, and consent, oh, let us beware of refusing or doubting their profession, or of reproaching them when they fail; let us remember the promised fruit of the Spirit's working among the children is this: "I am the Lord's."

And are we then to think that there is no danger at all connected with it? And are we to rest content with the momentary impressions which speak the words without inquiring farther? By no means. As with those who have come to years, so with children: impressions may be temporary and profession superficial. We have been warning against the disposition that doubts the reality of all children's conversion and profession: God's Word teaches us what it is that will give them sincerity and reality. Let us consider well the second lesson our prophecy teaches: it is the Spirit's working that will make the "I am the Lord's" Spirit and truth.

And in what way is the outpouring of the Spirit that is to have this blessed result to be given? Blessed be God, the promise was fulfilled on the day of Pentecost. The Spirit dwells in the Church of Christ, in the hearts and the homes of his believing disciples. There may now still at times come special outpourings of the Spirit in revival movements of wider or smaller extent, when the young come forward in numbers to confess their Lord. But for this we have not to wait. In promising the Spirit to the offspring of his people, God would have us expect that parental instruction, that a consecrated home life, that his ordinances of family religion, are to be the means the Spirit is to use and bless for leading the children to Christ. The Spirit ever works in the Word; to the child the parent is the God-ordained minister of the Word. The blessing of the new dispensation is this: that the parent may count on the Holy Spirit for his children, too, from their youth up, and that all his teaching and training, his word and work, though it be in weakness and in fear and in much trembling, may be in demonstration of the Spirit and of power.

But then everything depends upon the parent himself as a minister of the Spirit. He must live and walk, he must be led and sanctified by the Spirit, he must speak and pray in the Spirit, and he must in faith claim and accept the promise of the Spirit for his child. It is possible, we said, that a child's profession, "I am the Lord's," may be of no value. This depends greatly on the parents and those who surround it; he takes the meaning of the words very much from them. If to them it be the language of a joyous faith and consecration, the child unconsciously catches the meaning from the spirit in which he sees them lived out. If they watch over his weakness and continually speak words of help and encouragement, even the little child can, amid childlike stumblings and failures, prove the reality of the change of which this profession was the token.

Dear parents! Let God's thoughts for your children enter your hearts and rule there. These two thoughts especially:

- God's Spirit and my children belong to each other; I may in faith claim the Spirit's dwelling and working in them.
- And my child may know and say that he is the Lord's; the fruit of the Spirit is the faith of the heart and the confession of the lips, "Jesus is mine."

Let this promise be your strength as you deal with God, your strength as you deal with your child: "They that wait on the Lord shall not be ashamed."

O Lord God! We draw near to you to claim the fulfillment of this promise on behalf of our beloved children. Lord, may they from their very youth have your Spirit poured out upon them, that even in the simplicity of childhood they may say, "I am the Lord's."

O Lord, be pleased to this end to fill us your servants with your Holy Spirit. May all our home life and our parental influence be a channel through which the Spirit reaches each child. God, help us so to live that the life that breathes around him may be life in the Spirit.

Especially we ask you, gracious Lord, to give us great singleness of aim in training our children for you alone. Oh, that the indwelling of the blessed Spirit may not be thought of as something hardly to be expected, but as the one gift the Father loves to bestow, and the first thing the child needs to grow up into a noble man and Christian. Lord, let our training of him, as your exclusive sacred property, to know and say he is yours, be our one desire. And we can count on this: that each child we so consecrate to you, you will by your Spirit consecrate for your own. May we so experience how wonderfully the parent's work and the Spirit's work blend in securing the seed of your people for yourself. Amen.

TWENTY-FIFTH DAY

From Generation to Generation

"My righteousness shall be forever, and my salvation from generation to generation."—*Isaiah 61:8*

WHEN WE SPEAK of a generation in the history of man, we think of the shortness of human life and the continual change among men. "One generation passes away, and another generation comes: but the earth abides for ever." What a contrast between man and the heavens above or the mountains around him—always the same. What a contrast, still more, between man, whose life is but a span, and the unchangeable, the everlasting God.

We will find in God's Word that it loves not so much to contrast as to link together these opposites; it lifts man out of the transitoriness of life, to find his refuge in the unchangeableness of God. "As for man, his days are as grass; but the mercy of the Lord is from everlasting to everlasting upon them that fear him, and his righteousness unto children's children." "O God, take me not away in the midst of my days: your years are throughout all generations. The earth and the heavens shall perish, but you shall endure. You are the same, and your years shall have no end. The children of your servants shall continue, and their seed shall be established before you." Death may separate one generation from another but God's mercy connects them, passing on from one to another; his righteousness, which is everlasting, reveals itself as salvation from generation to generation. At every point where God meets and acts with man, there are two sides to be regarded—the Divine and the human. So it is here, too, in the transmission of God's salvation from generation to generation. God's faithfulness inspires that of man, and therefore demands and rewards it. In some passages it might almost appear as if everything depended upon man and his keeping the covenant; and so it does indeed. But not as if this keeping of the covenant were to be his work, by which he secures the blessing. No, but it is in the mercy and truth of God, as these are known and trusted, that human faithfulness has its strength and security. To know God's purpose, to believe God's promise, to adore God's unchanging faithfulness, communicates to the soul the very spirit of that faithfulness and binds us firmly to him, so that he who is all in all can work out his purpose in us.

Let us first look at the Divine side of this salvation from generation to generation. In Isaiah, from whom we have these words, the truth is expressed with great frequency and distinctness: "As for me, this is my covenant with them, says the Lord; my Spirit that is upon you, and my words which I have put in your mouth shall not depart out of your mouth, nor out of the mouth of your seed, nor out of the mouth of your seed's seed, from henceforth and forever" (Isaiah 59:21). This speaks of New Testament times. When God made his covenant with David, he anticipated generations in which there would be disobedience, and therefore punishment (2 Samuel 2:14; Psalm 89:30–33). But here the promise of the Spirit and the Word in the mouth of God's Anointed One and his people is not to pass from the mouth of the seed's seed. And, blessed be God, there are families in which for generations, and even for centuries, the Word and the Spirit have not departed from the mouth of the seed's seed. Let us only open the heart to take in the promise, and to let it grow within us.

Then we have that other beautiful promise: "I will direct their work in truth, and I will make an everlasting covenant with them. And their seed shall be known among the Gentiles, and their offspring among the people: all that see them shall acknowledge them, that they are the seed which the Lord has blessed" (Isaiah 61: 9). Or, as it is otherwise expressed (Isaiah 65:23), "They are the seed of the blessed of the Lord, and their offspring with them." The covenant with Abraham and David was also an everlasting covenant, but its fulfillment was reached over the heads of generations that proved faithless. But here, in the power of the promised Spirit, believing parents may claim and expect, from child to child, to see the blessing of the Lord. This is to be the fruit of the outpouring of the Holy Spirit; the promise, "You, and your son, and your son's son," is to have its literal fulfillment. And this not only for our comfort and joy, and the blessing on our children, but that God may be known and glorified. "Their seed shall be known among the Gentiles." To be God's witnesses on earth, if need be, among the Gentiles to the end of the earth: it is for this that the Word and the Spirit are not to depart from the mouth of our seed from henceforth and for evermore.

Let us look now from the human side at the fulfillment of this promise: "My salvation from generation to generation." Most strikingly God's purpose is set forth in the words of Psalm 78:4–7): "We will not hide them from their children, showing to the generation to come the praises of the Lord, and his strength, and the wonderful works he has done. For he established a testimony in Jacob, and appointed a law in Israel, which he commanded our fathers, that they should make them known to their children; that the generation to come might know them, even the children which should be born, who should arise and declare them to their children; that they might set their hope in God, and not forget the works of God, but keep his commandments." And then we read (Psalm 145:4), "One generation shall praise your works to another"; the triumphant joy of that psalm of praise being the spirit in which the parents tell their child of God's glory and goodness. Here we have the human side. Parents who know God show his praise, and his strength, and his wonderful works to their children. Parental instruction is in the ministry of the Spirit, not less but more than in the old covenant, a testifying for God in the spirit of praise, telling what he has done to us, his strength and his wonderful works. And so the children are taught not to forget the works of God, but to set their hope on him and keep his commandments, to trust and to obey him. And so his righteousness, which is from everlasting to everlasting, becomes salvation from generation to generation.

Parents! It is God's will that his salvation should be from generation to generation in your family, too; that your children should hear from you, and pass on to their children, the praise of the Lord. Oh, let us seek to enter into God's plans, and with our whole heart labor earnestly to secure the blessing and to please our Father! We know what is needed—nothing but wholehearted devotion to God. But nothing less will do. God's salvation must not be a secondary thing, something to be enjoyed along with the world. It must be the first thing. We must set our whole heart upon it, even as God does. It must be the one thing we live for, to glorify this God; it is such a life—proving to the children what the joy of God's salvation is, a blessedness and a delight that will influence them to come with us—that we may do them good. It is this wholehearted devotion that will give strength to our faith and confidence to our hope. Under its inspiration our prayers will be persevering and believing. It will impart to our instruction the joyful tone of assurance, and make our whole life the model for our children. It is one generation living for God that will secure the next for him; I may ask and expect that my wholehearted consecration to God will, in his infinite mercy, be blessed to guide them; his salvation is from generation to generation.

Gracious and most blessed Father! I bow before you once again with the prayer to open my eyes and my heart, that I may fully understand your holy purpose with an earthly parentage, to transmit through it your blessing. O my God, let your word, "My salvation from generation to generation," so fill my heart, that my calling and duty, with your promise and purpose, may be equally clear to me, and the salvation of my children be as sure as my own.

And grant, Lord, that in your light I may realize and manifest fully what salvation is—salvation from sin and its power unto the holiness and the service of God. Let it be in me a salvation that fills the heart with gladness, and the lips with praise, and the whole life with purity and love. Let the salvation in which I walk, and in which I train the children, indeed be, not what man calls so, but the salvation of God.

O my God, I beseech you, give me grace that this be the one heirloom of their parents my children cherish, the one thing transmitted in our home from child to child, the salvation, the love, the joy, the service of God. Yes, Lord, you are the Eternal and Unchanging One; let it be from generation to generation. Amen.

TWENTY-SIXTH DAY

The Crowning Blessing

"I will pour out my Spirit upon all flesh; and your sons and your daughters shall prophesy."—*Joel 2:28*

THIS IS THE PROMISE of which the day of Pentecost was the fulfillment and the interpretation. The coming of the Comforter, the baptism with the Holy Spirit and with fire, the endowment with power from on high, the receiving the power of the Holy Spirit to be his witnesses to the end of the earth—all these precious promises of Christ were comprehended and fulfilled in the fulfillment of Joel's prophecy. It contains the title-deeds of what the birthright and the baptism of Christ's Church secures to her: the Holy Spirit from the throne of the exalted Savior, as her power for testimony and for suffering, for triumph and for blessing, is the heavenly sign with which she has been marked and sealed.

In this foundation promise, what a place is given to the children! "Your sons and daughters shall prophesy; your old men shall dream dreams; your young men shall see visions." The seed of God's people have such a place in his heart—when he deals with his people their offspring are so continually in his thoughts—that even in the promise of Pentecost the first thing introduced is not the disciples now anointed to preach, but the sons and the daughters prepared to prophesy. Let us try and take in what it teaches us of God's purpose, of a parent's hope, and of a child's education.

1. *God's purpose*. With the gift of the Holy Spirit to his Church, God had an object, and that object was power—power from on high for her work of testifying to the ends of the earth. The very last words

of the Master (Acts 1:8) speak only of this. All the other blessings of the Spirit—assurance, joy, holiness, love—have this as their aim: influence, fruit-bearing, the power to bless. It is because so many Christians do not understand this that there is often such a weary and fruitless seeking for the blessings of the Spirit, when they would come as unsought if there were but a wholehearted surrender to what the Spirit is given to qualify for—God's service and work. No wise man wastes power: he economizes it and puts in just sufficient for the work. According to the work our will undertakes, and our faith expects to perform, is the power, the measure of the Spirit, God gives.

This is true of our children, too. In Joel's prophecy God reveals his purpose with our sons and daughters. Under the mighty breathings of his Spirit they are to prophesy. What this prophesying is Paul tells us: "If all prophesy, and there come in one unbelieving or unlearned, he is reproved by all, he is judged by all: the secrets of his heart are made manifest: and so he will fall down on his face and worship God, declaring that God is among you indeed." This is prophesying in the power of the Spirit, convicting even the unbelieving and unlearned. And for such prophets God wants our sons and daughters. And for such prophets we ought, in this dispensation of the Holy Spirit, to educate our sons and daughters.

The world is in sore need of them. The Church is suffering for want of them. Supply always creates demand. Because there is so small supply, the Church thinks it has done something great when there is annually some increase in the amount of its subscriptions and the number of its agents. But, oh, if there were a heart to enter into God's purpose, and the Church and parents understood what glory it is definitely to train our sons and daughters to be prophets of the Most High, witnesses and messengers for Jesus our Lord, what a change it would bring in our modes of operation! As the children of this world do their utmost to obtain some high commission in the army or navy, some good appointment in the civil service or in business, why should not the children of God press around the throne of their Father, seeking no favor so earnestly as that he would fulfill this promise in their children, and make them his prophets wherever he has need of them. God's purpose is that the Holy Spirit should take possession of our sons and daughters for his service; that our sons and daughters should be filled with the Holy Spirit of consecration and power for service. They belong to him, and he to them.

2. *The parent's hope.* Just imagine believing parents entering fully and heartily into this purpose of God, acting upon it as a settled thing that they are training their children for the service of God's Spirit. Could any doubt still arise in their minds as to whether they might count on the conversion of their children? Aim high is a daily maxim; you will accomplish more than he who is content with a lower range. This is the blessing of full consecration: while it aims at the highest that God has promised, the secondary gifts that others struggle life-long for in vain fall unsought to their share. Nothing will give such confidence of the salvation of our children, of the Spirit's working for conversion and renewal, as the consciousness of having surrendered them undividedly to the service of God and his Spirit.

And it will equally inspire us with confidence in regard to fitness for parental duty. We have no conception of the extent to which self-interest enfeebles faith and self-sacrifice emboldens it. If I know I am very much seeking the salvation of my children for their own and for my sake, the soul cannot find the strength to rise to the confident assurance that all grace for training my child will be given. But let me lose all selfish thought of myself and them in the childlike, generous placing them at God's disposal, and it will become impossible to doubt that my Father will give me grace for the work I do for him.

And then, though there is a diversity of gifts, and I may not see each child used in the direct service of the Master, I may be sure that the heart's purpose is accepted, and the effort to train all my children to be the vessels of God's Holy Spirit has had its elevating influence on my own soul, on my home, on each of my children, whatever their external calling in life may have to be. The more distinct my acknowledgment in family religion that in this dispensation the Spirit claims all, the more may I depend upon his presence with me and mine.

3. *The children's training.* Such a purpose in God's heart, and such a hope in the parent's heart clearly apprehended—how they ought to, how they *will*, influence the children's training!

Cultivate every mental power with the view of having a sharp instrument prepared for the Master's use. Cultivate, even what are counted natural virtues—diligence and decision, order and method, promptness and firmness—with the high aim of having the child the fitter for the work to be done. Cultivate every moral power to be the form prepared for the Holy Spirit's filling. Let obedience to conscience and to law, let self-control and temperance, let strict integrity and justice, let humility and love, be aimed at in education, that the Holy Spirit may have them to form a noble Christian, an efficient servant of the Lord, a true prophet. The prize that parents aim at for their children is often counted worthy of any sacrifice; there have been those who have willingly suffered want to give their sons a liberal education, or to secure their daughters a position in the world. Oh, let us so set our hearts upon the promotion we seek for our children, that all thought of sacrifice passes away as we study and labor, as we pray and believe, to have them in very deed counted worthy of a place among the separated ones whom the Spirit of the Lord anoints for his work.

And now we close our meditations on the Old Testament testimony as to the place children occupy in the purpose and promise of God. We have seen what God would be for our children—a God in covenant, with the covenant blessing of the blood and the Spirit of Jesus. And we have seen what he would have our children be to him—a covenant seed, to receive and transmit and multiply the blessing through the earth. And we have seen what he would have parents be, as standing between him and their children—the ministers of the covenant, to sprinkle and plead the blood with him, to receive the Spirit from him, and by example and training and life to communicate the blessing to them, to be the channels for the Spirit's training them for his service.

God help us to learn these three lessons. God help us to believe and receive all he is willing to be for our children through us. God help us to give and train the children for all he would have them be. God help us to be faithful sureties for our children, to seek for them nothing less than God seeks, and so to live that from our homes may go forth sons and daughters to prophesy in his name.

O Lord our God! We thank you again for the institution of the family, as your Divine appointment for transmitting your salvation to all generations. And we thank you for the revelation of yourself as the covenant God of the children of your servants, pledging yourself to fulfill all your promises of blessing. And we thank you most of all for the promise of the Spirit, of your Holy Spirit, of the Spirit of your Son, to dwell in our sons and daughters.

O Lord, fulfill your promise to our children. Give us grace to train them for you, in the faith of the Spirit's working, of the Spirit's coming with power. Give us grace to prepare them to be meet for the Master's use, every gift cultivated and consecrated for your service. Let our sons and daughters prophesy in the power of the Holy Spirit.

O Lord, bless all believing parents. Let your claim on their children, let your promise of the Spirit, let the inconceivably high privilege of offering their children to you for service, let the power promised to parents, let the crying need for laborers, let the Spirit's seeking for those whom he can use as the prophets of the Most High, so fill their hearts, that all their training may be in harmony with your purpose, "Your sons and daughters shall prophesy." Amen.

TWENTY-SEVENTH DAY

The Heavenly and the Earthly Father

> "If you, being evil, know how to give good gifts unto your children, how much more shall your Father which is in heaven give good gifts to them that ask him?"—*Matthew 7:11*

WE BEGAN our meditations on the Old Testament with man created in the image, after the likeness of God, and the home on earth the picture of the home in heaven. The glory of the New Testament is its fuller revelation of the Father in heaven: we can have no better beginning for our New Testament studies of what God means family life to be than to see what light the fatherliness of God casts upon our own fatherhood, and upon what we are to be to our children.

1. And first we note how Jesus wants us to rise from and through the experiences of fatherhood on earth to know the Father in heaven aright. Not as if our fatherhood were the original and the reality, to be used by way of comparison and illustration to make God's relation clear to us. By no means. God is the true Father: from eternity, in his very nature, as the God of Love. Fatherhood was the glory and the blessedness of the Divine Being. And our fatherhood on earth has been given as a reflection of his, and to lead us to a participation in its honor and joy. We, too, are to taste the blessedness of begetting a son in our likeness, having in him the object of our love, the reflection of our image, a companion and helper in all our work.

But because this fatherhood in heaven is so high above us, we are to study the father-heart on earth, and from it continually rise into a truer and fuller apprehension of what God is to us. Home life is a school as much for training parents as children; the deepest mysteries of God's love are best studied by a parent in his own bosom. As we think of our love to our children, the joy they give us, the tender sympathy their troubles awaken, the patient kindness their dullness or waywardness requires, the ready response their needs and requests meet with, Jesus wants us to look up and calculate how much more than in us who are evil all this must be in God, the Good and Perfect One, the Fountain of love. He wants us to banish every shadow of unbelief from the heart, and live our life in the sunshine of God's love. As we see what influence a parent can exert on his child, breathing his disposition and even his will into him, securing his unbounded trust, he would have us be sure that the Father does love, and is able to breathe his own mind, his own disposition—what Jesus calls his own Spirit—into us. And as we claim and strive to secure the love and obedience of our children, as we long that they should find their happiness in our will, our friendship, our company, he asks us to remember that the Father loves to meet us in secret, that the voice and the trust of his child are his joy and will meet a rich reward. What a study for every father, and every mother, too, in each pulse of love and joy that swells the heart to mark the revelation of a love and joy that is bending over them, and longs to meet with the response of their childlike love and joy. And so, in the light of the fatherhood of earth, we rise to what fatherhood in heaven is.

2. But then again, the fatherhood in heaven will also cast its light on the fatherhood of earth and teach us what it ought to be. In giving us the place and the name and the power of father, God has in a very real and solemn sense made us his image-bearers. He asks and expects us, in doing our work as such, in every way to copy him, to act as like him as possible. The parents who desire to bring a full blessing to their children must make God's fatherhood their model and their study.

They must enter into God's purpose, make it their own, and give themselves to pursue it with their whole heart. The heavenly Father seeks to educate children into his likeness: he has nothing higher to bestow on them; with nothing less can he be content if they are to have a place forever in his home. God has appointed parents on earth to be his ministers and fellow workers, to carry out his plan: how can they, unless they understand it and make its realization the first object of family life?

From the Father in heaven they must learn, too, the way in which that purpose is to be attained. In his dealings with his people they will see how he first came, as with Abraham, in love and kindness, securing trust and confidence; then with law and its authority, to lead on to self-knowledge and self-renunciation; then with the gospel of full liberty in the Spirit, that we might no longer be children, but men. From him parents will learn to combine love with authority, and through them to aim at the free and hearty surrender to all God's will. In the tenderness and patience and self-sacrifice of the Divine love, in the firmness and righteousness of Divine rule, the parent will find the secret of successful training.

From the Father must above all be learned what a very personal thing such training is. How the Father has come down to us in Christ; how in his own example he shows us that he only wants us to be as he is; how in giving us his Spirit he would have us understand that fatherhood longs to draw the child into perfect likeness and oneness with itself. As the earthly father gazes and studies, it will dawn upon him how the highest duty of our fatherhood is just to be what the child is to be. A father must breathe his own spirit into the child; he that as a child of the heavenly Father receives his Spirit day by day, can breathe this into his child, too. Is it not a solemn but most blessed thing to be a parent? First a child of the heavenly Father, and then his image, his substitute, his picture to the child on earth.

3. This brings us to a third lesson. The earthly father must not only take the Father in heaven as his model and guide, but he must so reflect him that the child may most naturally rise from him whom he sees to the unseen One whom he represents. A child loves its parents by natural instinct: as the child sees in the father all that is holy and worthy of honor, natural love becomes the homage of an affectionate and enthusiastic admiration. In a Christian father a child ought to have a better exposition than the best of sermons can give of the love and care of the heavenly Father, and all the blessing and joy he wants to bestow.

But to attain to this, the parent must consciously and distinctly aim at making himself, and the name he bears, the ladder by which the child can climb to the Father above. It is when the bright, living, happy piety of the parents, a mingling of holy reverence to God with childlike love, shines on the children from their early youth, that the name of God as Father will become linked with all that is lovely and holy in the memory of a child. Not so much as a matter of reflection or thought, but as the life-breath taken in all unconsciously, the fatherhood of earth will have been the gate of the Father's home above.

And is it possible so to live that all this shall be true? The one thing the Father loves to give, the sum and center of all his good gifts, is his own Holy Spirit—his Father-Spirit to be in us the spirit of a son. And we have only to believe, and as we believe, to receive, and as we receive, to yield to and live in the Spirit, and he will make our fatherhood the image of God's, and from us, too, there will flow streams of living water to bless our children.

What a world it would be if every Christian father set himself in true earnest to realize and fulfill his calling, and in his little home circle as God's vice-regent to bear God's name—the holy name of father; if, in a holy partnership with the Father in heaven, he yielded himself by him to be taught, and sanctified, and used to train children for the Father who is in heaven. Shall we not, all who are fathers, join, and shall not all mothers, with whom the fathers are so truly one, and on whom they so depend for what they are to be as fathers in the family, join too in the fervent prayer that the Father would make us all the worthy bearers of that name?

Our Father in heaven, we unite in an earnest prayer for all your children who bear the holy name of father. Give us, we beseech you, more insight into your Fatherhood, and what unspeakable riches of blessing for us and our children it includes. Let us, from the wonderful traits of your own likeness in our own feelings toward our children, rise up to believe and enjoy the Divine fullness of love which your heart and your name offer to us. Let our fatherhood so teach us the blessedness of being the children of your Father-love.

And then, our Father, give us to see how really you do command and expect that our fatherhood shall be nothing less than the reflection and the outflow of your own. Oh, may they indeed be one: one in purpose, one in method, one in principle, one in spirit. O God, we want to be fathers to our children, just as you are to us: make us such, so that you can fully use us as the channels for your Father-grace to our little ones. May they see in us true pictures of him to whom we teach them to say, Our Father who art in heaven.

Father, we look to your Son, and the "how much more" he taught us, for the answer to our prayer. We count upon the tenderness and the faithfulness of your love, and upon your mighty power and Spirit, to bless the parents of your Church who cry to you. Amen.

TWENTY-EIGHTH DAY

The Children of the Kingdom

"But the children of the kingdom shall be cast out into outer darkness."—*Matthew 8:12*

IN WHAT CLOSE UNION we have here before us the wonderful privilege and the terrible danger that attach to the place our children have in the Church of Christ. They are children of the kingdom: what more glorious! They can be cast out into outer darkness: what more awful! The only way certainly to avoid the latter is fully to grasp the former—to let it be not a name but a power ruling and renewing the whole life. To this end, let us try to apprehend all it implies.

Children of the kingdom! What kingdom? The answer is simple: the kingdom of God! And where is this kingdom? In heaven. It is that Divine rule or dominion which obtains in heaven and the whole heavenly world. Its center is the Throne of God, on which he dwells who is the Holy One, from whom all life and all law and all love flow forth. Around that Throne are powers and principalities and dominions, with their untold myriads of holy spirits who do his will and are the messengers of his power. Of that kingdom the mark is that, in God, everything is love and blessing; in his subjects, everything obedience and joy.

And how can this heavenly kingdom be here on earth? When God created the heavens and the earth, it was with the object of securing new territory in which his heavenly empire might be established. But the power of another kingdom, the kingdom of Satan, interfered, and in the fall of man the coming of the kingdom was delayed. For four thousand years it was promised and hoped for, but the kingdom of heaven was not yet on earth.

And how did this kingdom come? It was in the fullness of time, when the King himself came to earth, that the message was heard: The kingdom of heaven is at hand, the kingdom of heaven is come unto you. He came, first in his own life as a subject and a servant, to show us what the spirit is that animates all the subjects of the kingdom—implicit obedience, delight in doing the will of God. In that obedience unto death he broke the power of Satan and of sin, showed forth the wondrous love with which as our King he loved us, and set us free for the blessed life of serving and obedience like his own. And then, when as King ascending to heaven, he took his seat upon the throne, the kingdom could come. In the outpouring of the Holy Spirit the kingdom came in power, and was set up in the hearts that had been prepared to receive him, and to enter the kingdom.

And who were the subjects of this kingdom? Jesus had said: "Except a man be born again, he cannot see the kingdom of God." Nothing less than the Spirit of God, the Spirit of heaven, coming in and taking possession of a man could fit him to enter or even see the kingdom, or to live as one of its subjects. But with this solemn message Jesus had also spoken: "Blessed are the poor in spirit, for theirs is the kingdom of heaven." To become an heir of the kingdom, nothing was needed but the consciousness and confession of poverty; having nothing, we might possess all.

And the marks of those who truly belong to this kingdom? Nothing less than the marks by which the King was known on earth: obedience and love toward God, obedience to the uttermost, an absolute surrender to his will. And toward man, love, giving itself to live and die, to bring the blessings of the kingdom to all around. "The kingdom is not in word but in power." The kingdom of heaven above everything is in the infinite power of the eternal life: as the kingdom comes down, the Holy Spirit, the power, comes also to give the strength to live as members of the kingdom. In each one of whom the kingdom truly takes possession, the prayer, "Thy kingdom come," becomes the desire of the heart, and everything is subordinate to its extension and the manifestation of its glory.

And who are the children of the kingdom? Jesus spoke this word even of the Jews who rejected the kingdom. God had in his great mercy committed the promise of the kingdom to Israel, and all its children were its heirs. And now our children, born under its influence, destined for its blessings, baptized into the fellowship of the Church, which is the nursery and training school of the kingdom—our children are children of the kingdom—"of such is the kingdom of heaven."

And what is needed to secure for them the possession of the kingdom to which they have thus been made the heirs? That they may lose it, we see—children of the kingdom may be cast out into outer darkness. What is needed above everything is this: that they be so educated and trained under the influence and power of the heavenly life, in the very spirit of the kingdom, that the blessing which their name, as expressive of their destiny, brings, may become their own personal and everlasting possession.

And who is to train them thus? Christian parents! This is our holy privilege. As children of the kingdom, they are entrusted to us to keep and nourish. The keynote of our education, the watchword in all our desires and efforts on their behalf, our plea with God for them, and with them for God, must be this: They are children of the kingdom. To parents God has entrusted the high commission of leading their children on from the place where their title is only yet a name and a promise, to the life of possession and full enjoyment.

And what is needed to enable the parent to do this? Nothing less than that with his whole heart he himself live in and for the kingdom of heaven. The atmosphere of the home must be the spirit of heaven; Christ's command, "Seek first the kingdom of God," must be the ruling principle of all its conduct: unconsciously the child must receive the impression that not only personal blessing, but the interests and extension of God's kingdom, are the hope and the joy of life. Parents whose citizenship is in heaven, who have in truth entered the kingdom, and live in it, will alone be found worthy or fit to train the children as heirs of the kingdom.

And how are parents able thus to live? "My kingdom," Jesus said, "is not of this world: my kingdom is not from here." It is from above, from heaven, from God, the kingdom comes; it is from above, from heaven, from God, the Spirit and the life and the power of the kingdom must come each day. Coming out of the world, daily rising upward and entering into the Holiest within the veil through the blood, the believer must tarry in God's presence in worship and surrender, until the anointing is fresh upon him so only can he come down into his home, and consecrate it as the nursery for children of the kingdom. So long as we are content with just religion enough to save ourselves and our children, we must not be surprised if they remain unsaved: it is only in seeking to be filled with the Spirit, to have our whole life, like Christ's, sacrificed for the kingdom, that we may count on the blessing of a successful education. "My kingdom is not of this world": the spirit of the world, perhaps unconsciously, ruling in the parents, destroys all that they hope to effect by their purposes, their precepts, or their prayers. In Christ's command, "First the kingdom," we have the secret and the certainty of a successful education.

Parents! Your children are children of the kingdom, the kingdom of God in heaven! Hold and love and train them as such, for God alone! From God alone be your hope. From above, from *above* must be your help. Seek it in much prayer. Accept it in childlike faith, that believes that have what you ask. Yield yourself to it, denying self, not allowing self any say in the guidance of your life or home. Yield yourself to it, keeping the ear open every hour to hear the voice of the Holy Spirit, through whom alone the laws aid the powers of the kingdom can work in us.

Above all, remember Jesus! He said, "Suffer little children to come unto *me*, for of such is the kingdom of heaven." He is the King: in him we have the kingdom as a Presence. Live with him, on him, in him. He loves our children and looks after them; his presence and love will more than anything fill us and them with a holy enthusiasm for the kingdom: so will they grow up in the kingdom and for the kingdom. And we shall taste the joy unspeakable of having our home, with its life and love and training, within the kingdom; yes, of having the kingdom of heaven within our home.

Our Father in heaven, Thine is the kingdom, and the power, and the glory. Blessed be your name, that by your Almighty power your kingdom, the kingdom of heaven, has come to this earth, and will come, until the whole earth is filled with your glory. Blessed, too, be your name, that we and our little ones are the children of the kingdom. O Father, we look to your Father-love to give us who are fathers and mothers grace to realize how sacred our calling and our home is, because we are training children of the kingdom for you. Teach us, we pray you, never to put asunder what the words of our Lord have joined together—the children and the kingdom. May all our love and communication and influence help to link them inseparably with the kingdom. May they never know that they are not living and growing up in it.

Blessed Lord Jesus, who says of the little ones, "Of such is the kingdom," we beseech you, reveal to us what your kingdom is in its spiritual reality and glory; what it is even here on earth as the rule of God by the Holy Spirit in the hearts and lives of his people. May the kingdom of God be within us in such power, and we within it in such truth, that our children may not only have the name, but that the very atmosphere they breathe in our home be such as will really make them children of the kingdom. Amen.

TWENTY-NINTH DAY

A Mother's Persevering Prayer

> "A woman of Canaan came and cried unto him, saying, Have mercy on me, O Lord, you Son of David! My daughter is grievously vexed with a devil. . . . Then Jesus answered and said unto her, O woman, great is your faith: be it unto you even as you will."—*Matthew 15:22, 28*

IN THE OLD TESTAMENT we found God's promises of blessing on the godly training of children most clear and sure. Nor were his threatenings on the neglect of this duty less distinct. And in more than one terrible example, we saw with what relentless power the threatening came true. In the sons of Aaron and Eli, in the family of David and Solomon, proof was given that the personal righteousness of the father could not save the ungodly child. And we found no answer to one of the most solemn questions that can be put, and which has been as a burning fiery furnace to many a parent's heart: Is there still hope for a child grown up in sin, and passing out from beyond the reach of a parent's influence?

It is in Christ Jesus that God has revealed how completely the power of sin and Satan has been broken. It is in Christ Jesus that God has shown us what it is possible for his grace to do. It is in Christ Jesus, too, we must seek for the answer to every question of a parent's heart. And as it is his earthly life in which we have revealed all that the unseen Father, and he now too in his exaltation, are willing to do for us, so there we must find what a parent may hope for from his mighty saving power on behalf of a wandering child. As we study this carefully, we shall be surprised to find how many of the most precious and encouraging words of Christ in regard to faith have been spoken to parents in reference to their children. "Fear not, only believe"; "All things are possible to him that believes"; "O woman, great is your faith: be it unto you even as you will." Such words, which have countless times been the strength and comfort of the penitent seeking pardon, or the believer pleading for some spiritual blessing, are in the first place the parent's property; the blessed assurance that there is no case in which a child, now in Satan's power, is beyond the reach of a Savior's love and a parent's faith. Let us see how wonderfully this will come out in the well known story of the Syrophenician mother, as we think of her daughter's misery, her prayer's refusal, her faith's perseverance, and her rich reward.

Her daughter's misery. "My daughter is grievously vexed with a devil." How many a mother is there who has to pray this prayer for a child possessed with an evil spirit far more terrible than that of which we read there. In this case it was more sickness than sin; it was the power of Satan in the body more than the soul. But, alas, how many of the grown-up children of Christian parents there are who are under the power of Satan, given up to pleasure or worldliness, to self-will or to sin. Let our story encourage them to believe that, however hopeless their case appears, there is One who is mighty to save, the parent's Friend, the children's Redeemer. Let them come to him with their need, and cry out in prayer, "My child is grievously vexed with a devil." Let them make full confession of their child's lost estate. Beware of excusing their sin by the thought of what is good or lovable about them, or by laying the blame on circumstances or companions. Bring them to Christ, and say it out that they are lost, under the power of Satan, that they have deserved and are on their way to be with him forever. Hide not their wretchedness. Ask not only that they may be saved and made happy and taken to heaven. Ask nothing less than that they may turn from the power of Satan unto God, that they may be translated from the power of darkness to the kingdom of God's dear Son. Ask that they may be born again, changed from being the children of the devil and enemies of God to be his friends and children. Honor God by confessing their sin fully and clearly, and acknowledging his righteous judgment; ask distinctly and definitely for a full salvation.

Her prayer's refusal is the second lesson this woman has to teach us. Christ appeared to turn a deaf ear to her prayer. At first he did not answer her a word. When he did speak, his answer was worse than his silence; it cut off all hope. He was not sent to the heathen. A second answer, given as she had come nearer and had again worshiped him, saying, "Lord, help me!" appeared to heap contempt on her misfortune: she was not only a heathen, but a dog. A true picture of what passes in the heart of many a pleading parent! They hear of Christ's love and power, and begin to pray with great urgency. But he answers not a word: there is no sign of thought or change on the part of the lost one. Still they pray, and it is as if the power of sin grows stronger, and the loved one only wanders farther off. Conscience begins to speak of parental sin and unworthiness. Others, who are holier and have more power with God, may be heard, but how can we expect that God should work a miracle for us? And the parent settles down in a quiet despondency or a vague hope that tries to shut its eyes to its own wretchedness. Oh, the dark, heartrending uncertainty as to the salvation of that child!

Her faith and perseverance. It is for this specially that the mother's example is held up to us. She refused to be denied. She met silence and argument and contempt alike with one weapon—more prayer, more trust. She had heard of the wondrous Man and his compassion; she saw it in his face; she heard it even in the voice that refused her; she would not believe he could send her away empty. She hoped against hope; she believed against appearances, and, what is more, against his very words; she believed and she triumphed. And now, mother—you who are pleading for your prodigal child—you have her example. And not only her example, but a thousand words of promise, and a revelation of the Father's will and the Savior's power and love such as she never had. Let her faith and perseverance put your unbelief to shame. In the face of all appearances and all doubts, let your faith rise and claim the promise of an answer to prayer in the name of Jesus. Yield yourself to the Holy Spirit to have everything searched out and brought to the light that you must confess and cast out. Trust not to the fervency of your desires or the wrestling urgency of your petition; seek your strength in God's promise and faithfulness, in his power and love. Let the soul, in restful deliberate confidence in Jesus, praise him for his promise and his power to save. In this confidence let nothing shake you from the continuous and persevering prayer of faith. The prayer of faith is always heard.

The wondrous blessing she obtained is for us, too. There was not only her daughter's deliverance from this grievous trouble; there was something almost better—a spiritual blessing—our Lord's delighted approval of her faith: "O woman, great is your faith! Be it unto you even as you will." Yes, it is in the earnest, believing supplication for a child that the parent's heart can be drawn out toward the Lord, can learn to know and trust him aright, can rise to that insight into his love which is most pleasing to him, and bring down into the soul the consciousness of his good pleasure. Mother, who are pleading for loved ones far from the fold, come nearer—come nearer to Jesus. He is able, indeed, to save them. He waits for your faith to take hold of his strength, to accept their salvation. Oh, let not your child perish because you refuse to come and take time with him, until his love has inspired you with faith. Mother! Come nearer, tarry with Jesus in prayer, trust him: your child can be saved.

Blessed Lord Jesus! I, too, like the Syrophenician woman, have a child grievously vexed with a devil. Like her I come pleading, "Have mercy on me, O Lord, Son of David."

O Lord, I would confess the sin of my child. You know it all: unconverted, and an enemy to you by nature, he has rejected your love, to choose the world and sin. I confess my sin, too. Lord, you know how bitter the thought is that, had my life been less in the world and the flesh, purer and holier, more full of faith and of love and of you, my child might have grown up differently. Lord, in deep sorrow I confess my sin; oh, let not my child perish. Son of David, have mercy on me.

Blessed Lord, I put my trust in you. I look in faith to your Almighty power; the things that are impossible with man are possible with God. I look in faith to your promise to hear prayer. Lord, I believe you hear me; help my unbelief. I lay this perishing child at your feet, and plead your love. Savior, I do believe in your love, and claim deliverance for my child. In this faith I will praise you for your grace. I will tarry at your feet day by day in the rest of faith, praising you, and looking out for your fulfillment. Make haste, O my Lord, for your name's sake. Amen.

THIRTIETH DAY

The Heavenliness of a Little Child

"Whosoever shall humble himself as this little child, the same is greatest in the kingdom of heaven. And whoso receives one such little child in my name, receives me."—*Matthew 18:4–5*

THE DISCIPLES had come to Jesus with the question, Who is the greatest in the kingdom of heaven? He spoke so often of the kingdom; to them it suggested the idea of power and glory; they could not but wonder who would have the highest place. How utterly strange and incomprehensible must have been the answer Jesus gave to their question. He called a little child, and set him in the midst of them. He told them that as long as they were thinking of who would be greatest, they could not even enter the kingdom; they must first become as little children: and then in the kingdom the humblest and the most childlike would be the highest. And whoever should receive one such little child in Jesus' name, should receive himself. The deeper the sympathy with the child-nature, recognizing Jesus and his name in it, the closer and more complete the union with himself.

How wonderfully applicable to parents is what Jesus spoke to his disciples. In creating a family, with father and mother, God sets a little child in the midst. And in that little child he opens to them the mystery of the kingdom of heaven and the spiritual world. He tells them that if they want to know about heaven, and what will prove their fitness for its highest place, they must study the child-nature. On earth they will find nothing so heaven-like as a little child, and no surer way to the highest enjoyments of heavenly dignity than in receiving little children in his name, for in doing this they will receive himself in whom the kingdom is. These are the three lessons we parents must learn.

First, the heavenliness of the little child. Wherein does this consist? Our Savior uses one word: "Whosoever shall humble himself as this little child, the same is greatest in the kingdom." The greatest will be he who thinks least of being greatest, because he loses sight of himself in seeking God and his kingdom. The great beauty of childlikeness is the absence of self-consciousness. The true child loses himself in that which is around him. The curse of sin is that it makes man, every man, his own center; even when he seeks the kingdom of heaven, he is still thinking how he can be greatest in the kingdom. In the true child, self does not yet manifest itself; it lives and is at rest outside of itself in the parent. It loves, and rejoices in being loved; it is truthful, and trustful to all around, showing itself as it is, counting upon others to be what they appear. This naturalness and simplicity of the child, Jesus tells us, is something heavenly, the thing in nature most allied to the kingdom. And the lesson we need to learn is that there is nothing a parent should seek to preserve and cherish more carefully than this heavenly childlikeness. It is the secret of that beautiful calmness and serenity which is the image of the peace and the rest of heaven.[2]

The spirit of the world is the very opposite; with its rivalry and its ambition, its seeking excitement and possessions, it destroys all that is so beautiful and heavenly in the child, to make way for the show and self-seeking that are its marks. Especially Christian parents who have the means for gratifying taste and pleasure at their disposal are in danger of destroying the simplicity and tenderness of the child-life by stimulating the desires which are of the earth and draw thither. And so, in the midst of a great deal of Bible-teaching and hymn-singing, the very heart of true religion may be eaten out by the artificial and unchildlike spirit of the homes in which the children are reared.

Parents: make a study of it to find out what the thought of Jesus' heart was when he spoke so strongly of the need of being childlike as the only path to heaven and heavenly greatness. Value the childlikeness and simplicity of your little one as its heavenly beauty; realize that the little one, in its tender susceptibility of impressions, is all alive to what surrounds

2. See Note B on the value of this serenity and tranquility in a child's character.

it, to the fostering influence of the heavenly life or the withering effect of a worldly life. Believe that between the Holy Spirit, who brings heaven down to us and reveals it within, and the heavenliness of childhood, there is a wonderful suitableness for each other; train your children in that holy, happy stillness which keeps the heart open to his workings.

But how shall the parent succeed in doing this? Our Lord's words have a second lesson. If we are to watch over the heavenliness of our children, we must ourselves be childlike and heavenly-minded. Christ put a little child in the midst of strong men to teach them. Parents often owe more to the teaching of their children than these to them. Our children lose their childlikeness so soon because parents have so little of it. The atmosphere of the home is so little that of simple, happy, trustful living in the Father's presence. Amid many of the proprieties of religion, the spirit of the world too often reigns. To be great in the kingdom of heaven is all too seldom the object of earnest desire. To be the greatest, as Jesus puts it, by being humble and childlike, the least and the servant of all—this is hardly dreamt of. No wonder if parents, instead of maintaining and strengthening the spirit of the child and of the kingdom, hinder and quench it.

Let parents study to be childlike. There are very few studies more difficult; very few that will bring a richer reward. The little treasures entrusted to us have a higher worth than we know; their very littleness, of which we often think only in connection with their weakness, and their future value, is what to him, who looked at things in the light of God, constitutes their greatest attraction. It is only the childlike life of the parent, living in great simplicity of truth and trust with the Father in heaven, that can maintain the childlikeness in the child, too.

To this end let us take in the third lesson our Savior has: "Whoso receives one such little child in my name, receives me." Let us at their birth receive our children in the name of Jesus, in his Spirit, with his appreciation of their simplicity and humility. Let us receive them in his name, as those whom he loves and blesses, and of whom he says, "of such is the kingdom," to be kept and trained for him and his kingdom alone. Let us receive them in his name, as sent by Jesus to remind us of his own childlike humility and obedience to the Father. Let us receive them day by day in his name, coming as a gift from the Father and the heaven from which he came, to draw us there, too. Let us receive them and cherish them in his name, just as he would receive them, as he did receive them, and bless them. Let us receive them in his name, just as we would receive himself.

Yes, just as we would receive himself. This is not saying too much, for he asks and promises nothing less. "He that receives one such little child in my name, receives me." He that recognizes and loves the humility, the childlikeness, the Christlikeness of the little child, and on this account receives and treasures the child, receives Christ himself. This is the promise. With every child something of heaven and of Christ comes into the house. In many cases it is not noticed, not cared for, and all of heaven is pushed aside by the world. Blessed they who know truly to receive the child in Jesus' name, a being from heaven, and like heaven, and for heaven—they receive himself. He comes to such with the little one to be its and their Savior. "Whosoever receives one such little child in my name, receives me." With the child he sets in their midst he takes the parents afresh into his training, to teach them how to be great in the kingdom of heaven. He comes to make their child a blessing to them, that so they may be prepared to be a real blessing to it. He comes to bless parent and child together, and make the home what it was meant to be—the picture, the promise, the pathway, to the Father's home in heaven.

Dear parents! Shall we not ask our Lord Jesus most earnestly to open our minds to take in his Divine thoughts about the heavenliness of our children, to open our eyes to see him in them, to bring our hearts into perfect sympathy with himself, so that our little ones may day by day be the blessed messengers that lead us to heaven, that bring to us Jesus himself, the life and the light of heaven?

Blessed Lord! Open our ears to hear what you speak, and our eyes to see as you see. Give us hearts to beat in sympathy with yours at the sight of every little child; and above all, our Lord, to understand and experience how surely and how blessedly you fulfill your promise, "Whosoever receives one such little child in my name, receives me."

Lord Jesus, we ask you for a childlike spirit. May the simplicity and restfulness, the love and the loveliness, the trustfulness and truthfulness, of the child-nature so dwell in us, that in communion with us the heavenly childlikeness of our little ones may not be lost, but cherished and maintained through advancing years. Give us to feel very deeply that we cannot truly fulfill our parental calling except as in simplicity and godly sincerity our walk with God is that of little children.

Blessed Lord, we thank you that however feeble we be, and however far short our attainments fall of what we should be, in receiving a child in your name we receive you. You come yourself to be our Teacher and our Helper. We pray you to strengthen us and all parents in this faith, that we may rightly understand that nowhere are you nearer or more ready to bless than in the home where the children are received in your name, to be saved by you, to be trained for you. Amen.

THIRTY-FIRST DAY

Suffering Children to Come to Jesus

"But Jesus said, Suffer little children, and forbid them not, to come unto me, for of such is the kingdom of heaven."—*Matthew 19:14*

WHAT DEEP SIGNIFICANCE there is in this word, "Suffer little children to come unto me." We suffer, or allow, or permit that which we are not naturally inclined for, which we would prefer to be otherwise. The mothers had probably heard of the words Jesus had just spoken (18:3–5), and brought their little ones to be blessed of this wonderful Teacher. Jesus saw the disciples rebuking them. They found it so hard to understand and to follow the Master: what could the little children have to do with him? Jesus hears them and says: "Forbid them not; allow them to come unto me, for of such is the kingdom of heaven." Among his disciples he loves to have the children: they are nearest the kingdom, the fittest for it; the kingdom needs them as the teachers of the wise and the great, to show the path through which alone heaven can be entered.

"Suffer little children to come unto me"—the word reminds us how, now still, our wisdom cannot understand that the kingdom and the little ones are specially fitted for each other. It is only, as it were, by sufferance that the religion and the faith of a child is borne with; a thing not to be too much trusted or rejoiced in. No wonder that with such a spirit in parents or the Church, the youthful grace is quenched, and that the child's religion becomes very much as that of the majority of older people. Let us hear the words of the Master today. If you cannot understand or fully approve, still do not forbid or hinder the children coming to Jesus; just bear with it, until you see how he can bless them, until his word, "of such is the kingdom," has entered your heart, and you learn to receive them as he did. Then only and truly will you have right views of what child-religion is: its nature, its dangers, its needs.

Child-religion must consist of that which constitutes the very center of God's revelation—coming to Jesus. In his own well-known words, "Come unto me," our Lord spoke of the blessed rest he would give to all who came to him to exchange their weary burdens for his loving yoke. This simple gospel is just what a child needs. Its faith is ready to believe in the unseen One, so kind and loving. Its humility finds no difficulty in confessing its sin and its need of help. And nothing appears more simple and natural than that this loving Savior should be obeyed and followed. As by instinct it reconciles faith and works, it sees at once that trust in him should beget obedience. But, above all, the child at once takes in what older people often cannot apprehend: that all religion and salvation center in a living Person. To a child, Jesus—Jesus loving and to be loved, Jesus trusted and obeyed, Jesus himself—is religion. Would that it were so all our life! Coming to Jesus in prayer, in surrender, in love, would be the spontaneous exercise of our faith. Oh, let us not hinder, but help our children to come to Jesus!

For this child-religion can be hindered. The words of Jesus suggest the thought. The child is weaker than the older disciple, is under his influence, can be kept back by him. God has given the making of the children into the hands of their elders. And the natural religiousness of the child, his simple faith and sense of love and duty to Jesus, may be terribly checked by the example and conduct of those around him. And so Jesus says, "Forbid them not." The word means (as it is elsewhere translated), "Hinder them not." The religion of the child is feeble, and can so easily be hindered. Christian parents are appointed as guardians, to watch and foster its growth. All growth comes from within, and depends upon a healthy life. But young and feeble growth needs to be preserved from danger from without, and to have provided for it the sustenance it demands. Often parents have been bitterly disappointed in their children: when young they could feel so deeply and speak so beautifully; they had not lived long before all was lost. It was probably because parents trusted to what was a blessed, but still only a feeble, beginning. They did not watch over the evil influences which the young plant could not yet resist. They allowed the spirit of the world in their own religious life or their friends; they allowed company and pleasure and the enjoyment of the world to choke the good seed. Or they failed to supply the needful nourishment. There was not, as the child grew up, anymore the personal speaking of this blessed Jesus, the helping of faith and obedience by the fellowship and example of a warm, living Christianity, a living love to Jesus. The child's religion disappeared because the parents hindered it in coming to Jesus.

How different the result is where this coming to Jesus is in a right spirit, fostered and encouraged not only in the little ones, but in the growing boy and girl through the years that lead to maturity. We need to be kept from right-hand as well as left-hand errors. On the one side, we must beware of despising a child's religious impressions as of little value. Like all beginnings of life and growth, they may be feeble and easily lost; they are still of infinite value as the preparation for that which abides ever. We must, on the other side, be kept from over-estimating or trusting in it. We must remember that the tender plant needs unceasing watching, and that only in the congenial atmosphere of a home holy to the Lord, and wholly dedicated to his service, can we count on its ripening fruit to eternal life.

We have already suggested what a child's religion needs. Just suffer the child to come to Jesus, and remove every hindrance. Believe deeply what Jesus says, "of such is the kingdom," and allow this heavenly element in the child's nature to show itself and to reach out after the Son of God. Let, in your education, Jesus and the coming to him to be saved from sin, to have the heart sanctified and satisfied, be your chief end. Beware of coming in between the child and Jesus; let the child under your leading have free access to Jesus. Beware of hindering it by distrust or coolness. Let the warmth of your love to Jesus, your holy example of obedience, your teaching and praying, in one word, your whole living—be a daily help to the child to see Jesus, to live with him, and to long for him. Jesus Christ is meant to be our every-day friend, our every-hour companion. Let all the wondrous influence you possess in forming your child and fixing his destiny be wielded for this one thing—to satisfy the desire of the Savior's heart and make your child wholly his.

These words of Christ's were spoken to disciples who knew him and confessed him the Son of God. They were sound in the faith, Christ's chosen friends. But they understood not his thoughts about the children:

this was too high for them, because the love of childlikeness is one of the highest things in the kingdom. Many a theologian and preacher and parent is not yet in sympathy with Jesus. Dear parents, who have taken the Savior as your only teacher in the revelation of the mysteries of Divine love, let him teach you the preciousness of your little ones. Learn to see in them what he does; in his light your care of them will become a blessing to yourself and to them.

Blessed Savior! Again we beseech you, open our eyes to see in our little ones what you see; to think of them as you do, as belonging to you and the kingdom. Make this so clear to us that it may become impossible to do otherwise than to lead them to you. Let your claim on them, your love to them, be the secret principle that inspires all our education.

And we ask, Lord, for a heavenly wisdom to know how to guide them in coming to you, and to help them to abide with you. Teach us to estimate aright a child's impressions, both in their weakness and in their worth, as the seeds of the eternal life. And may our faith in your love to them, and in their share in the kingdom, be the power by which their young hearts are made strong.

Blessed Lord, you are the parent's and the children's Friend. "Come unto me" is your one call, in every need and for every blessing. We come now, Lord, and ask grace to enable us to bring our children. Grant us your Holy Spirit, that day by day, and year by year, we may possess and train them for you alone and for your glory. Amen.

THIRTY-SECOND DAY

A Father's Tears

"And straightway the father of the child cried out and said with tears, Lord, I believe: help my unbelief."—*Mark 9:24*

WHEN JESUS spoke to the disciples about the mothers who were coming with their little children to him, his word was, "Suffer the children to come, and forbid them not." In this story he uses a stronger word. When the father of the lunatic had told him that the disciples had not been able to cast out the evil spirit, and Jesus had reproved their unbelief, he spoke, "Bring the child to me." The expression is a stronger one, still setting forth the same truth. The little ones were quite ready and willing to come to the loving Stranger to be blessed. This poor child, at times all unconscious or rebellious, had to be brought, whether he knew it or not. There can be no evil spirit in a child so strong, no resistance so desperate, but the parent has the liberty and the power to bring him to Jesus. To every disciple, to every father and mother, in every extremity of sin or need, Christ's voice is heard calling, "Bring the child to me."

And then, if we want to understand what it is really to bring a child, on whom Satan has a hold, to Jesus, we have this most wondrously set forth in the further communication of this father with Jesus. When, in answer to Christ's question, he had told the touching story of how ever since his childhood the boy had been the prey of this terrible trouble, and had pleadingly added, "If you can do anything, have compassion on us and help us," Jesus threw all the responsibility of the issue of the case upon the father, and said: "If you can! All things are possible to him that believes." It was not the question whether Jesus could and would do it, but whether the father could believe. If he did, the healing was sure; if he did not, it could not take place.

"If you can! All things are possible to him that believes." These words are one of the well-known expressions in which all the blessings of God's mighty saving love are put at the disposal of faith. "By faith we understand, both what God has done and will do. By faith we see him who is invisible, in the reality of his almighty power and his love toward ourselves. By faith we receive his word into our very heart as a quickening power, which works in us the very thought and sentiment that was in his heart when he spoke it. By faith our heart, our nature, our life is opened up to give place to God, so as to let him be and do in us what he pleases. By faith we become fully conscious of what the purpose of his will is, and of himself as waiting to work it in us. By faith we forsake the visible, ourselves, with our own thoughts and strength; we look to God to do what he has promised, and so give him the glory. Faith is the exercise of a will that yields itself for God's holy will to take possession of it and work out its pleasure. "All things are possible to him that believes," because "with God nothing shall be impossible," and faith is union with God.

In speaking these words to the father of the lunatic, Jesus gave to us for all time the secret of successful parental training and prayer. He tells us that it is not only the ministers of his gospel, the watchmen, and the workers in fields of special danger or difficulty, but every Christian parent, that needs to exercise strong faith, and in strong faith may most assuredly secure the salvation of his child. It teaches us that his compassion and power are longing to help us, if we can believe. If not, it is our blame if our children perish.

There are parents who think this is a hard saying. They seek the cause of unconverted and unsaved children in God and not in themselves. Has God's sovereignty nothing to do with the salvation of our children? Is there not such a thing as election? And if so, how can all the responsibility be thrown on our unbelief? Scripture reveals to us most clearly God's sovereignty; his grace is electing grace; the final decision of the destiny of each man is in his hands. Scripture reveals as clearly man's responsibility, and the all-prevailing power of faith. True humility accepts both statements without reconciling them; it bows under the solemn truth Jesus utters here, that if the parent can believe, the child can be saved.

How this truth ought to affect us, our text tells us. With tears the father cried, "Lord, I believe! Help my unbelief." In the agony of the thought that his unbelief may keep the blessing from his child, in the consciousness of how strong unbelief is still in himself, he bursts into tears, and casts himself to confess at Jesus' feet that unbelief, and ask deliverance from it. It is amid these tears of penitence and confession that the faith is exercised to which the victory is given. The devil is cast out, and the child is saved. Christ's blessed and most heart-searching word had done its work; it had revealed the unbelief, but also wakened the faith that brought the blessing.

Christ's word must do the same with every parent, with every father, who pleads for a child's liberation from Satan's power. A father's tears have power. There must be confession and humbling wherever there is to be strong faith. There must be the conviction and confession of the sin of unbelief: that it has been the cause of the blessing being withheld, and that we are verily guilty in being unbelieving. When the disciples asked the Master why they could not cast out this devil, he told them it was because of their unbelief, and that this unbelief was caused by their life not being one of prayer and fasting. Unbelief is not, as many think, a weakness, inexplicable and beyond our power. Unbelief has its reasons: it is the indication of the state of heart. The world, the worldly man, cannot believe. The self-righteous, the proud man, cannot believe. It is only the pure in heart, the humble, the soul that thirsts for God and forsakes all to follow Christ, that can be strong in faith. And therefore the first step in the path of an overcoming faith is the confession of its sinfulness, and the sins of which it is the index and the symptom.

I have heard parents plead very earnestly with God for the conversion of their grown-up children, when I secretly feared that they could not be heard. I saw no sign of confession of parental sin. There are parents whose worldliness, whose lack of living faith, whose self-indulgence and neglect in the education of their children, have simply sown the seeds of which they are now reaping the fruit in the departure of their children from God; and yet they wonder why their children are not more religious. They sometimes pray earnestly for them, and try to have the faith—perhaps think they have it—that their children will be saved. They may be deceiving themselves. True faith sanctifies. It searches the heart. It confesses the sin of unbelief, and all the sin in which that has its root and strength. It casts itself weeping and helpless at the feet of Jesus. There, and there alone, bowing in its weakness, resting on his strength, it obtains the blessing he loves to bestow.

Fathers who have sons you would gladly bring to Jesus to be saved, come and hear the lessons the Lord would teach you. Let these children first bring you to Jesus in confession and prayer and trust; your faith can then bring them in truth. And in yourself and in them you will experience what the all-prevailing power and truth is of the word: "If you can! All things are possible to him that believes."

Blessed Son of God! Look in mercy upon a parent who now comes to you with a child still unconverted and under the power of the Evil One. O Lord Jesus, have compassion on us and help us! Let the child be delivered from Satan's power; oh, make him a child of God.

Lord, I have heard your voice—"If you can believe!"—and it has filled my heart with trembling. I have to confess how little my life has been a life of faith, and how my unbelief has hindered the blessing from my child. I have to confess the worldliness and selfishness, the want of entire surrender and obedience to you, which made a strong faith impossible. I bow in shame at the thought of all the unbelief that even now comes up in me. Lord, I do believe! Help my unbelief.

I do believe, Lord, in your mighty power. I do believe in your infinite Love. I do believe in you as my Savior, my Friend, my Covenant Redeemer. I do believe, my Lord, that you hear me now for this child. Lord, I believe! Help my unbelief. I look to your word and hold it fast. I yield myself to a life of entire surrender to you, to be yours alone. Blessed Lord Jesus, I do believe you hear and save my child. In this faith I praise your holy name. Amen.

THIRTY-THIRD DAY

The Sacredness of Motherhood

"He shall be filled with the Holy Spirit, even from his mother's womb."—*Luke 1:15*

MAY GOD grant us his grace to meditate in holy tenderness and reverence on the truth revealed to us here, a truth of unspeakable preciousness and power to a believing parent: the mother's womb is the workplace of the Holy Spirit. Our Lord has taught us that the least in the kingdom of heaven is greater than John the Baptist; if he could be filled with the Holy Spirit from before his birth, how much more, now that Christ is glorified and the Holy Spirit given, the child of those who have become partakers of the full redemption and the indwelling of the Spirit of Christ.

We find here, at the very opening of the New Testament history, the same truth that came out so strongly in the laying of the foundations of the covenant with the patriarchs. In preparing and securing servants to do his work, God loves to begin at the very beginning, and from before the birth, from the very first conception of life, to take charge and to sanctify the vessel he is to use for his service. The more distinctly we apprehend this part of God's plan with his Church as one of the root principles of the economy of redemption, the better we shall understand the holy privilege and duty of parentage. Very specially will mothers be encouraged and strengthened in faith to yield themselves, with all the hopes and joys of motherhood, to be God's chosen vessels for the fulfillment of his purpose and the perfecting of his Church.

Let us look first at what Scripture teaches us of the mother in whom the Holy Spirit is thus to work. Of John's parents it is testified: "They were both righteous before God, walking in all the commandments and ordinances of the Lord blameless." It is the God of nature, who in this world of cause and effect has ordered that like begets like, who is also the God of grace. With omnipotence at his command, ready to work any miracles he pleases, he yet most carefully observes his own laws, and when he wants a holy child, seeks for holy parents. Throughout Scripture, specially in the New Testament, the blessed indwelling and inworking of the Holy Spirit is promised to the obedient. Man must, in obedience to Divine command, and under the preparatory moving of the Spirit, build the house; then does the Holy Spirit as the glory and the presence of the Lord take possession and fill it. And so it was of parents, walking in all the commandments and ordinances of the Lord blameless, that he would be born who was to be filled with the Holy Spirit from his mother's womb, and the forerunner of him who should baptize with the Holy Spirit. It is of holy parents that God would take a holy child.

The double lesson for every parent, and especially for every mother, is of the deepest interest. A righteous and blameless life prepares for, and may also count upon, the power of the Holy Spirit in the unborn child. Let expectant mothers who would fulfill their holy calling as the ministers of their Lord's purposes study Elizabeth's character: "Righteous, and walking in all the commandments of the Lord blameless." It is to such a life that God chose us, "that we should be holy and without blame before him in love." It is to such a life Jesus redeemed us: "He has reconciled you in his body through death, to present you holy and unblameable and unreprovable in his sight." It is no more than what every child of God ought to be and can be: "Blameless and harmless, without blemish in the midst of a perverse generation." But it is specially what every mother should be, who would offer her body as the temple of the Holy Spirit, that in her the very first beginnings of life may be overshadowed by the Holy Spirit. Oh, that mothers, and fathers too, understood to what a terrible degree the spirit of the world and the flesh, a life in which blamelessness before God is never expected or sought after, in which sin and selfishness are allowed to have rule, hinder the influence of the Spirit and entail upon the child, more than is needed, the heritage of unholy appetite and passion. Let them believe that a life which, in deep humility and the faith of Jesus as our sanctification, seeks to walk in obedience and righteousness, blameless before the Lord, will be accepted and honored of him. Let them believe that they have a right to ask, and most confidently to expect, the Spirit that is in them to take possession of the life God gives through them. Let them cherish this as the highest and the brightest hope of a holy motherhood: "He shall be filled with the Holy Spirit, even from his mother's womb."

Let us now look at what the angel's message teaches us of the child thus conceived and born: "You shall have joy and gladness, and many shall rejoice at his birth, for he shall be great in the sight of the Lord"—three marks of a child born under the covering of the Holy Spirit. The parents are to have joy and gladness. Alas, how many a Christian parent has had reason to say in bitter agony, "Would God my child had never been born!" Would you have divinely given and divinely secured joy and gladness in the children that are given you? Oh, let the Holy Spirit take possession of them from before their birth. Yours will be the holy joy of heaven in them, as you see the beauty of the Lord upon them, a joy that none can take away.

"And many shall rejoice at his birth." Alas, how many children of Christian parents have been the curse of their fellow men! Would you have your child blessed and made a blessing, with many to thank God that ever they knew him or that he was born? Study the story of John's birth. Study it in connection with the story of Jesus' birth. It was for Jesus' sake, in the power of the Son of God coming in the flesh, in virtue of his connection with Jesus, that John was thus filled with the Holy Spirit from his mother's womb. Plead the coming, and the birth, and the redemption of Jesus on behalf of your child; claim the outpouring of the Spirit upon all flesh, and the promise of the Spirit to you and your children, and your faith will be strengthened to perfect confidence that your child, too, may in his measure be filled with the Spirit, and shall make many to rejoice at his birth.

"And he shall be great in the sight of the Lord." This sets the crown on the whole. A joy to his parents, a blessing to his fellow men, and great in the sight of the Lord, is the Spirit-born child. Among men he may not make a name, in gifts and talents he may not be great, but great he will be in the sight of him who sees not as man sees. He will be a vessel God can use for his work, a true way-preparer for the coming of the Lord in his kingdom.

Mother! God gives you this picture of Elizabeth and her child of promise, with the double lesson: live as she did; believe and receive what she did. Young mother, your motherhood is in God's sight a holier and a more blessed thing than you know. If you are indeed God's child, you have in everything been placed under the leading and the rule of his Holy Spirit. Be sure that all the tender interest and solemn thought, all the quiet trust and joyful hope, which expectant motherhood calls forth, may be sanctified and refined by God's Holy Spirit, and you be united with your little one under the overshadowing of his heavenly grace.

Ever blessed God! Once more you have shown me your way in preparing a seed to serve you, and what a deep interest you have in securing a holy and blameless motherhood. I have seen you training a mother for your service. You fill her heart with the thought of the Divine destiny of her child. You stir her faith to the confident expectation of your Divine Spirit and blessing on her seed. You call her in righteousness and blamelessness of life to her holy work. You do in all things teach her that the life she is to bring forth is a holy gift from you, to be received and borne in a pure and holy vessel.

O great and glorious God, in deep humility and trembling your handmaid bows before you, to offer herself to your service. O my Father, who much more surely than fathers on earth give good gifts to their children, give your Holy Spirit to your children, to make even their body your temple, fulfill your wondrous promise to your child. Let your Holy Spirit dwell in me. If it pleases you to make me the mother of a child, oh, let him be filled with the Spirit from the womb. Let me be filled with the Spirit. And let my child be born only for this one thing: that he may be great in your sight and a blessing to all around him. Amen.

THIRTY-FOURTH DAY

A Mother's Surrender

"And Mary said, Behold the handmaid of the Lord; be it unto me according to your word."—*Luke 1:33*

WE HAVE OFTEN had occasion to notice the wonderful oneness of mother and child, and to what extent the former, in her life and character, influences and decides what the child is to be. The life she imparts is her own life, in the deepest meaning of the term. When God gave his Son to be born of a woman, this law was not violated, and the mother he chose for his Son was doubtless all that grace could make her to be the fit vessel through whom he should receive his human nature and disposition.

And so, just as Jesus himself is in everything our example, so we may naturally expect that in his mother God has given us one of his servants who may be an example to our mothers. If the child Jesus is an example to our children, there will be something for mothers to learn from his mother. She to whom the heavenly messenger said, "Hail, you highly favored, the Lord is with you: blessed are you among women," and to whom Elizabeth, filled with the Holy Spirit, also said, "Blessed are you among women, and blessed is the fruit of your womb, and blessed is she that believed," will surely in her words and ways have left an example for every mother who yields herself like Mary to the Lord, to bear a child that can be called a son of the Most High. Were there more mothers like Mary—this we may confidently say, without forgetting the infinite distance between her child and ours—there would be more children like the holy Child Jesus.

And what, looked at from the human side, constitutes the most marked feature of Mary's motherhood? It is the childlike simplicity of faith in which she surrenders herself to the Divine purpose: "Behold the handmaid of the Lord; be it unto me according to your word." She calls herself the Lord's slave or bondwoman; she gives her will, herself, up to him, to do what pleases him; in quiet trust and expectancy she will look to him to do what he has said. It is the same spirit of obedient faith, which had once fitted Abraham to be the father of the promised seed, which now prepares her to become the mother of him in whom the promise is to be fulfilled. Not that there were no difficulties or questionings. We read, "She was greatly troubled at the saying of the angel, and cast in her mind what manner of salutation this should be." When again he had spoken, she feared not to ask, "How shall this be, seeing I know not a man?" But when once the angel had spoken to her of the power of the Most High overshadowing her, she yielded herself to the Divine word. And she became an example to every mother who would like her share the benediction, "Blessed is she that believes, for there shall be a fulfillment of the things which have been spoken to her from the Lord." It is the surrender of faith that makes a blessed motherhood: "Blessed are you, and blessed is the fruit of your womb."

"Behold the bondmaid of the Lord." Mary teaches a mother to yield herself to God for the service of his kingdom, that in her his purpose and glory may be made manifest. It was not by the birth of Mary's son alone that God's kingdom was to come. Believing parents may look upon their children as the stones of the great temple of which Jesus was the cornerstone. Not less than with the birth of Isaac, and every child of the chosen race down to Christ, is the birth of each of our children under God's guardianship a link in the golden chain of the good pleasure of God's will. Over all the impulses of human love and the instincts of a God given maternity, there hovers a Divine purpose using them for the carrying out of his plan. And nothing will do more to sanctify the life of the wife and the mother than when she realizes herself to be the Lord's bondwoman, redeemed for this, too, that from her the chosen seed may be multiplied, that from her may be born a generation to serve the Lord. Human love will receive a Divine consecration; what otherwise appears to be only nature and earthly is elevated into the heavenlies, the region of God's will and God's favor; the expectant mother knows herself to be like the angels, one of his servants, doing his commandments, hearkening unto the voice of his word.

"Be it unto me according to your word." Such is the faith that gives the strength to surrender oneself to God's service. It looks no longer at difficulties or impossibilities; it counts upon God to carry out his purpose and to give the grace and the strength for the work to which he has called us. And it is just this faith that above everything fits for the blessed duties of motherhood, that gives that quiet rest of body and spirit which to mother and babe is health and strength. Or what mother is there who, as she first becomes conscious of her new vocation, is not at times with Mary "greatly troubled," and does not feel the question come many a time, "How can all this be?" She finds no rest so sure or sweet as to cast her troubles on her Lord—let him do what seems to him good. If the God of nature has created her for a calling, and the God of grace has redeemed her to fulfill that calling in the interests of his kingdom, she assuredly may trust his power and love not to forsake her in her hour of need. "What hour I am afraid I will trust in you; in God have I put my trust, I will not be afraid"—such words have a thousand times over been the stay of the trembling but trusting handmaid of the Lord.

"Be it according to your word." To understand fully the teaching of Mary's example here, there is one trait of her character we must not omit to notice. Twice it is said of her, "Mary kept all these things and pondered them in her heart." It is in the holy quiet of meditation and reflection on what God has said that the spirit of trust is cultivated. It is only as God's words are kept and pondered in the heart that they can quicken and deepen a living faith in him who spoke them. Every mother who searches Holy Scripture will find there many a saying of God with reference to her sacred calling, which, if truly drunk in, will fill the heart with confidence and joy. They will teach her to regard everything connected with the birth of the child as a matter of deepest interest to the Father in heaven, and of great importance to his kingdom, as the ushering in of a new member into its number. She will see how all the exceeding great and precious promises may be claimed by her for the little one, before ever yet it has seen the light. She will see how her receiving the little one in the name of Jesus has the promise of Jesus' presence for herself and for it. She will find that all the ordering and training of the child has been provided for in regulations of Divine wisdom and love, and that all the grace needed for carrying out these orders is most surely given to each one who, like Mary, will but be a bondmaid of the Lord, and will believe what he has spoken. All of care and fear, of danger and pain in the life of motherhood, all the help and joy and rich reward God has connected with it—all is written in the Book of the Lord; the mother who listens, and waits, and believes, will, in view both of what she fears and what she hopes, be able to say, "Behold the handmaid of the Lord; be it unto me according to your word." As she bides her time, let quiet retirement, in which she not only hides herself from the world but opens her whole being to the rays of heaven; let thoughtful, trustful pondering of God's words engage the heart; she will find how true the word is, "Blessed is she that believed."

What a holy and what a blessed thing the birth of a child becomes in the light of the birth of Jesus! What a holy and what a blessed task that of the mother becomes in the light of the favor of the Most High God, as the means of the fulfillment of his purpose, the promotion of his glory, the experience of his special grace and mercy! As the mother ponders these things, she will understand something of the deep meaning of that word of Paul, "She shall be saved through the childbearing, if they continue in faith, and love, and sanctification, with sobriety." Just as labor in the sweat of his brow was given to man, to be in his fallen state one of his greatest blessings, so the labor of childbearing to the woman, that through it and its blessed discipline the salvation of Christ might the more effectually be inwrought into her whole character and disposition. It calls and helps to a continuance in that blessed life of faith and trustful dependence, of love and gentleness and motherly kindness, of holiness in the indwelling and sanctification of the Spirit, of sobriety and self-restraint and temperance, in which true blessedness is found. It helps, to them who are rightly exercised thereby, to form that perfect womanly character which is one of God's most beautiful gifts on earth. It is in this path of loving acceptance of God's appointment, and trustful resting in his promise, that the word will come true, as a greeting to each expectant mother: "Blessed are you, and blessed is the fruit of your womb."

Behold the handmaid of the Lord! Yes, Lord! As you have already looked upon her in your mercy, and set her apart for the sacred work of bearing and bringing up a seed for you, still continue to look upon her to give her all that she needs, and to work in her all that is well pleasing in your sight. As the eye of a maid unto the hand of her mistress, so our eyes look unto the Lord our God, until he have mercy upon us. Grant to your child an ever increasing clearness, the blessed assurance that in this holy calling of motherhood she is indeed your handmaiden, called to the fulfillment of your purposes, set apart for the service of your kingdom. Let this thought teach me to look upon everything connected with the birth of my child as of deepest interest to my Father. Let it encourage me to cast every fear and burden, every care and pain, on him in whose service they come. Let it sanctify all the hope and joy with which you do so wonderfully sweeten the sorrow with which sin had filled our cup.

And so let it be unto me according to your word. In childlike faith, O my Lord, I would take your blessed Word, with all its teachings and its promises, as my light and strength. In the time of patient waiting, or in the hour of anguish, your Word shall be my stay. Let your Holy Spirit unfold to your handmaiden what treasures your Word contains for her as mother, that she may know at the right time to receive what you have provided for her. May she so be prepared that the child which has been received according to your word may be trained according to that Word, and enter into the full enjoyment of all that your Word holds out in promise to the seed of your people. Behold the handmaid of the Lord! Be it unto me according to your word. Amen.

THIRTY-FIFTH DAY

A Mother's Thanksgiving

"And Mary said, My soul does magnify the Lord, and my spirit has rejoiced in God my Savior. For he has regarded the low estate of his handmaiden."—*Luke 1:46–48*

THERE IS perhaps no such moment of exquisite joy, of deep, unutterable thanksgiving taking the place of pain and sorrow, as when a mother knows herself to be the living mother of a living child. Our blessed Lord used it as the fittest type of that wondrous surprise, that strange resurrection joy, with which his disciples should find him whom they mourned as crucified and dead to be the Living One. "A woman when she is in travail has sorrow, because her hour is come, but as soon as she is delivered of the child she remembers no more the anguish, for joy that a man is born into the world." A mother will find no more fitting expression for her joy than in thanksgiving to him to whom she owes so much. And for the expression of that thanksgiving she will find in many portions of Holy Scripture the most suitable language. How often, for instance, has the mother almost instinctively asked for the words of Psalm 103: "Bless the Lord, O my soul; and all that is within me, bless his holy name. Bless the Lord, O my soul, and forget not all his benefits: who forgives all your iniquities; who heals all your diseases; who redeems your life from destruction; who crowns you with loving-kindness and with tender mercies; who satisfies your mouth with good things, so that your youth is renewed like the eagle's." But as the simple summary of all a mother has to say, no words will be found more beautiful than these of the mother of our Lord: "My soul does magnify the Lord, and my spirit does rejoice in God my Savior. For he has regarded the low estate of his handmaiden."

In his holy providence the Father has so ordered it that the first week after the birth of the little one is a time of weakness, in which nothing is so much needed as quiet and rest for the restoration of nature's exhausted powers. The arrangement is one of wondrous grace, giving the mother time to prepare herself again for the new duties devolving on her. While household duties and ordinary relation are kept at comparative distance, the Lord would keep his child for a little while in the secret place of his Holy Presence, to encourage and instruct her for the solemn responsibilities now again awaiting her. And there is nothing that will be more pleasing to her Lord, and more refreshing and strengthening for her own life, and a fitter preparation for blessing to the little one, than that the spirit of thanksgiving should give its bright tone to all her thoughts and hopes, and the song of praise, from the lips of the model mother, be repeated day by day, and from hour to hour: " My soul does magnify the Lord, and my spirit does rejoice in God my Savior. For he has regarded the low estate of his handmaiden. For he that is mighty has done to me great things, and holy is his name; and his mercy is on them that fear him, from generation to generation."

It is hardly necessary to remind a mother of what all there is to stir her to praise. She has but to think of the anxious thoughts and fears that would sometimes come up as the solemn hour of her trial rose up before her, and her song is, "I sought the Lord, and he heard me, and delivered me from all my fears." She looks at the precious little treasure that has been given her, with all the love and joy it brings into heart and home; and the words come spontaneously, "What shall I render to the Lord for all his benefits toward me?" She sees in the little one, as she looks upon it in the light of God's purpose and promise, an immortal being, fitted for showing forth God's glory on earth, and sharing that glory in heaven, as a jewel in Jesus' crown; and her soul bows in trembling wonder at the thought that the charge of keeping and forming such a treasure should be committed to one so feeble. She remembers that, though the little one has inherited from her an evil nature, yet through her, too, it has the promise of the covenant and the earnest of the Spirit: her child is holy, because she is one of God's holy ones in Christ. She thinks of all the grace and wisdom and strength provided her in Christ to secure to her and her child all that God's love had prepared; and as she listens to the voice, "My grace is sufficient for you: my strength is made perfect in weakness," she can only sing again, "My soul does magnify the Lord, and my spirit does rejoice in God my Savior; his mercy is on them that fear him, from generation to generation." It is not only God's mercies, but God himself, in whose love they have their value and their continuance; it is God himself in whom Mary, in whom the believer, in whom the grateful mother, is glad and rejoices. True praise uses God's mercies only as the steps of the ladder along which it rises to leave them behind and rejoice in God alone.

This spirit of thanksgiving, in which, not content with the blessings alone, we rise up to the God who gave them and rejoice in him, is of greater worth than can well be expressed. It elevates and sanctifies both the joy, the gift that causes it, and the glad possessor, because it lifts all out of the sphere of nature into the fellowship of the spiritual and the Divine. And in this way it is the true preparation for all the work the mother has before her. We saw in Mary's surrender of herself to her God, that he might fulfill in her the good pleasure of his will, how there were combined in it two elements, the surrender to the work she had to perform, "Behold the bondmaid of the Lord," and the trust that counted on God to do for her what he had promised, "Be it according to your word." In both of these aspects the thanksgiving and joy of the hour of deliverance, if cultivated and kept up, will be guidance and strength.

"Behold the bondmaid of the Lord." The labor of bearing a child is but the beginning of that labor of love to which God has appointed and set apart the mother. The whole work of rearing and guarding and training the child is now to follow. The spirit of thanksgiving is the best preparation for the altar of consecration. If the mother is indeed to receive grace for the right and successful fulfillment of this new charge, it will need on her part a very distinct consciousness and confession of unfitness, a very definite giving up of herself to be henceforth the Lord's willing, loving slave for this holy work. As she looks at how much there may be that has to be parted with and put away, how much that she will have to struggle against and overcome, to be the holy mother of a holy child, entirely consecrated to God, the thought may conic up that the sacrifice and the strain will be too great, that it is impossible to live so strictly, so entirely and peculiarly given up to God's service. We fear to be too different from others; God could bless us and our children even though we are not so very holy. Oh, that a mother, if such thoughts come up, would just pause and think of what God has done! There is the new life given to herself, and the life of her precious little one; there is the love and mercy of God, and all the promise of more love and mercy to be poured out. Has the thanksgiving been so unreal, has the joy been so selfish and earthly, that there can be any hesitation as to whom these lives shall belong to? God forbid! If the thanksgiving has been true, it cannot but lead the mother to say that utterly and entirely she will live for God, that she may have grace to train a child who, too, shall utterly and entirely be the Lord's. "The joy of the Lord is your strength": a mother's joy is the power for a mother's work; the spirit of thanksgiving leads to the altar of consecration where mother and child are laid as living sacrifices to be the Lord's alone.

"Be it unto me according to your word": this word of faith and trust, looking to God to do all that he has promised, gets new meaning after the experience of the first part of its fulfillment. In all the work that waits the mother in the future, the goodness just experienced teaches her to trust. Let her but yield herself heartily, not to her work, but to her God for his work; she may depend upon it that his teaching and his help and his strength are realities. Let her in the joyful spirit of praise take his word, and, as she studies what it says of a mother on earth, note what it says of the Father in heaven and the abounding grace he has undertaken to supply, and her faith will grow strong that her vow of surrender has been accepted, that its fulfillment is possible and certain, and that the joy of a child born into the world is but the beginning of a joy that shall know no ending. Let thanksgiving lift the heart to God in praise; there faith becomes easy. Let faith lift the heart to God, too; there thanksgiving becomes natural, and the life of mother and child may become one unceasing song of faith and love, of surrender and obedience, of thanksgiving and praise.

Blessed be the Lord! For he has showed me his marvelous kindness! Bless the Lord, O my soul, and forget not all his benefits! What shall I render to the Lord for all his benefits toward me?

O my Father! In this the time of her weakness and gladness of heart, your handmaid draws near to praise your mercy and your love. Here am I and this precious child you have given me, the witnesses of your power and your goodness; may our lives, all our days devoted to you, be the sacrifice of thanksgiving we bring you.

Oh, hear the prayer of your handmaid, and let my life, now received anew as from your hand, indeed become wholly new. In daily relation with my Father, in close following and fellowship with my Lord Jesus, in a very tender yielding to the leading and sanctifying of the Holy Spirit, I desire henceforth to live only and wholly as your handmaid.

And with myself, Lord, I offer you my precious child. Let the grace I have implored of you fit me from its very birth to hold it as your property, a sacred trust from you to nurse and train as yours. It comes from you, O my God, a gift to me; accept it from me again, a living gift to you. Come to your handmaid, I pray you, in this her time of weakness and thanksgiving: let in this time of holy quiet your presence overshadow me, and give me the assurance that my prayer is heard; that you have accepted her and her little one to keep as your own forevermore. Amen.

THIRTY-SIXTH DAY

Jesus the Children's Surety

"And they brought him to Jerusalem, to present him to the Lord, as it is written in the law of the Lord, Every male that opens the womb shall be called holy to the Lord, and to offer a sacrifice according to that which is said in the law of the Lord."—*Luke 2:22–24*

According to the law of God in Israel, a child was circumcised when eight days old; this was done in its home. On the fortieth day the mother was to appear in the temple to bring the sacrifice of her purification, and to present her child to the Lord. If the child was a firstborn, then its presentation had special reference to the firstborn belonging to the Lord, and it had to be redeemed. The Child Jesus had thus also to be presented to the Lord, as being made under the law, and made like unto his brethren in all things. Made like in all things, not only that he might have experience of everything we pass through, but that we might know that every state and condition has been sanctified by his Holy Presence and merit, and that he now, by giving us the spirit which was in him when passing through them, might impart to us the blessing and the sanctifying grace that flow from fellowship with him. This truth has thoughts of wonderful joy and comfort for parents as they bring their little ones to God's home, to present them before the Lord in baptism.

Let us study this presentation of the holy Child Jesus. There he is, presented to his Father in heaven by his earthly parents; a helpless infant, but yet a pleasing sacrifice, a sweet smelling savor. There, too, he comes as the firstborn among many brethren, the Forerunner, through whom our little ones, too, can be acceptable to the Holy One. For now, when we bring our child to present him to the Lord, he looks down from heaven on the offering and gives, in answer to the parent's faith, to our child the spirit of his holy childhood. He was indeed made like us, that we might become like him; he was made like unto our children, that they might be made like him. He was not only Mary's firstborn, but the Father's first-born among many brethren. Where the first-fruits are holy, the whole family is holy. The presentation of the Child Jesus to the Father gives us a right to present ours, and makes them acceptable, too. Blessed thought! To place my child beside the holy Child, and in faith to claim that in him my child is holy and accepted, too. In Israel the presentation of the child was accompanied with a sacrifice to cleanse away the defilement of sin clinging, at every birth, to both mother and child. This we need, too. And what a mercy that the mother now can look to the blessed Jesus, the great sin-offering and atonement (Leviticus 7: 6), for her cleansing from all sin, so that she may be accepted and fitted for being a true mother to this God-devoted child! And what mercy that the children, too, share in the efficacy of that great sacrifice before they know it! That from their birth they now are holy to the Lord, and may receive that Holy Spirit which is the lawful inheritance of the seed of God's believing people. We present our little one to the Lord, with Jesus as the great sin-offering making us acceptable and clean and holy to the Lord.

The object of this presentation in the temple of the children was very specially to acknowledge God's claim upon them, and to devote them to him as his property. With what gladness and confidence parents do this when first they have seen Jesus presented in the temple. Or what does this mean? Has the Eternal God indeed not spared his only-begotten Son, but given him up for us and our children? Has he in very deed given his Son, the Lord of glory, to be our and our children's possession, to enter into all their feebleness and misery, to be like them subjected to a birth needing purification and presentation with sacrifice, and to a death like ours under the curse, and shall we now withhold our children from him? Or shall we not most gladly present them before him to be only and wholly his, devoted to his service and glory? Shall we not place our little one beside this holy Child, and on his merits, and say, "Father, through your holy Child Jesus, with him, in him, like him, I present my child to you, to be the Lord's only and forever"?

Be assured that in such a presenting of your child, after the example, in the power and spirit of God's Child, there is a rich and sure blessing. Presented to God in Jesus, accepted in Jesus, it may now grow up with and like Jesus. Let your faith lay hold of the holy child-life of Jesus as belonging to your child, as communicable by the power of the Holy Spirit. Let your faith maintain and renew daily the solemn act in which you as parent appeared before the Lord to present your child to him, before you took it back to your home to rear and train. Let your faith rejoice in that definite Divine transaction in which, when you presented your child in the name of Jesus, it was accepted of the Father as his own. What we present to God, "according to that which is said in the law of the Lord," that, in accordance with his word, God takes. And what he takes he keeps. And our faith has only ever to look to God's taking and keeping to have the joyful assurance that the matter is finally settled between God and us. Let this faith make you strong to train the child for God, in a strength and grace which he will give, to secure his property for himself. Let this faith speak to your child, as he can receive it, of his having been presented with Jesus, like Jesus, in Jesus, to the Father, and of his fellowship in the life and spirit of him who became the children's Surety. Let the holy childhood of Jesus overshadow and sanctify the childhood of your little one. Let your children grow up in the friendship and the footsteps of the holy Child. Live in everything as those who are going to train children who are to be like Jesus. If the thought appear too high, let it but constrain you to ask the Father whether he does indeed desire your child to be wholly like his, and whether he does expect of you to train it to be so. The answer will not be withheld, and the presentation of Jesus in the temple will become to you a pledge of the grace that enables you to see how Jesus is in everything the promise of what your child can be, and to train him accordingly.

We all know how, in the economy of grace and in the work of salvation for man, there are always two powers in action, the Divine and the human. To the former corresponds faith, that ever looks to God's promise and power; to the latter works, without which faith cannot be perfected, and which obey and fulfill the will of God. In our study of the teachings of God's Word on the parent's calling, we have ever found how these two aspects of truth are presented by turns, and how, while at one moment everything appears to depend upon a parent's faith in what God does, very soon after a parent's character and conduct appear to decide all. The two are inseparably interwoven: the more intently we pursue the one line of thought, the clearer will the other become. And we shall see that the deeper our insight into the indispensable necessity of either, the greater will be our felt need of the other as its complement.

We have here again been meditating on the spiritual side, and apparently speaking less of the practical training of daily life. Let all parents be assured that there is nothing more intensely practical than an act of real faith. If our presenting a child to the Lord is the deed of an intelligent, childlike, heartfelt faith, it will have its mighty influence on our daily treatment of the child. If it is renewed from day to day, it will have its effect on our whole relation to the little one growing up under our care. As we think of it as God's devoted and accepted property, as we regard ourselves as trustees to whom it has been committed for keeping and training, as we realize how God never would expect of our feebleness to take charge aright of an immortal spirit without providing the grace to do it well, and give ourselves with the child to a life of consecration and holiness, our faith will be the vital principle ruling all our conduct.

THIRTY-SEVENTH DAY

The Baptism with Water and the Spirit

> "John answered, saying, I indeed baptize you with water; but there comes he who is mightier than I, the latchet of whose shoes I am not worthy to unloose. He shall baptize you with the Holy Spirit and with fire."—*Luke 3:16*

MAN has a twofold nature: there is the external and visible; there is the internal, unseen, spiritual. Sin brought both equally under the power of the curse. In redemption both are to be made partakers of the glorious liberty of the children of God: "We wait for our adoption, to wit, the redemption of our body"; the whole man, body and spirit, is to be saved. All God's dealings with us have respect to both sides of our nature; through the external he seeks to reach the inner man; the inner again is renewed that thence the blessing may stream out and take possession of the outer man.

It is on this ground that we have the twofold baptism of which our text speaks: the baptism with water, and the baptism with the Holy Spirit. The Baptist teaches us the relation existing between the two; the insufficiency of the baptism with water in itself, and its high value as the pledge and the preparation of what was to come. In his words, ministers and parents, through whom together the little ones receive their baptism of water, find the clearest light on their duty toward the baptized child, and on the spirit in which they themselves, and afterward the child under their guidance, are to regard its baptism.

And first we note the faith which the baptism with water warrants and demands as a sign and seal of the baptism of the Spirit. It is a sign in which God sets forth the working of regeneration, the cleansing of our nature by the renewal of the Holy Spirit. It is also a seal, an assurance that, where God has given the water, he most certainly gives the Spirit, too, to the faith that claims and takes it. When John had come, the coming of Christ was certain; when John had baptized with water, the baptism with the Spirit was certain. God gave the one to awaken faith and expectation for the other. So intimate is the connection that our Savior did not hesitate to speak of being "born of water and the Spirit"; thus closely does he join and make them one. God would teach us that what he has meant to be one, and made one in promise, our faith can make one in reality. As in the whole economy of grace the connecting link between God's promise and his fulfillment is our faith, so here too. The promise of God is no empty word, though our unbelief may make it of none effect. In his purpose the water and the Spirit are inseparably united: "What God has joined together, let not man put asunder"—let not a parent's unbelief rest content with the water without the Spirit. Claim and accept with the most assured confidence the baptism of the Spirit for your child; and in faith praise for it as the divinely secured heritage of your little one.

Let us now observe the work to which the baptism with water calls and pledges us. The whole history of John teaches us that the Spirit could not be received until the way had been prepared for him. The Baptist knows how little his labors avail until the baptism of the Spirit is given. And yet he labors. He does the double work of preaching repentance of sin and faith in the Lamb of God. A most blessed lesson for the Christian parent. In some children the workings of the Spirit are given from the very birth. In others they become manifest at very different stages of later growth. But in all, the manifestation of the Spirit needs a parent's education in the lines of John's preaching. The child needs to be taught what sin is and what repentance is, what the giving up of everything that is not according to the will of God. And it needs to be pointed to Jesus, the Lamb of God, through faith in whom the full influx of the Spirit is to come. So that, just as in the parent there is to be the harmony of faith and work, so the child no less from its earliest youth has to be trained for a God who asks to be trusted and obeyed. It is by the obedience of faith that parent and child are prepared for the fulfillment of the promise.

Learn one more lesson from John. The secret of the wondrous union between faith and work in him you will find in his deep humility. His preaching had been with mighty power. A great revival of religion was taking place; all men were flocking to him; no prophet in Israel had ever preached as he had done. And yet he says, "The latchet of whose shoes I am not worthy to unloose." It is ever thus. The more the soul has received of the vision and the fellowship and the power of the Holy One, the deeper the sense of its utter nothingness and absolute dependence. But then, also, the deeper its confidence in the truth and power of him whom it has seen, and the greater its courage for his work, because it knows whence its help most surely comes. The thought might rise, or we might even hear others say it, that the assured confidence of the Spirit's being given to our children may lead to pride, or may slacken exertion in their behalf. He that understands what faith is knows the answer. True faith and deep humility are inseparable, because faith is the becoming nothing to let God be all. And so true faith and faithful labor are no less inseparable, because faith yields itself to God to use and to work through us. Let it be with the parent as with John; there is nothing that makes us so strong to honor God as when we are bound by the threefold cord of strong faith, earnest effort, and deep humility.

Christian parent! Have you accepted the promise of the Spirit with the water? Oh, hold that promise fast in a living faith. Praise God unceasingly for his gift to your child, even when you do not yet see its fulfillment. In your daily home-life, let everything be subordinated to the high destiny for which your God has entrusted a child to you: he is to be a vessel filled with his Spirit. Labor earnestly and hopefully with this blessed prospect in view. As often as these labors teach you your impotence or your unfaithfulness, look to him whose servant you are, and who has made you the messenger of the Spirit. He will fit you for the work he has given you to do. Jesus has said, "He that believes in me, rivers of living water shall flow out of his belly." Believe in Jesus! Try again, and once again, and ever more again the unexhausted fullness of that word; live your life by the faith of the Son of God. Through you the Spirit will flow out to your child. And each baptism you witness will be the glad reminder of the riches of the inheritance of your child, too.

And, you ministers of Christ, if any such read these lines—to whom is committed the ministration of this holy baptism—seek, oh, seek, like John, with every baptism to testify that he who has sent you to baptize with water has said to you that there is One coming after you to baptize with the Holy Spirit! Let us pray God to make all his servants indeed ministers of the Spirit, that they may have grace in all their ministrations to speak and act as men who have realized that the Spirit has been given to follow and to seal the message and the work of faith. And especially that they may have grace to lead and train both parents and children into the apprehension of that presence of the Holy Spirit in their home-life, through which the family can again take its place as God's first and choicest ordinance for the maintenance and the extension of the kingdom of heaven. It is as ministers and parents, as the whole Church, awakes to this truth, that the baptism of little children will no longer be, what it has too often been, a religious form, or a promise that is never fulfilled; but a sacrament, mighty and efficacious, of the presence of the Holy Spirit in the Church and in the home.

Gracious God! I thank you for the holy ordinance of baptism, with its Divine assurance of the baptism of the Spirit. And I thank you that as our little ones are with us children of the covenant and its spiritual promises, they also share in the seal of the covenant. And I thank you that their baptism is the token of their being holy to the Lord, and the heirs of the promise of the Spirit. Lord God, teach me—teach all believing parents, teach your Church—to believe that, wherever in your name the baptism of water is received, you wait to fulfill your engagement to give the baptism of the Spirit, too. In the great gift of your Son, you have given us him who baptizes with the Holy Spirit.

Blessed Lord Jesus, I come to you with my children. I bring them to you. I claim for them the baptism of the Spirit. In faith I accept of it. In that faith I would train them to believe in you, that they may by faith in you come into the personal possession of what I have received for them. Yes, before they can yet believe, I offer myself, that through me and the influence of my life your blessed Spirit may rest upon them.

Blessed Savior, give me grace in this faith to train them wisely, and according to your will, preparing in them the way of the Lord. Amid the consciousness of unworthiness and impotence, may this be my one hope and aim: that my children may daily live under the rule of your Holy Spirit. Amen.

THIRTY-EIGHTH DAY

A Faith Home

"One comes from the ruler's house, saying, your daughter is dead; trouble not the Master. But when Jesus heard it, he answered him, saying, Fear not; believe only, and she shall be made whole."—*Luke 8:49–50*

FEAR NOT; only believe! To how many thousands that word has been the messenger of comfort and hope, as they struggled under the burden of sin, or sought for help in trial or difficulty! It told them that there was deliverance from fear in believing in Jesus; faith can banish fear. And yet, how many who have found a blessing in the word have forgotten that it is a word that especially belongs to parents. In every other use it is but a loan; it is as parents that we have full right to it. It is Jesus, the Lord of the home, of parents and children, who speaks: "Fear not; only believe." The word reminds of the needful double lesson: in our children there is every reason for fear; in Jesus, every reason for faith.

When we look at our children, there is every cause for fear. When we think of the evil nature they inherit from us, and the mighty power Satan has in this world into which they are entering, we may well fear. When we see, both in Scripture and in the world around us, how often the bright promise of childhood is blighted, and the children of a religious home depart into the ways of evil and of death, we may well fear. When we think of the dangers to which they often are exposed, in the very nurses that surround their infancy, in the little friends of their childhood, in the schools through which they must pass, in the spirit of the world with which they must come into contact, in the literature and the amusements and the business from which they cannot be kept separate, we may well fear.

And then, when we think of our children and realize how feeble and unfit and unfaithful we are to take charge of them, the fear grows stronger whether they will indeed secure the blessing prepared for them. We know how the atmosphere we create and breathe through our home is stronger than all precept or external practice. We are deeply conscious of how much there still is of worldliness and selfishness, how much that is not in the fullness of the Spirit and the love of God; and we tremble at the thought of how our children may suffer from our lack of grace. We have reason to fear: would God that there were more of earnest, hearty fear of the power of sin and death!

To such the word of Jesus comes: "Fear not; only believe." Only believe: for faith is the one condition through which the power and the salvation of God are given. Only believe: for it is by faith that we throw ourselves and our children on Jesus and secure his blessing. Only believe: let faith look upon God's covenant with us and our seed, and see how he engages to give us all the grace we need as parents, as well as all the grace our children need. Only believe: it is faith that is the mighty renewing power in a man's life that teaches him to obey and do all that God has commanded. Only believe: this is the one thing Jesus asks of the parent who truly seeks his child's deliverance from sin and death, and fears lest he fail of securing it.

This is now the one lesson we must seek to learn: that of a parent who has come to Christ with his child, the first duty is faith. Just as with the penitent sinner, or the believer seeking more grace, all things are possible to him that believes. Our domestic, as our personal life, must be a life of faith. We must not only have the heart, but the home, too, purified by faith. Faith is the one thing God asks for in his children. It was in each case faith that made it possible, made it simple and easy, as parents, to do what made them the channels of a Divine blessing to their children.

And so still the power to understand God's purpose with our children, to save our household, to obey God's will in all its rule, to offer our children to God, to bless our sons, and to save them from the destroyer, depends upon our faith. The living Christ, in whom is our salvation and our strength, every needed blessing and grace for us and our children—it is he who speaks, "Only believe." It is in the knowledge of what he is, it is in his presence, that such a faith is possible and must prevail. Has he not, if we are indeed his, redeemed our children as well as ourselves from the power of sin? Has he not come to make the covenant of promise, "Your God and the God of your house," a brighter and fuller reality than ever it was to Abraham? Has he not secured for us, in the Holy Spirit, a power from on high to fulfill every obligation that rests on us as God's children, this one, too, of keeping our children for him to whom we belong? Has he not made true all the promises given of old, of God's Spirit upon our offspring, of God's Word not departing from the mouth of our seed's seed for evermore, in that one word on the day of Pentecost, "The promise is to you and to your children"? Can we not count upon him to give for us and each child just what we need, if only we believe?

"Only believe"—let us take the command literally; faith has never yet been disappointed. Living faith will teach us to see new beauty and preciousness in our children. Living faith will awaken in us new earnestness and desire in everything to hold and to train them for God alone. Living faith will give its own hopeful and confiding tone to all our relation with God for them, and all our relation with them, too. The name of "Faith Home" has been appropriated to certain special institutions; we shall boldly claim it as the name of our own dear home because everything is done in the faith of Jesus. The birth of our children, and our love to them, our prayer with and for them, our watching against their sins and our reproving them, our teaching and training, their lessons and employments and pleasure—all will be under the inspiring and regulating power of this: Only believe.

It need hardly be said that such a faith life in the home is not possible without the faith life in the heart. We cannot be to our children more than we are to God. "It is no longer I that live, but Christ that lives in me; I live by the faith of the Son of God": this must be the language of the father, the mother, who would have theirs a faith home. It is not only in moments of special need and prayer, or when we are in direct contact with the children, that Jesus says, "Only believe." No, day by day, hour by hour, it must be, "I live by the faith of the Son of God."

Christian parent! This life is for you. Learn only with each new morning to say: "For this day I accept Jesus for all my duties as believer and as parent." Commit simply, commit fully to him every duty, every difficulty, every circumstance, every moment, and say then confidently: "I know in whom I have believed. It is he who spoke to me as parent the blessed word, 'Only believe'; and I am persuaded that what I have committed to him he is able to keep." This is the blessed secret of a faith life and a faith home.

Blessed Savior! I thank you for this precious word. I have long heard and understood that it is by faith alone the sinner is saved. I have begun to understand and experience something of what it is that a saved sinner is to live entirely by faith, and every hour to receive from you the life you have engaged to live in him. Lord, teach me the additional lesson that in the home-life faith is just as much the power of blessing, and that in all my relation with my family your word still is, "Fear not; only believe." O Jesus, you are not only the sinner's, but the parent's, Friend; in nothing will you delight so much to reveal your saving and sanctifying power as in the family life which you have redeemed to the service of your kingdom.

O my Lord! I do pray that you to teach me and all parents how impossible it is to train our children aright, or be a blessing to them, except as we live the life of faith. Open our eyes to see all that you offer to our faith, and how our love to them, our influence on them, our education and our training, may all be inspired and purified and perfected by the faith in the power of your finished redemption and your abiding presence. Show us how all our own feebleness and our fears, all the waywardness of our children and all the wickedness in the world that tempts them, can be fully met by your power and your love, if we only trust you. O Lord Jesus, teach us to know you as the Savior of our children from their very birth, and in the homes we have to form for them. And let our whole life and relation with them, day by day, every day and all the day, be in the faith of the Son of God, who loved us and gave himself for us. Amen.

THIRTY-NINTH DAY

The Chamber of Death

"And all wept and bewailed her. But Jesus said, Weep not; she is not dead, but sleeps."—*Luke 8:52*

IN GOD's great school of tribulation there are many classes. In the department where God trains parents, there is one room which all greatly fear to enter. Many, as they are led into it, are seen struggling and murmuring. As its darkness closes in over them, they almost refuse to believe that God is love. Many pass through it, and come out of it, with hardly anything of the Divine comfort or holiness the chastisement was meant to bring, because they knew not why they were there and were not silent to wait for the teaching and the blessing Jesus gives. Others, again, who entered trembling, can testify that the chamber of death—for of this we speak—was to them the gate of heaven; it was the death of a little one that first led them truly to know Jesus. As truly as to Jairus with his dead daughter, the child's death was the parent's life.

Let us see how Jesus meets the sorrowing parent in the chamber of death. The first thing he asks is silence and solitude. Jesus comes to the house, and finds "the crowd making a great tumult." At once he puts out the crowd and goes in alone, with the parents and the three disciples. One of the things that most effectually hinders the blessing of affliction is that it is too much spent in the relationships with men, and comfort sought in their sympathy. One of God's great objects in chastisement is, by clouding the light and the brightness of visible things, to draw the soul to himself and the Unseen. "My soul is silent unto God"; "I will hear what God the Lord will speak": such is the disposition God would gladly have in those whom he visits. He has lessons, often difficult lessons, to teach the parents whose little one death has taken away; it is only when there is the teachableness that really looks to God himself, and waits on him, that the trial becomes fruitful in blessing.

What the lessons are in the dying chamber of a child it is not difficult to say. The parent is led to ask: "Have I loved my child in the Lord, or looked upon it and treated it too much as my own possession? Has the spirit of my life and my home been truly an educating of my children for heaven and its holiness? Is there not worldliness, selfishness, sinfulness, of which this affliction must remind me? Has it indeed been, in all I seek for my family, 'the kingdom first'?" Affliction never can profit without heart-searching; and heart-searching is impossible except in the holy stillness of soul that is found in separation from man and meeting with God. Oh, let parents beware, in their time of trial, of the dissipation that comes from too much seeing of friends, from seeking and finding comfort in their company. God wants to see us alone; without this he cannot bless or comfort us. Jesus waits to reveal himself in the power of his great salvation as the Surety of the parental covenant too—the Redeemer in whom the parent will find all the grace and blessing the covenant God has promised; but he cannot do it except the crowd is put out. He takes his three disciples with him, that all his servants may learn in their ministry to remind us that by the bedside of a dying or a dead child, Jesus wants to be alone with the parents. Even his ministers are only to come in as they come with him, and point to him.

And now that he is alone with the parents, now comes the comforting. "Weep not," he says. Jesus does not condemn weeping. He wept himself; weeping ever touched his heart. And yet he says, "Weep not." "Woman, why do you weep?" was his very first resurrection word. It is as the Lamb, which is in the midst of the throne, leads his redeemed, that all tears are wiped away. Jesus came to dry our tears. He says, "Weep not." Weeping is often self-indulgence, a nursing of our grief, the fruit of being too absorbed in ourselves, the object we mourn, or the suffering we endure. Weeping often hinders the voice of God being heard, hinders altogether the blessing the affliction was meant to bring. We are only occupied with what we suffer, and God would have us think of the cause of the suffering, the sin with which we have made him suffer. By taking away a child, God meant to take us away from ourselves, and to make room in the heart for himself. Weeping often only fills us with ourselves. God would have us in the affliction learn to bear, and love, and worship his will. Weeping is often the homage—yes, the adoration—of our own will.

Beloved mourner! Hear the voice of Jesus say, "Weep not." He does not say it without a reason. It is not enough that the tumult of the crowd outside is put away, and that there is silence in the room; the tumult of thought and feeling must be hushed, too; within the soul there must be silence. At the bidding of Jesus, the gush of tears must be restrained, and the heart must turn to him, to ask who this is who thus, with authority, bids us cease our weeping, and what he has to say to justify his injunction. Obedience to the command is the path to the comfort he brings.

And what is the comfort Jesus gives? He leads from the visible to the invisible; where we only see death, he speaks of life; he comes to rouse us to faith, and to it he reveals himself as the Living and Lifegiving One. "Weep not: she is not dead, but sleeps." With these words Jesus draws near to the lifeless form of each little one over whom a mother's bursting heart is weeping, to remind her that death has been conquered, and that the loved one is not dead, in the terrible meaning which sin gave that word, but truly sleeps, in the deep and blessed sense which that word now has in his mouth.

Your little one is not dead. Judge not by sight. There is a better life than the life of this earth—the eternal life in which God dwells. In that eternal life there is a sleep provided for those who are in Christ Jesus, the blessed waiting time till he comes to gather all his own. As the life itself, and the glory in which it shall be fully manifested, is something that has not entered the heart to conceive, so this sleep, too, is something that passes knowledge. We only know for certain that it is a most blessed rest, rest in the bosom of Jesus. And Jesus asks if this is no comfort, to know that your little one, whom with yourself he took into his covenant before it could know him, or your child, grown up and trained in the faith of the covenant, is now resting with him. He took it that he might draw you heavenward. He took it that he might empty your heart, to make more room for himself. He took it that you might be drawn to him in your need, and be prepared for receiving the new revelation he has to give of his power, of his love, of himself as your life.

It is Jesus himself who comes to you to speak of all this. As in the Old Testament it was the God of the covenant who came to one believing parent after another with his promise of what their children should be; so in the New it is Jesus, the Surety of the children, in whom the parent will find the grace for all he needs to train a seed for God. Jesus said, "Believe me that I am in the Father, and the Father in me: he that has seen me has seen the Father." In the incarnation of Jesus, all that God of old had promised of blessing to parents and children is now fulfilled. If we but learn to know Jesus aright, to believe on him fully, to live in the faith of him, our home and family life will be holy to the Lord. No sacrifice is too great if we only learn to know Jesus aright. It was in the chamber where Jairus' daughter lay dead that her parents learnt to know Jesus.

Weeping parents! This is God's one purpose and desire; this is God's one great thought of blessing and comfort: in his Son Christ Jesus he has come near to bless and take possession of you. Let this your time of affliction not pass without a hitherto unknown experience of what Jesus is as the parents' Friend, their Teacher, Comforter, and Sanctifier. And so the loss you have sustained will be restored tenfold in the blessing it is made to yourself and the children still left you. Or even if it were the only one, in the power and blessing which this new knowledge of Jesus, the Living One, the parent's and the children's Friend, will enable you to bring to others, you will yet be led to confess how that death has become your greatest gain. The presence and the power and the love of Jesus can more than compensate for the absence and the loss of the child.

Blessed Lord! In this my hour of deep sorrow I come to you, my Savior and the Savior of my little one. Condescend, I beseech you, to come in with me, my Lord, to the chamber of death, where your weeping child waits for you. Oh, come in and be yourself my Comforter and my Teacher. Put out, I pray you, the tumult of the crowd, all the sad thoughts and uncontrolled feelings that keep me from hearing your voice. Speak yourself; say to the storm, "Be still!" and let your presence be the great calm. O my Savior, speak: I desire to hear.

Speak, Lord, if it pleases you, of your holy will, and your right to do with your own even what pleases you, and teach me to say, "Thy will be done." Speak, as you see it is needful, of my sin and wandering from you, of my love of the creature, of my lack of love to you and delight in your fellowship, and make me see how this chastisement of your love was what I needed to make me partaker of your holiness. Speak, Lord, and teach me.

Speak, Lord, and comfort your child. Reveal yourself to me as the Resurrection and the Life, the Shepherd who has taken his lamb into his bosom. Reveal yourself as my Shepherd, who will see to it that the blessing of the affliction is secured, by coming nearer to me with your abiding presence. Reveal yourself as from henceforth more than ever the house-Friend, making yourself at home with us, to sanctify our family life more than ever into the blessed experience of your care for the homes of your people. Come in, Lord Jesus! Come in to me in the chamber of death, and, as you have taken my child to yourself, take me and my beloved home, and make us entirely yours. Amen.

FORTIETH DAY

The Widow's Child

"There was carried out one that was dead, the only son of his mother, and she was a widow. And when the Lord saw her, he had compassion on her, and said unto her, Weep not."—*Luke 7:12–13*

ANY ATTEMPT to set forth the teaching of Scripture on the education of children would certainly be incomplete, if it had nothing to say on what always is so sad and difficult, and yet often has been so blessed and successful a work—a widow's training of her orphan children. There are few sights which so claim and attract sympathy, both human and Divine. It is indeed one of the sorest trials that can befall a woman. The husband for whom she left her father's home, on whom she counted and leaned as her guide and guardian, in whom her life and her love found their joy, to whom she looked as her help and strength in the training of her children—her husband is taken from her, and she is left alone and desolate. The stricken heart seeks in vain for the object of its affection; in temporal prospects there is perhaps nothing to which to cling, and the sight of the beloved little ones still left her, instead of being a treasure to which her love now clings, at first only gives new bitterness to the trial. It is not only the heart of man that is touched by this thought: the heart of God, too. Throughout Scripture, from the repeated commands in the law of Moses down to James's testimony that pure religion teaches us to visit "the fatherless and widows" in their affliction, God never forgets the widow. "A Father of the fatherless, and a Judge of the widows, is God in his holy habitation"; "He upholds the fatherless and the widow"; "Leave your fatherless children, I will preserve them alive; and let your widows trust in me" (Psalm 68:5, 146:9; Jeremiah 49: 11): Such words reveal to us the very heart of God.

And now, when Jesus came, how could he fail of showing in this, too, that he was the Father's image, that God was in Christ. It is as if the picture of the Master's life would be incomplete without the story of the widow of Nain. In what he said of the widow's mite, we see how his eye watches over a widow's poverty, and he values what men would call her little deed of love. At Nain we see him as the Comforter of widowed motherhood. Let us go to Nain, the sacred spot to which so many a widow has resorted to find in Jesus her Friend and Lord, to learn what Jesus, the Friend and Savior of our children, has to say to a widow weeping over her child. Not only when the tears are those of sorrow over one taken away, but those of anxious love or sad distress at the sight of those still left behind, Jesus meets us with his "Weep not."

Weep not, widowed mother, as you look at your little ones, and the heart almost breaks at the thought of their being fatherless. Weep not, but come, follow me, as we seek him who has been anointed "to comfort all that mourn." Weep not, as you tremble to think of how you are to train and educate them all alone in your feebleness. Let your soul for a little be silent unto him who came from heaven to say to the widow, "As one whom his mother comforts, will your God comfort you." Weep not.

Weep not! And may the wounded heart not have at least the comfort that the unrestrained flow of its tears does often bring? Just think for a little moment. As little as the widow of Nain knew why Jesus spoke thus, do you know it yet. But let it be enough that Jesus says it. All the other parents, whose children Jesus blessed, came and asked for help; he speaks to the widow without being asked. Her widowhood is her sufficient plea: "When the Lord saw her, he had compassion on her, and said, "Weep not." Jesus is looking on you; do not let your tears keep you from looking and listening to him. Be sure that if it could have been, he would have spared you that cup; that now that it has come, he is looking on you in compassion, waiting to comfort and to bless; in the tenderest love, but with the voice of authority Jesus says, "Weep not."

But Jesus was not one who comforts only with words; his words were always followed by deeds.

And so, if you will look up and see, he will show you what he will do. To the widowed mother at Nain he gave back the dead son, who had been to her in the place of a husband. And his believing people know that, though it may last a little while, the departed ones who have died in the Lord will be given back to them, in glory and forever. Look up to Jesus, the Resurrection and the Life, weeping widow, and believe; them which sleep in Jesus will God bring with him. The resurrection, the meeting again, the being ever with the Lord, are realities, as real—more real, more mighty—than the separation and the sorrow. Look up in faith; it is Jesus who speaks, "Weep not."

But, oh, the desolation that meantime fills the heart and the sense of utter feebleness and unfitness to fulfill my charge with these boys, these girls, who still live, and who do so need a father's wise, firm, loving rule. Dear mother! When Jesus says, "Weep not," he never speaks without doing; he gives what can dry the tears. What do you think? If Jesus were to take the place of the father to these children, would not this make you smile and sing even through the tears. If, as a living reality, Jesus would undertake the responsibility of educating those children, of being your Adviser and your Strength and your assurance of success in your work, would this not be enough to stay those tears? And just this is what he comes to do. What God spoke of old, "Leave your orphans to me, and let your widows trust in me," "The Lord upholds the fatherless and the widow," Jesus comes in human tenderness, and in the nearness of the Holy Spirit, to fulfill. You may trust your fatherless children to him; he will preserve them; he will, in a Divine fullness and power of meaning, be the father of the fatherless.

It may be that a widowed mother reads these words, to whom they have but little meaning. Though a Christian, she has so little yet learned to live by faith, to count the unseen things of faith surer and clearer than the things of sight, that the promise appears all vague and distant. She hardly dares hope that it ever will become a reality, that she may be quite sure that Jesus will do it for her. She does not feel as if she is good or holy or believing enough, that her children should receive such a wonderfully special and Divine guidance.

My sister! Would you learn what Jesus would have of you, that you may with confidence depend upon your children being preserved and blessed by him, and your tears pass away in the sunlight of his love and care, come and listen. Of a widow he asks but one thing—"Let your widows trust in me"; "She that is a widow indeed trusts in God, and continues in supplication and prayer night and day." Trust me! This was what he claimed from the widow of Nain; this is what he asks of you. Trust Jesus! This is the message I bring you this day in your weeping, anxious widowhood. Trust Jesus! Trust him for yourself. Let each thought of your departed one lead you to say, "I have Jesus with me—I will trust him." Let the consciousness of sin and shortcoming, of unfitness for your mother's work, awaken the prayer, "Jesus! I will trust you, to make me what I should be." Trust him with your children, with their temporal and their eternal interests. Only remember, the life of trust just needs a life of undivided, of simple, childlike surrender. Be wholly his, and he will prove himself wholly yours. Tarry in prayer and supplication, in the silent, restful committal of every care and fear to him. Really trust him; in every prayer make this the chief thing. I have now entrusted my need to him, I trust him with it; I am confident he is mighty and faithful to keep that which I have committed unto him. Trust him wholly; they who wholly trust him, find him wholly true.[3]

And if ever the double trial of the widow of Nain should be yours, and you have to mourn the loss not only of a husband, but an only son, oh, remember that there is still Jesus, the Comforter of the widow doubly desolate! This will be the time in which you will find him become doubly precious, and you will have grace to say, "My flesh and my heart fail; but God, but Jesus, is the strength of my heart, and my portion forever."

Blessed Lord Jesus! How shall I praise you for that thoughtful love which would not give us the record of your life without the story of the widow of Nain. Blessed be your name for the revelation of the special place the widow has in your heart, and the tenderness of that compassion which drew near to her before ever she knew that she might look to you! Lord Jesus, for every widowed mother we now pray to you. Teach her to come to you with her fatherless children. We bless you that there are thousands of widowed mothers who have proved how wonderfully you can bless the feeble, and how richly you have blessed their children.

Teach the widow, we pray you, to put her trust in God and in you. You are able and you are willing to do what man dare not expect, what man counts impossible, if we honor you by trusting your love. O Savior, help the feeble faith of every widow. Let her desolation and her sorrow and her feebleness compel her now wholly to cast herself with her children

3. See Note C at close of volume.

on you, to depend upon you alone. Draw near, O you compassionate One, and reveal yourself. Speak into the depths of the sorrowing, anxious heart your word of comfort, "Weep not!" Oh, let your widowed child hear you speaking, see you come to take charge, and provide, and care for the education of her children. Teach her that her one work is to trust you, in separation from the world, in holy devotedness to you, to trust you for a more than human, a Divine guidance and blessing on her children. Let her continue in prayer and supplication, in daily communion with you the Unseen One, the portion of her children. Let her then fully know how truly you are the widow's Friend, the Savior and the Friend of her children. Amen.

FORTY-FIRST DAY

The Sick Child

> "There was a certain nobleman, whose son was sick at Capernaum. He went unto Jesus, and besought him that he would come down and heal his son; for he was at the point of death."—*John 4:46–47*

HERE IS AN EXPERIENCE that almost every parent passes through. In the wonderful training of the parent through the child, God uses a child's sickness as one of his special means of blessing. And in the parent's training of the child, the sickroom has often been the place when the parent first fully found his way to the child's heart, to guide it to Jesus and the distinct confession of faith in him. Let us prepare ourselves for the children's sickrooms by the lessons the beautiful story of the nobleman of Capernaum teaches us as to how sickness is to be met, to be healed, to be blessed.

How is sickness to be met? God's great gift to sinful men is Jesus; in his Son he meets our every need. And the one great thing God asks of in us, as the spirit in which we are to meet him in Christ, is faith—the trustful surrender to let this blessed Jesus be to us all that the Father would have him be. And because he has been given to us, not only as individuals, but as parents, for us to accept and to use on behalf of our children, until we can lead them to accept him for themselves, the one thing that God asks of the parent is faith—trust in Jesus. As faith in God was the one thing by which the saints of old pleased God and did all that was pleasing to him, and to which God therefore sought to train them, so faith in his Son is the one supreme grace by which the Christian parent can please

God and obtain his blessings on his children. And all God's leadings and dealings have this one object and purpose: to make us strong in faith, giving glory to God.

When God allows sickness to come upon the child of one of his believing people, perhaps still young or an infant, and the parents' hearts are agonized by the sight of its pain or the fear of losing it, the question comes with terrible force, "Why does God permit all this suffering?" The answer Scripture gives is for the trial, and so for the purifying and the strengthening, of faith. God's one purpose with parent and child is to exercise and increase faith in them. By faith they become capable of receiving the revelation of God's glory and showing it forth again; by faith God can dwell in them and work through them. God's one desire is that they should more fully believe in his Son; and our one desire should be to meet the sickness by faith in Jesus.

This is the one great lesson the story of the nobleman teaches us—the growth and increase of faith in the dealing with Christ. It begins as a general faith in what he has heard of Christ's compassion and power; this brings him into contact with Christ. He believes in Jesus as a healer. It becomes a distinct faith in the promise he received of healing: "The man believed the word that Jesus had spoken unto him." He believes in Jesus as the Healer of his child. And then the faith in Jesus the Healer is perfected in the faith in him as Savior and Lord: "Himself believed and his whole house." This is God's one purpose with sickness; let it be ours, too. Let the chastisement discover to us our unbelief, and that fleshly and worldly spirit, that unholy life, in which unbelief has its root and its strength. Let us look from the hand that holds the rod to the face of him whose is the hand; to see that face in truth makes trust easy and real.

How the sickness is to be healed? This is the second question our story suggests. The answer it gives is very simple: By the power of Jesus. In Matthew, Christ's healing work is spoken of as the natural result of his atoning work of which Isaiah had spoken (Isaiah 53; Matthew 8) as a bearing of our sickness. He took upon him our human nature in the flesh, and, having redeemed it, lifted it into the glory of the eternal life in heaven. When on earth, he delighted in healing the sick, as something his loving heart could do for them even when he could not save their souls. In his Word he left among the heritage of the exceeding great and precious promises which are the riches of his Church, the assurance that the prayer of faith would save the sick, because the prayer of a righteous man avails much. He has a thousand times over by his Spirit led his children, applying the promise of an answer to believing prayer, the promise of his doing whatsoever we will if we abide in him, to believe and receive the healing of a sick child. His great desire in sickness is to educate us into that simple, child-like faith, which, while it cannot give account of its assurance to reason, yet through the Holy Spirit has the assurance that its petition is granted—that it has what it asks. Let us but see that the lesson of the chastisement has been accepted, that the sin, or the want of entire harmony of our life with God's will, has been confessed and pardoned, has been cast out and conquered; let us claim the life of the beloved sick one for God's glory in him and in us as parents: the word of Jesus can come to us as real as to the nobleman: "Your son lives."

And we shall learn how sickness is to become a blessing. The Lord Jesus used it as a means of drawing to himself; when it had done this he took it away, that the healing might bind to himself. When the sickness had done its work, the healing perfected what had been begun. The sickness had brought the nobleman to Jesus in hope and expectancy; the healing left him a confirmed believer, with his household. There is a very prevalent opinion that sickness is better than health for true piety; in the life of Christ and in his work we see no token of this. Health obtained direct from Jesus in the prayer of faith, health received consciously as a gift of redeeming love, is one of the most wonderful spiritual blessings: a bearing in the body the mark of the hand of Jesus. Let each parent, whom our Lord leads into this school of sickness, realize this fully, that health, indeed asked and received in faith, may be a token of even more intimate contact with Jesus than the blessing of the sickbed ever has been. As this is understood, we shall feel courage to make known our desire for a health in which there is to be power for God's glory. The new revelation of the power and the love of Jesus may make us and our household believers as never before—full of faith and devotion to him who has blessed us.

Parents! Our sick children are God's messengers to lead us to Jesus and to faith in him. The sickness has a message and a blessing. It calls us to remember parental sin, and to confess it. It calls us to search the heart and life and home as to whether we have held our children wholly for God, trained them as holy to the Lord. It comes to make the heart tender and humble, and to draw it out to Jesus. Oh, let us beware lest in all the care or sorrow the sickness occasions, in all the means to which we flee to seek deliverance, in all the fear of losing our child, we miss God's purpose. He wants to bring us, subdued and quiet, in faith and hope to Jesus. Let us pray God very earnestly that we may not miss the blessing of the sickness.

And, much more, let us accept the greater blessing of the healing. The exercise of faith honors God more than anything. The availing ourselves of our privilege, the trusting of Jesus' word and power, the learning to know him as indeed our Helper, the experience of his healing power in distinct answer to our faith—it is this that binds to Christ. We learn to know him as the Living One. We have the token of the acceptance of our surrender and our trust. Our home has become the scene of the display of his kingly power. It has sealed afresh the parental covenant. We and our home become the Lord's as never before.

Blessed Redeemer! We come to you to learn the lesson that sickness has but this one purpose—to draw us to yourself. When you went on earth, the sickness of a child was one of the cords with which the Father drew men to you. And still he takes parents into the sickroom of their little ones, that there they may learn to seek and find you, to wait for and to receive the revelation of your power and love.

Lord Jesus, teach us, we pray, in all the time of our children's sickness to learn the blessed lesson of coming to you and trusting you. We may be most sure that you are watching over us to teach, to comfort, to sanctify, and to heal. Teach us especially that you are still the same as when on earth, mighty to bid the sickness depart, and to free from the power of death. To spare the life of a child for your service, to gladden and sanctify a parent's heart by your grace, and for the Father's glory, you are still ready to hear the prayer of faith and raise up the child. Oh, grant us this faith, that we may honor you, and not hinder you from proving with what compassion you hear a parent's cry.

And grant, Lord, when you graciously have heard, and given back a child to the parent's faith, that the blessed fruit may be that the parents with their whole house believe in you as never before. May all see that Jesus is now Lord and Master, the beloved Friend of the home. As the sickness leads to seek you, may the healing bind to you and your blessed service. Amen.

Feed My Lambs

"Jesus says to Simon Peter, Do you love me more than these? He says unto him, Yes, Lord; you know that I love you. He says unto him, Feed my lambs."—*John 21:15*

PETER was a fisherman. After the first miraculous draft of fish, the Lord had said, "Follow me, and I will make you fishers of men." Peter's work on earth was made the symbol of his heavenly calling. After the second miraculous draft of fish, in the days preceding the ascension, our Lord no longer calls Peter a fisherman, but a shepherd. There is a deep meaning in the change. One great point of difference between the fisherman and the shepherd is that while the former catches what he has neither reared nor fed, and only seeks what is full-grown, casting away all the little fish out of his net back into the sea, the shepherd directs his special attention to the young and the feeble; on his care for the lambs all his hope depends.

The type of the fisherman gave no place for the Master to give special charge concerning the children of his Church. The shepherd's calling at once suggested the words, "Feed my lambs," and sets forth the deep importance and the blessed reward of giving a first place to the little ones of the flock. Peter, and Christ's ministers, were not only to feed the sheep; the prosperity of the Church would specially depend upon their feeding the lambs. What was said to them is very specially applicable to parents as under-shepherds, who each have their little flock of lambs to keep and rear for the Master. Christ's commission to his Church through Peter shows the place the little ones have in his heart, and teaches us to think of the weakness, the value, the need, and the hope of our children.

"Feed my lambs," Jesus says, and reminds us of the feebleness of our children and their religious life. I was once leaving a sheep-farm in company with its master toward evening. There were threatening clouds; just as we had left he hurried back to call his son and cry out: "Take great care of the lambs! There is a storm coming." The Lord was just about to ascend the throne; one of his last words is, "Care for the lambs." The sheep is a weak and helpless animal; how much more the little lamb! It cannot care for itself. The Master would have every minister and every parent think much how utterly dependent the child is on the care of those to whom it is entrusted. It cannot choose the company under whose influence it comes. It knows not yet to choose between good and evil. It knows nothing of the importance of little words or deeds, of forming habits, of sowing good or bad seed, of yielding itself to the world or God. All depends upon its surroundings: parents especially have the children in their power. What a solemn responsibility to lead and nourish them carefully, to feed them, not with the husks of this world's thoughts and pleasures, but with food convenient, the milk for babes which our Father has provided, to lead them only in the green pastures!

"Feed my lambs": the words remind us of the high value of the little ones. In the lambs the shepherd sees the possibilities of the future: as the lambs, so the coming flock. The Church of the next generation, the servants with whom, in but a few years' time, Jesus has to do his work of converting and saving and blessing men, are the children of today. No wonder he says—alas, how little we have understood or heeded the voice—"Feed the lambs." He says more; he says, "Feed my lambs," "of such is the kingdom." Not only for what they are to become, but for what they already are in their childlike simplicity and heavenliness, he loves them and counts them of great worth. For the lesson they continually have to teach grown-up people, for all the influence they exert in making their parents and elders gentle and humble and trustful, for all the blessings they bring to those who receive them in the name of Jesus, they are to him of unspeakable worth, the most beautiful part of his flock. Let us try to catch his spirit as he cries, "Feed my lambs." Oh, let us learn to look upon our children in the light in which Jesus looks upon them! Let us pray for the Holy Spirit to make the familiar words, "Jesus' lambs," a deep spiritual reality to us, until our hearts tremble at the thought. Our little ones are his lambs: we are daily to feed them as such, that they may grow up as the sheep of his pasture.

"Feed my lambs": the children's great need is here set before us. Food is the condition of growth. Food is something received from without, to be assimilated and taken up into our very life. The body has its food from the visible world. The mind is nourished by the thoughts that enter it. The spirit feeds, through the mind, on the thoughts, the words of God. The little ones cannot seek pasture for themselves; Christ looks to parents to bring to them day by day, not a chapter of the Bible just read over, and in most cases beyond their comprehension, but some of the thoughts of Divine wisdom and love, without which the soul cannot possibly grow. Not less carefully than the mother studies daily how to let the child have something to eat, and what it is to eat, ought she day by day to feed each lamb entrusted to her care. The one desire and aim must be to rear it for him. The consecration of the child to the Lord must be the chief thing in its life. The idea of its being his, and growing up entirely and alone for him, the absorbing desire—this will make the duty easy.

"Feed my lambs": the words tell the provision Christ has made for his feeble ones. To whom were the words spoken? To one of whom the question had been asked, "Do you love me?" and who had answered, "Yes, Lord, you know that I love you." It is only one who is inspired by love to Jesus who can truly take charge of the lambs. This is the examination of fitness for the duty of parent and shepherd of the lambs—"Do you love me?" This is the provision Jesus has made for the lambs: true love to Jesus can do the work.

Let every parent who longs to know how he can obtain the needed qualification for his work, give in his name for this examination. Let Jesus search your heart—once, twice, a third time—until the remembrance of past unfaithfulness brings tears, and the answer comes, "Lord, you know all things; you know that I do love you." Alas, it is this that is the blight of so many a Christian home—the conscious, fervent, and confessed love of Jesus is wanting. Nothing influences a child like love: the warmth of a holy love to Jesus will make itself felt. There may be a great deal of religion, and of teaching, and of praying; it is only love that will conquer. Love to Jesus will lead to obey him very carefully, to walk with him very closely, to trust him very heartily. Love to Jesus will make the desire to please him very strong, and the charge he gives us to keep very precious. Love to Jesus will make our testimony of him very personal.

The food with which we feed the lambs will have the warmth of a Divine love about it. Jesus wants parents who love him, who love him with their whole heart and strength: this is the provision he has thought out for his little lambs.

The religion of Jesus is a religion of love. Of the Father it is said, "God is love." Jesus himself is the gift of a love that passes knowledge. His own life and work is one of love—love stronger than death. When the Holy Spirit comes to us he sheds abroad in our hearts the love of God. Our whole relation to the Divine is to be one of love. And our relation as parents and children was meant to be one of love. It was to restore this that Jesus came. And he does it by calling parents to love himself, and then, receiving the little ones in his name, for his sake, and in the fervor of his love, to take charge of them. The love of earth he purifies and elevates by the love of heaven. And the home is consecrated by the light of Jesus' love resting on the children, and the power of his love dwelling in the parents, and the whole of education being made a work of love for him.

Christian parents! See and accept your blessed calling; you are the shepherds of the Divine love, to tend and feed the lambs. In his Church, the Chief Shepherd has many shepherds to care for the flock, but none who can so care for the lambs as the parents. "He makes him families like a flock"—it is to parental love, inspired and sanctified by redeeming love, that Jesus looks for the building up of his Church. Let us pray very earnestly to have, in the first place, our eyes opened to see things as Jesus sees them, to realize by the Holy Spirit what he feels for our little ones, what he expects of us and is ready to do for us in giving us wisdom and strength. "Feed my lambs": when this word is made the law of a parent's duty, what gentleness and love will it inspire, what heavenly hope, what faithful, watchful care, and what an unceasing life of faith in the love and grace and blessing of Jesus on our home! Let us often wait for the voice to say to us: "Do you love me? Feed my lambs."

Blessed Savior! You are the good Shepherd, of whom my soul has said, "The Lord is my Shepherd, I shall not want." I bless you for the tender love that did not forget the little ones, but did so carefully commit them to the charge of your servant Peter, at his installation to the office of shepherd, in your precious, "Feed my lambs." I bless you for the holy privilege you have bestowed on me of being a parent, and also bearing your commission, "Feed my lambs." I bless you with my whole heart for the honor and blessedness of being, in my little sphere, what you are in yours, of being to others what you are to me, a gentle, loving shepherd. O my Lord, may my daily experience of the way in which your shepherd-love does its work on me be a daily lesson to teach me how to feed my little flock of lambs.

Blessed Master, the servant of whose love I am to my children, I beseech you to open my eyes to look upon my children as you do, to regard them always and only in the light of your claim upon them. Open my eyes to see what a holy life of fellowship with you.

FORTY-THIRD DAY

The Holy Spirit in the Family

"To you is the promise, and to your children."—*Acts 2:39*

WE HAVE NOT FORGOTTEN the frequent use in the Old Testament of the words in which parents and children were joined together as being together partners in God's covenant and blessings. "You and your house," "you and your seed," "you and your children," "me and my house"—such were the expressions of the blessed bond that made the whole family one in God's sight. God be praised, the expression is found in the New Testament, too: "You and your children." And nowhere could it have found a place of deeper significance than where we have it today. On the day of Pentecost, as the Church of Christ, which had just been born by his resurrection from the dead, receives its baptism of the Holy Spirit, the word is heard, "To you is the promise, and to your children." All the blessings of the new dispensation, the ministration of the Spirit, are at once secured to our children.

"To you is the promise, and to your children." The promise is of the Spirit of the glorified Jesus, in all his fullness, the baptism of fire and of power. When we are baptized in the name of the Father, and of the Son, and of the Holy Spirit, we confess our faith in the Holy Trinity, and in the Holy Spirit, not only as one with the Father and the Son, but as being the third person, as alone bringing the full and perfect revelation of the Divine glory. All that in the Old Covenant had been promised by God, all that had been manifested and brought near to us of Divine grace in Jesus, the Holy Spirit is now to make our very own. Through him all the promises of God are fulfilled, all grace and salvation in Christ becomes a personal possession and experience. God's Word calls our children "the children of promise"; it is especially of this promise of the Holy Spirit that they are the heirs. And the secret of a godly education is to bring them up in the faith and for the fulfillment of this promise. In the faith of the promise we must learn to look upon the aid and the presence of the Spirit in our daily training as absolutely necessary and indispensable, but also as most positively secured to us. In all our praying for them, and living with them, in our family religion and daily life, we must learn to count upon and expect the direct working of the Holy Spirit. So we shall educate them for the fulfillment of the promise, that their lives more than our own may, from their youth up, be in the power of the Spirit, holy to the Lord.

To you the promise is, and to your children. The very thought of training children every day in dependence upon the Holy Spirit's presence, and with the expectation of his filling the children, appears to some too strange and high: the thing is impracticable. The reason of their thinking thus is simply that they have not yet learned to understand and enjoy the abiding of the Spirit as essential to a true Christian life. The promise of the Spirit is to you: it is just as parents realize in their own personal experience that it is only the continual leading of the Spirit that enables to live as God would have us, that they will have the capacity for believing, in its full meaning, the promise of the Spirit for their children. So only can they become the ministers of the Spirit to their families. Oh, that the Church of Christ understood the place and the power which the Spirit of God is meant to have in every Christian, and in every Christian home! All the complaints about the neglect or the failure of religious education have their root in this: the Holy Spirit is not expected, is not accepted as the only, as the sufficient strength, of the believer for all God asks of him. As you parents receive the promise, and live and walk in the Spirit, will you receive it for your children also?

For to you is the promise, and to your children. As in nature, so in grace, you and your children have been linked together for good or for evil. Physically, intellectually, morally, they are the partakers of your life. Spiritually it may be so also. The gift of the Spirit and his gracious workings, to you and to them, does not consist of two distinct separate acts; no, but in and through you he would come to them. Your life, your daily influence, is the channel through which his quickening and sanctifying grace would reach them. If you are resting content with the thought that you are saved, without seeking to be truly filled with the Spirit—if your life is still more carnal than spiritual, with more of the spirit of the world than of God—do not think it strange if your children grow up unconverted. It is nothing but what is right and natural. You are hindering the Holy Spirit. You are breathing day by day into your children the spirit of the world. You are, it may be unconsciously, but most effectually, using all your influence to train them into man's religion, in its harmony with the spirit of the world, instead of God's religion, in the power of the Holy Spirit sent down from heaven. The promise is to you and to your children: in spite of your evil influence, through the faith of others the blessing may reach them, but you have no reason to expect it, except as you yield yourselves to be the channel for its conveyance. If nothing else has yet awakened us, would that parental love might lead us to see that for our children's sake nothing less is needed than for us to be filled with the Holy Spirit.

To you is the promise, and to your children. The promise! Would God that all parents understood what is implied in the promise. Too many look upon a promise of God as a mere word or thought—something that is without power until they from their side do what is needed to make it effectual. They do not know that the word of God has in it a living, mighty energy, a Divine seed-life, and that if they will but hide and keep it in their hearts, it will beget the faith through which the blessed fulfillment comes. I come this day to every parent who reads this with a wonderful message. The promise, the promise of the Holy Spirit in his fullness and his power, is to you and to your children. A promise means that God in his infinite power has bound himself to do what he has said, and that he will most certainly do it for us, as soon as we claim it in faith. And the promise here means that the Holy Spirit, with his quickening, sanctifying, and gladdening grace, is ours, waiting to come and to be, in our home, in our family life, all that we need to make it holy and happy. And however far our home life may yet be from God's ideal, and however impossible it appear to us that in our circumstances and with our difficulties we shall ever succeed in making it very different, if we will but claim and hold fast the promise in the prayer of faith, God himself will fulfill it. A promise needs two things: the receiver must believe and claim it; the giver must fulfill it and make it true. Let our posture be that of simple, trustful faith in God for ourselves and our children, counting on the promise: God is faithful, who will also do it.

Dear fellow parents! Let us humble ourselves that our home life has not more distinctly proved the truth and the glory of this promise. Let us confess with shame how much there has been that was carnal and not spiritual; of the spirit of the world, and not of the Spirit of God. Let us open our hearts to take in the promise of God as something that has a Divine quickening power, and that will itself beget in us the very state of mind which God requires before the fulfillment comes. Let us look upon ourselves as the divinely appointed ministers of the Holy Spirit, to prepare and train our children under his influence from their youth up, and let us yield ourselves wholly to his guidance and working. To train a child aright means training him to be a temple of the Holy Spirit, means living ourselves in the power of the Spirit. Let no sense of short-coming or feebleness discourage us: to you is the promise, and to your children. Let us place our lives as parents under the leading of the Holy Spirit. That will mean placing our whole life under his leading: because we can be to our children only what we really are to God. Let the spirit of praise and thanks unceasingly fill us, that God should have bestowed the wondrous grace upon us to make our family life the sphere for the special working of his Spirit; and let it be our unceasing prayer and our confident expectation that, by the power of the Holy Spirit from heaven, our home on earth shall be coming continually nearer to the home in heaven, of which it is meant to be the image and the preparation.

O you thrice-holy God! How shall we bless you for the promise that our home is to be your home, the abode of your Holy Spirit, and that in the happy life of love between parents and children which you give us on earth, the Spirit of your Divine love is to be the link that binds us together. Glory to your name, O my God, for the promise of the Holy Spirit to us and to our children!

O God, we come to set wide open the doors of our beloved home to you, and to place it with our whole family life at the disposal, under the rule, of your Holy Spirit. We beseech you, let him take possession. As parents we desire to claim the fulfillment of the promise. May our love to our children and our desires for them, our daily relations with them and our influence on them, all be under the continual overshadowing of your Holy Spirit. May our whole life, the invisible atmosphere that surrounds us and that fills our home, be that which your Holy Spirit breathes, holiness to the Lord.

We claim the promise for our children. We desire, in simple, child-like faith, to count upon it, as a settled thing between you and us, that they are the heirs of the promise of the Spirit. Give us grace, O Father, as often as we see in them signs of evil that make us sad, tendencies and dispositions that make us fear, or influences around them that bring danger; oh, give us grace to plead the promise in the assurance of faith! O our Father, we would live ourselves, we would guide our home life, we would train each child day by day under the leading of the Holy Spirit. Teach us this yourself. May the holy reverence, the deep, quiet joy, the tender watchfulness, the death to self and the flesh, the life of faith in Jesus, which mark his presence, ever be ours. Amen.

FORTY-FOURTH DAY

Parental Self-Culture

"You therefore that teach another, will you not teach yourself?"—*Romans 2:21*

NOTHING can be more inconsistent and vain than the attempt to teach others without teaching ourselves. It is in ordinary instruction only what the teacher is really master of and has thoroughly made his own, that he can successfully communicate to others. In the higher sphere of the life-truth which a parent has to impart, it holds far more good: it is only the lesson I first teach myself that I can really teach my child. One of the first laws in the science of home education is that it depends far more on example than precept; what parents are, avails more than what they say. There is not one of the great lessons of child-life which the parent must not first himself learn. Let us look at some of them.

The great aim of education is to give the child, when grown up to manhood, the perfect mastery and the ready use of all the wondrous powers God has endowed him with. To this end a wise self-control is one of the first of virtues. As little as a state can prosper if there is no wise, intelligent ruler to make its laws and provide for its needs as they arise, can there be happiness in the little empire within man's bosom, unless everything is subject to a ruling power. The child cannot be too early trained to habits of quiet thoughtfulness in speech and act, giving time and opportunity for mind and will to hold their rule. This training comes far more through example than precept. It is the atmosphere of a well-regulated home, the influence of the self-control which parents exhibit, which unconsciously set their mark on the child. When parents give way to impulse and temper, perhaps at the very time when professing to reprove or restrain the child's temper, the effect of the good advice they mean to give is more than neutralized by the evil influence of the spirit displayed. It is the spirit that influences. The child may never look up and say, but God's Word on its behalf says, "You that teach another, will you not teach yourself?" If parents honestly watch themselves, they will often discover the causes or the helps to their children's failings in themselves. Such discovery ought to lead to very earnest confession before God, to a very hearty surrender to the teaching of Jesus and the Holy Spirit. We can depend upon the Divine renewal to fit us for true self-control; and what we so by grace teach ourselves will in due time influence our children also.

But the self-control must know its object and the path to reach that object. The child finds both in the word we have already repeated so often, "obedience." He must control himself to be able to render obedience to his parent, that in that he may be trained to what will be his liberty and his glory, obedience to God. But here again the parent's obedience will be contagious; it will inspire the child. If the parent's position is all one of privilege and liberty and command, the child may feel that the burden of obedience is all put upon him, the weaker one. "Johnny," said a father once to a child, who was hesitating about obeying his father's will, "whose will must you do—your own or Papa's?" "Papa's will," was the reluctant answer. But on it followed at once the question, "But whose will must Papa do, then?" The father was able at once to answer, "God's will," and to explain how he considered such obedience, to a wiser and a better will than his own, his greatest privilege. He could at once take his place by the side of his child as also having to give up his own will. The parent who can appeal to his daily life with his children, that they know how he in all things seeks to do the will of his God, and can in his prayers in their presence appeal to his God, too, will find in the witness of such a life a mighty power to inculcate obedience in the child. When, on the contrary, the seeking of our own will marks our relation with our children, we need not wonder if our education is a failure. Let us turn at once and hearken to the voice, "You that teach another, will you not teach yourself?"

Very specially does this hold true of that great commandment which is the fulfilling of the law. Family life has been very specially ordained of God as the sphere where love can be cultivated. In nothing is our self control to be more proved than in loving others, in restraining everything that is selfish or unloving. In the daily life of our children with each other and their companions, we have in miniature the temptations to which later life will expose them. For the exercise of the virtues of gentleness and forbearance, of forgiveness and generosity, of helpfulness and beneficence, continued opportunity will be found. Principles must not only be inculcated, but the trouble taken to lead the child to do the right thing easily and lovingly. Many a one wishes to help the poor, for instance, but does not undertake it, from not knowing how to set about it. It is one of the highest parts of a right Christian education to make beneficence the chief object of life, and awaken the desire to live to make those around us better and happier. But we feel at once how all this can only be attained as the parents teach themselves, and, for their own sakes, as well as their children's, cultivate the virtues they inculcate. In the daily life of the family the parents must seek to prove that love is the law of their life. It must be understood that unkind words, harsh judgments, unloving reports, form no part of their conversation. In the intercourse with each other, with children, with servants, with friends, and the world around, love—God's love—must be sought after and manifested. In the sympathy with the needy and wretched, in the thoughtful study of everything by which those who have none to care for them can be helped or comforted, in the actual loving self-denial exercised for the sake of the poor or the suffering, the example of Christ and his love must be reduced to practice in daily life. Thus alone can education to a life of love be truly successful.

"You that teach another, will you not teach yourself?" With what searching light these words ask whether as parents we are doing the first and most needful thing for being successful teachers of our children: teaching ourselves. Yes, parents, teach yourselves. If we are to train our children wisely, we must go through a new course of training ourselves. We have to put ourselves to school again, and to be teachers and scholars in one. Of the two scholars whose education has to go on simultaneously, the parent and child, the parent will often find that the child makes more progress. The lessons which the attempt to train a child teaches parents are often of greater importance and difficulty than those the child has to learn. It is especially well if the first lesson is learned—the need of self-teaching, the need of teachableness, the need of continual daily learning.

Let the parent who begins to see this realize what it means to become a scholar. All schooling requires time and trouble, patience and payment.

Teaching that costs nothing is of little value. No one can graduate as even fairly competent to train a child for eternity, without making sacrifices. Take time to study God's Word and what it says of a parent's duties. Study man's moral nature, with its wonderful capacities, as the sacred trust committed to your care. Teach yourself to cultivate that nature to its highest fitness for God's service: it will be the best preparation for teaching your children aright. And if you feel how much you need the help of some friend to stimulate and to guide—let Jesus be that teacher. He came and taught himself, that he might know to teach us; he learned obedience that he might show us the way. He came to show us the Father; he will so reveal the Father's love and grace, the fatherly tenderness of our God, that we shall be full of a joyful assurance that he will not refuse to teach and enable us to be true fathers and mothers to our children. And we shall understand that to be ourselves teachable, obedient, loving children of the Heavenly Father, is the surest way of having our children teachable, obedient, and loving, too.

Gracious God! I come again to seek the grace I need for filling rightly my place as a parent. I ask of you to imprint deep on my heart the solemn thought that I can effectually teach my children only what I really teach myself, and that I can only expect the truth that influences my own life really to influence theirs.

O my God, I think with shame of how much that I reprove in them is only the reflection of what they have seen in me. I confess how much there has been wanting of that spirit of childlike love and self-denial, of joyful obedience to you, and thoughtful self-sacrifice for others, which would have been to them the highest education. O my God, forgive me what is past, and give me grace in everything to teach myself what I want to teach my children.

Be pleased especially to make me feel deeply that it is as I live as an obedient child with my Father in heaven, that I can teach my children and expect them to be obedient to me. Lord, may childlike simplicity and obedience be the atmosphere my home breathes, the bond that makes parents and children one. As I think of my own slowness in learning, may I be very patient and gentle with my children, and yet full of hope that the lessons I impart to them will have their effect.

Jesus, Master, teach me yourself, that with your teaching I may teach my loved ones. Amen.

FORTY-FIFTH DAY

Baptized into Christ

> "We who died to sin, shall we live any longer therein? Or are you ignorant that all we, who were baptized into Christ Jesus, were baptized into his death? We were buried therefore with him, through a baptism into death; that like as Christ was raised from the dead through the glory of the Father, so we also might walk in newness of life."—*Romans 6:3–4*
>
> "In him you are complete, having been buried with him in baptism, wherein you were also raised with him, through faith in the working of God, who raised him from the dead."—*Colossians 2:10–12*

IN WRITING both to the Romans and the Colossians, Paul, in pleading with believers to live a life of separation from sin and the world—a life of holiness and liberty—uses their baptism into Christ as his great argument. He unfolds the spiritual meaning of baptism as a union with Christ both in his death and his life, and shows how this is both the obligation and the possibility of a walk like Christ's in newness of life. Baptism is the symbol of the deep spiritual mystery of our perfect oneness with Christ; as it is understood and believed, it is the pledge of an abiding union and the ever growing likeness to him.

It is a matter of deep importance to remember that baptism brings and seals to an infant nothing less than to an adult. All the believing parent receives in the covenant and its seal is by God meant and secured for the child, too. For a double reason, thus, the parent needs continually to remember what God meant baptism to be. Without this he cannot educate the child into the possession of what God intended for it in its baptism. Without this he cannot live himself, in the power of his baptism, that life which alone can lead the baptized child to the blessing God has in store for him. Let us try and understand what, in the full light of the Holy Spirit's teaching, baptism really is.

The great lesson we are taught is that in baptism the death and resurrection of Jesus Christ are set forth. We know that baptism originally was by immersion. Scripture teaches us how the old world, in the time of Noah, had been destroyed and renewed again by a fearful baptism of water. The old nature, mankind in its sinfulness, had perished under the water. From the water a new and cleansed world had emerged; Noah the believer had been brought forth, as begotten again from the dead. Scripture teaches us how, at the birth of Israel, God's firstborn son among the nations, that terrible baptism had not been wanting. Under Pharaoh's rule the Egyptians and the Israelites had been mixed up, very much one. In the Red Sea, Pharaoh, the old man, had perished; out of the waters that were death to Egypt, Israel came forth as God's firstborn, to sing the song of redemption. The Holy Spirit teaches us (1 Peter 3:20 and 1 Corinthians 10:2) to regard the waters both of the flood and the Red Sea as types of baptism and its spiritual meaning. As the Jew, at John's command, went in under the water, he not only thought of the water in its cleansing power. His life was so tainted by sin that nothing but the giving up, the death of the old life, the reception of a new life, could really cleanse him. Going in under the water meant the drowning, the death of the old nature, the putting off of sin in confession and repentance; the coming up out of it, the profession and the hope of a new life.

John's baptism of water was but a preparation; Jesus Christ alone could give the true baptism—the true deliverance from the old nature. But even he could not do this until he had himself undergone his own baptism into death. In him the two elements, the old and the new, which in the flood and the Red Sea were represented by two separate parties—in him they were united. The power of sin he bore in his own flesh—"Our old man was crucified with him." He descended into the great deep, where he had to cry, "All your waves and your billows are gone over me; let not the water-flood overflow me" (Psalm 40:69). It was this prospect that made him say, "I have a baptism to be baptized with, and how am I straitened till it is accomplished." And again, "Can you indeed drink of the cup that I shall drink of, and be baptized with the baptism that I am baptized with?" This was Christ's baptism, a terrible reality—a baptism into death.

But this was only the one half. There was also "the coming up out of the water," the entrance on a new life, redeemed from destruction. That new life, typified in Noah and Israel, symbolized in John's baptism, now became a reality. Jesus was raised from the dead, in the power of a new victorious life that can die no more. "We were buried with him, through a baptism into death; that like as Christ was raised, we also might walk in newness of life." "You were buried with him in baptism, wherein you were also raised, through faith in the working of God who raised him." Baptism is, in the power of the Holy Spirit, our participation with Jesus Christ in the deepest and most mysterious experiences of his life; as our faith ever looks to, and rests on, and claims, and yields itself to the working of God who raised him, we experience the power of his death and his life working in us; our life becomes conformable to his, that life of his which died and lives forevermore. Reckoning and knowing ourselves to be indeed dead unto sin and alive unto God in Christ, we have the power to walk in newness of life; we are made free from sin and live as the servants of God and of righteousness. And as often as the flesh suggests that we must sin, or tells us, with the Colossians, to seek our strength in carnal help and ordinances, God's Word reminds us of our strength: "We have been baptized into Christ, into his death and into his life."

What strong consolation this teaching of God's Word offers believing parents in bringing their children to baptism. The deeper our insight into the spiritual blessings which the sacrament seals, the more we shall value the grace which secures them to our infants. Our gratitude will be deeper; our sense of responsibility more solemn; our faith more stirred to effort; our whole life will be holier, as the appointed channel through which all this blessing is to be conveyed to the child. Yes, believing parent! Your life is the means of grace, the medium appointed and consecrated by God, through which the life of the Risen One is to become the life of your child. It is through your life—not your teachings, or your prayers, or your beliefs, for these are but parts of yourself—but through your *life*, representing the sum of all you are, and of the influences you do exercise upon your child, that God would have him inherit the blessings his baptism into Christ have made his.

What an urgent call for the parent to live truly the life of a baptized one—as one who has been made one plant with Christ in the likeness of his death and resurrection. Let no believing parent say or think that this truth, that this life, is too high for him. If he is a true believer, this Christ, who died but lives again, is his life, his blessedness. He cannot taste the true blessedness of the life of faith, he cannot praise or honor God aright, he cannot abide fully in Christ, but as he accepts him fully in all he is and gives. Parents, I beseech you: make it your firm resolve to educate your children for nothing less than all their baptism offers them. Live to this end yourselves under its full power, as people who have been baptized into the death of Christ, with the flesh crucified, yourselves crucified to the world, made free from sin, bearing daily the cross and the dying of the Lord Jesus. Live as those who in baptism have been raised again by the faith in the working of God who raised Jesus. Let your faith claim all the power of his resurrection life; all that God wrought in him, he will work in you (Ephesians 1:20, 2:6; 1 Peter 1:21). Let the whole of your education be in this faith in the working of God to make true to your child all he promised in raising Jesus from the dead. Live as one baptized into the death and life of Christ, taking charge of a child who is partaker of the same baptism.

And make that baptism the starting-point of all his education. Lead him to Jesus, to whom he alone belongs. Lead him to the cross, to take it up and bear it in the love of Jesus. Help him, as sin and self come up, as the flesh and the world tempt, to practice the blessed self-denial which Jesus links with the cross. Guide him in that path of bright and loving obedience, where truest happiness is found. Speak to him of Jesus, the Risen One, as a living Friend, as the power of his new life. Long before he can understand the theology of it, let the impressionability of his young heart have been won for Jesus and a life like his, devoted to his service. Pray for grace, that above everything you may be to your dear child the interpreter who teaches him to understand the wonderful baptism with which he has been baptized into Christ, the guide who leads and helps him to the full possession of all it gives.

O my God, with my whole heart I thank you for all the blessing and power that is secured to me by my having been baptized into Christ and into his death. And that my child is partaker of this baptism also. And that you have set me apart as parent so to live as one baptized into Christ's death, that first my life, and later on my teaching, too, may lead my child to know the blessed life in Christ which has been sealed to him.

FORTY-SIXTH DAY

The Heritage of Holiness

"Now are your children holy."—*1 Corinthians 7:14*

LET US BLESS God for this precious sentence. There is not a deeper or more distinctly Divine word in Scripture than "holy"; in this statement the whole treasure of holiness, with all that revelation teaches us concerning it, is made the heritage of our children. God's holiness and our children are meant for each other; as parents we are the God-ordained links for bringing them into perfect union. If we would do this, we must know to understand and apply this precious truth. The revelation of God's holiness was a very gradual one because it was the opening up of the mystery of the Holy Trinity. There was first holiness as seen in God, its source and fountain; then in Christ, the Holy One of God, our sanctification; then in the Holy Spirit, as the Spirit of holiness in the Church. It is only by gradual steps that we can rise from the lower to the higher use of the word and enter into the fullness of Divine meaning which the word has as used of our children.

"Holy." The word expresses a relation. Whatever was separated unto God and made his property was called holy. "The Lord will show who are his and who is holy: the man whom the Lord shall choose, he is holy." Apart from the moral character, even an inanimate object, whatever had been given to God, and taken by him to be his own, was holy. And so the first and simplest thought our faith must take in and fill with spiritual meaning is this: our children belong to God. The very fact of their being born of believing parents make them his in a very special sense. Just as in olden times the children of the slave were the property of the master as much as the slave himself, so the Lord's redeemed, who love to call themselves his bond-servants, have no desire to look upon their children in any other light than themselves—wholly and absolutely his. "Now are your children holy."

"Holy." The word suggests a destiny. It is of great importance, as we study the word "holy" in Scripture, to notice how everything that is called holy had a use and purpose; every holy day and thing, place and person, had its service to fulfill. Let the Christian parent beware of looking upon holiness as a mere means to an end, simply as the way to get safe to heaven. Oh, it is infinitely more. Let him consent to it, that his child is God's property, to be used in this world only as God directs, to be trained with the one purpose of doing God's will and showing forth God's glory. The more clearly this is apprehended and made the distinct object of the work of prayer and education, the more speedily shall we be led to grasp what the word "holy" contains in its higher meaning, and what the path is to realize the blessing it offers.

"Holy." The word is the pledge of a Divine life-power. Though we find that God himself uses the word "holy" sometimes of external relation or privilege, and at others of real spiritual blessing, we must remember that the former always had the latter in view as its aim. Let us beware of emptying the word "holy" of its Divine truth and power. If God calls our children holy because of the covenant in which he has taken them up, it is because they are born, have their life from a believing parent, who is holy in Christ, and therefore are holy, too. The child of true believers, having soul and body under the rule and indwelling of the Holy Spirit, inherits from his parents not only the sinful nature, but habits and tendencies and dispositions which the child of the heathen or the infidel does not share. These are the true seed-germs of holiness, the working of the Holy Spirit from the mother's womb. Even where it cannot be seen and is but very feeble, there is a secret heritage of the seed of holiness implanted in the child of the believer. And with this there is given, in the word "holy," the promise of the Divine life and power to make to the child a reality and a personal possession what is his in covenant and in the being born of a holy parentage. There is secured to him that Holy Spirit in whom the holiness of God has reached its full manifestation. In promising the Holy Spirit to his disciples, our Lord said he would be a river of living water flowing from them to others. The believer has a power to influence those with whom he comes in contact; his faith is to save his household, since the child born of him inherits a blessing in the very life he receives from one who is sanctified by the indwelling of the Holy Spirit. In the mother's womb the child can receive the Holy Spirit. Oh, let us be sure of it: when God gives our child the name of "holy," there is the beginning and the pledge of a Divine power, even the work of his own Holy Spirit. Let nothing less than this be what our heart reads in God's words: your children are holy.

"Holy." The word describes a character. God's holiness is his infinite moral perfection; that he hates and destroys the evil, that he loves and works the good. Holiness is the Divine energy of which perfect righteousness and infinite love are the revelation. It is correspondence with himself that God seeks and that he gives. "Be holy; I am holy; I make holy." In calling your children holy, God invites you to have them partakers of his holiness; without this, holiness is but a name and a shadow. It is the work of the Christian parent to train his children in such dispositions and habits, such ways of thinking and feeling and acting, as shall be in harmony with the faith, that they are holy in Christ and belong to the Holy Spirit, as shall be a preparation for his dwelling in them and using them as his temple. Holy in all manner of conversation is what your children are to be; their young child-life separated from the world, its spirit and its service; consecrated to God, his Spirit, and his will.

It is as we begin to understand the word, "Your children are holy," clearly, that we shall know to apply it rightly. We shall find it a word of great power in our dealings both with God and with our children. With God it will be the strength of our prayer and faith. We shall feel liberty to claim that we be not sent away with a mere possibility, a promise without fulfillment, a covenant right without a personal experience. No. We may be sure that when our children are called holy, all that is implied in the word "holy" is meant for them. As we study the wonderful word in the story of Israel, in the character of God, in the person of Jesus, in the work of the Spirit of holiness, we shall find in God's "Your children are holy" the assurance that it is all for them. As we plead for the conversion of our children, we shall say with holy boldness, "Have you not said they are holy?" As we plead still more earnestly that they may not only be saved, but truly and fully sanctified, vessels meet for the Master's use, we shall most confidently cry, "O you who have laid the name of holy on them, it cannot be your will it should mean anything less than all your power and love can give." As in its light we confess how little we have realized the holiness of our parentage and the holiness of our children, the blessed heritage of holiness they have in us as believing parents, we shall yield ourselves more than ever to train them as holy to the Lord.

And so the word will exercise its mighty influence in our dealings with our children. We shall think of our home and family as his home, the dwelling-place of his holiness. We shall learn to look upon sin in our children, upon the spirit of the world, or conformity to it, as at utter variance with a child which the Holy God has set apart for holiness. We shall write holiness to the Lord upon our door-posts. We shall realize that the first need of a parent, whose children God calls holy, is to *be* very holy—that personal holiness is the indispensable condition for educating a holy child. "Your children, holy" will lead us to look to our own position, "You are holy in Christ Jesus," and to our own example and conduct as the channel through which the knowledge and the love and the power of holiness are to come to them. And as we hear the words we have known only as spoken of Jesus used by God himself of each child as it is born, "that holy thing which is born of you," "your holy child," we shall realize that nothing but a life in the holiness of God, a life entirely under the leading of the Spirit of holiness, can fit us for watching over and training the children God has given us.

O my God! My meditations on this word of the Holy Spirit have made me feel deeply the need of his Divine light to teach me what it means to you. Lord, show me, I pray, what the thoughts and the purposes of your heart are when you say to your believing people, whom you have sanctified in Christ, "Your children are holy." Show me, my God, how in this word there is secured to my child all that treasure of sanctification which is prepared in Christ, and which the Spirit of sanctification makes our personal possession.

O blessed God, you are the Thrice Holy; the glory which the seraphim praise and worship without ceasing is the glory of your holiness; in it all your attributes have their perfection and their beauty. You have revealed yourself as the Holy One who makes holy, your Son as your Holy One, your Spirit as the Spirit of holiness. You call your people your holy ones, and even of their little ones you say, "Your children are holy."

O my God, your words are never like men's words, empty thoughts; they are full of meaning, of life, and of power. Oh, make these words of yours quick and powerful in our hearts, that we may understand and rejoice in and hold fast the infinite blessing they bring us. And grant, Lord, that as we love and train, as we pray and believe for, our children, it may all be with this one object as our motive and aim, that we and they may be holy to the Lord, realizing and showing forth the glory of his holiness. Amen.

FORTY-SEVENTH DAY

The Reign of Love

"You fathers, provoke not your children to wrath."—*Ephesians 6:4*

"Fathers provoke not your children, that they be not discouraged."—*Colossians 3:21*

"Love suffers long, and is kind; seeks not her own, is not provoked."—*1 Corinthians 13:4–5*

"Train the young women to love their children."—*Titus 2:4*

THE APOSTLE had noticed, in the houses he visited, how sadly education often suffers from a want of love. And so, in addressing different classes in his general epistles, he speaks especially to fathers, and, on the two occasions in which he names them, repeats the warning to them not to provoke their children to wrath. His words suggest the three thoughts: that a child is often very provoking; that a father often allows himself to be provoked; that then the result generally is that he again provokes the child to wrath. Instead of thus, by his reproof, being the help and the strength of his child in seeking what is good, he discourages and hinders him. Paul's warning opens up to us the whole subject of the difficulty of giving reproof or punishment in the right spirit, of the need of patience and wisdom and self-control, of the secret of a parent's rule being this: that it is to be a reign of love.

Let us mark, first, that fathers are here especially addressed. They are expected to take a part in the management of the children. There are many fathers who neglect this and seek to throw the work entirely on the mother. When returning home from the day's labor, they do not feel inclined to trouble themselves, and the children are regarded more as a burden and a weariness than as a charge entrusted by the Lord, to be met in the spirit of love and gladness. God has joined to the weakness and gentleness of the mother the firmness and strength of the father; it is as each takes his share in the work, and becomes the helper of the other, that the Divine blessing may be expected. On this account it is of such great importance that in addition to the daily united devotions at the family altar, there should be set times when father and mother join in reading and conversation and prayer on the training of their children. One half-hour a week set apart for this purpose, if it were only for one year, would bring a rich reward. It would supply the lack of a training-school for parents, and draw attention to many an important lesson which is otherwise not noticed in the presence of work. It would give the opportunity for a mother's calling for, and receiving a father's aid and guidance. It would bring the blessing on conjugal and parental love, of which Peter speaks: "You husbands, dwell with your wives according to knowledge, giving honor unto the woman, as unto the weaker vessel, as being also joint heirs of the grace of life; to the end that your prayers be not hindered." Let every father accept his calling to take his part in the training of the children.

"You fathers, provoke not your children unto wrath." The occasion of this taking place is ordinarily that the child has first provoked the father. A child is sometimes wayward, often thoughtless, always feeble and ignorant, so that even what was well meant may be the cause of annoyance. It is only when the nature of the child, and especially its weakness and sinfulness, is carefully and lovingly taken into account, that the parent will be able patiently to bear with it and rightly to train it. It is the privilege and honor of the parent to have this immortal spirit, with all its failings and with all the trials of patience it involves, entrusted to his charge, with the view of his being the artificer through whom God is to make of it something of beauty and of glory for himself. Let parents take into their consideration the weakness and the willfulness of their children; let them not be surprised or taken unawares by what may be trying to temper and to patience; they will see the need for preparing themselves for their holy work by faith in him who fits us for every work he gives us to do.

"You fathers, provoke not your children to wrath." There is much in some children that is provoking; there is much in some fathers that is easily provoked. Beware above everything of giving way to such provocation; it has been the ruin of many a child. To educate a child is impossible without self-control. If anywhere, in this that scripture is true, "You have need of patience," "Let patience have its perfect work." The whole life of the Christian is meant by the Father in heaven, under the guidance of the Holy Spirit, to be one of watchfulness and self-recollection. In home life these graces are especially indispensable. The sudden outbreaks of temper in children, the little vexations arising from their disobedience or neglect or mistakes, their little quarrels and naughtinesses, are all so many occasions on which a father needs the love that is not easily provoked. God meant the rule of the family to be like his own, a reign of law inspired by love.

"You fathers, provoke not your children to wrath." However provoking the child may have been, however much inclined the father may be to feel provoked, he must see to it that he does not provoke the child to wrath. One provocation calls forth another; an angry father, giving way to his failing of being provoked easily, makes an angry child. There is innate in each human bosom a sense of the dignity of government and the duty of submission to authority. The calm, quiet assertion of authority helps greatly to bring the offender to the acknowledgment of the justice of his punishment. When, instead of trusting to this, the parent gives way to anger and passion in the sharp reproof or the hasty punishment, the child's passion is roused, too, and he is angry and vexed at an infliction of which he does not understand the reason or perhaps the justice. Passion ordinarily incites passion; the parent is the teacher and example of the child appointed of God to meet and conquer outbreaks of his passion by the gentle firmness of love. How sad when the very opposite is the case, and a father's hasty anger inflames a child's passion, and he becomes his provocation to wrath!

"That they be not discouraged." In the struggle between good and evil that goes on in the child, there is nothing so much needed as that he should be encouraged to believe that the victory of the good is within his reach, that goodness is possible and pleasant. To inspire a child with a holy confidence in what, by God's grace and the aid of his parents, he can accomplish, is one of the blessed secrets of success in training. In training a horse the utmost care is taken never to overtax it, or give a load that might lead to failure; at each difficult place you see its master all alert with voice and hand to inspire it with confidence; it must not know that it cannot succeed. That the child may never be discouraged by thinking that its weakness is not taken account of, that its little reasonings are not regarded, that it has not received the pity or the help or the justice it expects, will need a love which children all too little receive, and a thoughtfulness which parents all too little bestow.

"You fathers, provoke not your children to wrath." The education of a child is a holier work than many think. It needs above everything self-training. This was one of the objects with which God created the family relation: it is one of its chief blessings. Without his knowing it, your child is God's schoolmaster to bring you ever nearer to Christ. Not only does the child, in his tenderness and lovingness, call forth the love of your heart; his waywardness and willfulness call for it still more, as they put it to the test and school it in forbearance and gentleness. Study to have every token of your displeasure, every reproof and every punishment, so marked by love that through it all the child may really be encouraged into goodness.

But it is not by reproof and punishment, however gently and wisely administered, that parents will keep their children from getting provoked or discouraged. This is but the negative side; the positive is of more importance. Prevention is better than cure. Cultivate ever in yourself and the child that state of feeling which takes away the opportunity of its coming into collision with you. Endeavor by your own tranquility, gentleness, and kindliness to promote the same feelings in the child. Count upon the wonderful ascendency and influence over children that sympathy gives, in both its aspects. Throw yourself in sympathy into their interests, entering into their state of mind and feeling. Expect them—for their nature is as keenly susceptible of sympathy for others as from others—to enter into your spirit and temper, and instinctively to yield themselves to its influence. And as you seek to maintain the rule of love, not the mere love of natural instinct, but of love as a principle of action, earnestly sought in prayer from above, and carefully cultivated in all your family life—you will find how the children will catch its spirit, and become your helpers in making your home the reflection of the life of love in which the Heavenly Father guides and trains his children.

Gracious God and Father! The longer we listen to the teaching of your Word on our duty as parents, the more deeply we feel the need of a Divine grace for doing that work aright. I come to you with the humble confession of my sin; how often sin in the child has only been met by sin in the parent, to call forth in the child new sin, and to discourage him in the battle with it. And you had meant the parent to be to the child the model of a holy, patient love, uniting and helping its feebleness, and by his example encouraging him into the assurance that he, too, can conquer.

O God, we beseech you to open our eyes that we may know our holy calling. Give us a deep conviction that nothing but your own Spirit, dwelling in us day by day, can fit us for training sinful beings in a life of holiness; that nothing but the most entire surrender to walk with you, and to be in everything guided and possessed by your Spirit, can prepare us for the work of parents. O God, we pray especially for a baptism of love, of your own love. May a holy wisdom and patience in meeting each little outbreak of the evil nature, may the power of a love that enables us to bear and yet to conquer, as well as to inspire our child with confidence in us and the victory of good, be given us. O God, we would train our children after your mind, and to be a pleasure to you; be you our help. Amen.

FORTY-EIGHTH DAY

The Nurture of the Lord

"You fathers, nurture your children in the discipline and admonition of the Lord."—*Ephesians 6:4*

We know of what great importance it is to attend to the distinction between instruction and education, between teaching and training. The former is the communication of knowledge, secular or religious; the latter is the development of the faculties, both intellectual and moral, helping the child really to do and to be what the teaching has set before him. The two words the apostle uses correspond exactly to our expressions: we might translate, "Nurture them in the training and teaching of the Lord."[4]

Let us first note the spirit which must pervade the upbringing of our children: "Nurture them in the discipline and admonition of the Lord." Our children are the Lord's; their whole education must be animated by this thought; we train them for him, according to his will and in his spirit: it is the Lord's own training of which we are to be his ministers to them. Jesus Christ, the Son of God, as our Lord and Master, with his personal presence, his love and rule in heart and home, must be our aim; we must educate our children as "unto the Lord." That they may know and love him, that they may be fitted to obey his will and to serve him, must be

4. It is difficult to understand why the Revised Version should have translated the first of the two words by "chastening." The Greek word παιδεία is the exact equivalent of our "education," and is only translated "chastening" where the context evidently requires it as being a part of education.

what all our education strives after. And it can only be this, as we very earnestly study his will, and the rules he has laid down in his Word for parental duty, as we wait for his Spirit to guide and to sanctify us for our work. Our whole nurture is to be the nurture of the Lord.

In it the two parts God has joined together may not for a moment be separated. In the life of the child its emotional nature, with all its sensitiveness and impressionability, is first developed. For the due regulation of this, the Creator has endowed it with two great powers, that of willing and knowing. Training seeks to influence the will, as the power which really makes a man; teaching supplies the knowing by which the willing is to be guided and strengthened. The nurture of the Lord is to bring up the child that he may be a vessel meet for the Master's use, with every faculty of spirit, soul, and body prepared for doing his will. The training and teaching must work in harmony for securing this blessed object. All instruction and admonition has the forming of the will, of character as a completely fashioned will, of the perfect man as its purpose.

The word "education" is so much used of what is merely instruction, that I have used the word "discipline" to give the idea the apostle intended. The foundation of a useful and happy life will be found in the habit of order and self-control, the ready submission to law and obedience to duty. When not impulse or circumstance, not our likes or dislikes, but the steady purpose and power of knowing and doing right rule the life, one of the chief objects of education has been attained. Discipline uses the means, and exercises the power needed for securing this result. The discipline of the Lord has not only reference to what may be considered more directly religious, but to the child's whole being—spirit, soul, and body. Whatever contributes to the healthy development of the powers God has bestowed on us is included in the nurture of the Lord. There are what may be called physical virtues, at the foundation of which is order. "Order is heaven's first law" throughout the immeasurable spaces of the universe, and in the minutest atoms that the mind can conceive there reigns a Divine order; everything owns submission to law. How little it avails that a child or a man is converted if the power of self-control, the power of at once doing what is seen to be the right in its time and place, has not been cultivated. Conversion will not give this: the parent has to prepare the home in which the Spirit of God is to dwell, and to find its servants. The habit of order cultivated in a little child in external things can pass on into his intellectual training and become a mighty power in his moral and spiritual life. And it leads to that other foundation—virtue, decision of character, firmness of purpose; strength of will. In submitting to order in the external, the child learns that for everything there is an ought and a must, and that his welfare will be found in entering at once and heartily into that ought and what it requires. Let every parent seek, in nurturing a child for the Lord, to discipline into a fixed habit the innate sense of the rightness of order and decision. They will become ruling principles, in the wake of which other natural virtues will easily find their place.

Then come what may be called the legal virtues—those distinctly commanded in God's law. Such are obedience, truthfulness, justice, and love. Parents cannot too often or too earnestly remind themselves of the power of single acts often repeated to become habits, and the power of habit to aid in giving ascendency to the principles that underlie the acts. Our moral, no less than our bodily powers, are strengthened by exercise. Conscience may in early life be so disciplined as, by the Divine blessing, to become habitually tender and ready to act. The innate sense of right and wrong, the feeling of guilt and shame following on sin, the authority of God's Word—all these the discipline of a wise training appeals to in nurturing for the Lord.

And then there are the virtues that belong more distinctly to the New Testament and the great redemption it reveals. These are the faith and love of Jesus, the indwelling and leading of the Holy Spirit, the self-denial and holiness and humility of a Christlike life. All this is not to be only matter of teaching in the faith of the promise of the Spirit, working all unconsciously in the children; they are to be trained into it. To be temples of God through the Holy Spirit, to bear the image and be fit for the service of the Lord Jesus must, from the outset, be the aim of the Divine nurture in which we seek to bring up our children.

For such training to be successful, it is absolutely necessary that there be authority; the nurture must be in the discipline of the Lord. To this end it is not enough that the parent as the superior assert the right God has given him; the authority derived from God must become a personal possession by the influence the parent acquires over the child. The parent must prove himself worthy of his place; his ascendency will depend upon the weight of his moral character. To acquire such influence must be a matter of study and effort and prayer. All who wish to govern children not by force, but by influence, not against their will, but by means of it, not in virtue of a position in which they have been placed, but in the power of a life that proves them worthy of that position, and that secures an instinctive acknowledgment of their authority, must make not only their own duty, but especially the nature and the needs of childhood, their careful study. Only then can the education of our children become, instead of being a series of experiments and failures that teach us wisdom when it is too late to benefit by them, the wise and well-ordered commanding of our household that they may keep the way of the Lord.

Of such influence, in which true authority has its root and strength, the secret is a life in which we exhibit ourselves what we ask of our children. A life of childlike trust in the Father's love, of submission to his authority, and surrender to his training, will make itself felt through the home. It will awaken our sympathy for their childlike needs and failings. It will awaken their sympathy with our teachableness of spirit and our quiet restfulness in the Divine rule. And the nurture of our children will be to ourselves and to them truly the Lord's nurture—God's nurturing us by means of them, that he may nurture them by means of us.

Blessed God and Father, who has appointed us your servants to bring up our child in a training and teaching which is to be your own, we come again with the prayer for wisdom and grace to perform our task aright. We ask of you to show us the difficulty and the sacredness of our task, to show us, too, the nearness and sufficiency of your help. We want especially to realize that it is as we yield ourselves to your training and teaching, and walk with you as loving, obedient children, that we shall have power to nurture them aright.

We ask for grace rightly to combine the admonition that points out the way, with the discipline that trains to walk in it. We would form our children's character to that order and self-restraint, to that submission to law and authority, in which is the secret of happiness.

FORTY-NINTH DAY

Home Rule

"The bishop must be one that rules well his own house, having his children in subjection with all gravity; but if a man knows not how to rule his own house, how shall he take care of the Church of God? Let the deacons be the husbands of one wife, ruling well their children and their own houses."—*1 Timothy 3:4–5, 12*

It is a most suggestive thought that among the qualifications for office-bearers in the primitive Church, bishop, elder, or deacon, in each case the state of their household should have been taken account of, and a failure there should have been considered sufficient to bar them from the office for which personally they otherwise might have appeared fit. It reminds us once again of the closeness of the link between parents and children, and the organic unity of the home as a whole. From the household you can infallibly judge of what the parents are: the parents make it; it is the outgrowth and the expression of their life, the mirror in which, often with startling faithfulness, their hidden failings are revealed.

Some may be inclined to doubt the truth of this statement. They have so often heard, they know, of pious parents whose children have turned out ill. Is all the blame to be laid on the parents? We have no power to change the evil nature; it is grace alone can do it. Is it not going too far to put the blame of unbelieving or unruly children on the parents, and count such a father unfit for holding office in the Church or household of God, because his own household is not what it should be? And yet just this is what the Holy Spirit does. He teaches Paul to connect unbelieving and unruly children with the failure of the home rule, and unfitness for Church rule. He thus stirs us to search out what the secret evil may be by which, in parents who otherwise appear fit to be leaders in the Church, the training of their children is robbed of its power and its promised blessing. We are to seek for causes of failure in the home rule.

The first answer may be suggested to us by the words of Paul, as he argues from failure at home to failure in the Church. We may go a step backward and argue from failure in the family to failure in the person; the wrong in the home reveals something wrong in its head. We have more than once seen that the secret of home rule is self-rule, first being ourselves what we want our children to be. The wonderful power of the will with which man has been endowed was meant to make him in the first place his own master. And yet how many Christian parents there are to whom real self-control in daily life is quite foreign! It is not the thought of God's will, nor the rule of their own will, that guides and decides their conduct, but in conversation and action, in likes and dislikes, they are led away by the feelings of the moment. Because they trust that they are God's children, and that Christ's blood pardons their sins, and that their prayers will be heard, they hope for the salvation of their children. And yet their education is setting up the most effectual barrier against God's grace. Pleasing themselves, allowing their inclination or temper to be the rule of language and conduct, they give the most effectual contradiction to their profession of being the servants of God's will. Would that all Christian parents might learn the lesson that a quiet self-recollection and self-control, that a calm stillness of soul that seeks to be guided by God's Spirit, is one of the first conditions of success in our own spiritual life, and so in the sacred influence we wish to exert on our children. "In quietness and confidence shall be your strength." Nowhere will the unconscious but strong influence of this restfulness be felt so soon as in family life.

But there may be other causes. A Christian parent may not be wanting in self-control, and yet fail. The reason will very possibly be found in neglect of the duty of ruling. With some this may come from an entire ignorance of the solemn place a parent occupies. They have never thought seriously of the extent to which the souls and wills and characters of the children are in their hands. They have never taken any trouble to think carefully of the work entrusted to them. They may pray earnestly at times that their children may be saved; they know not that it is of more importance to pray daily that they themselves may be fitted to guide their children aright. With others the neglect of the duty rests on wrong principles thoughtlessly adopted. They admire a strong will; in the waywardness or self-assertion of a child's will they often see nothing but cause of amusement or admiration. They wish to see their child grow up a strong, bold character, able to do and dare; they would not for anything weaken his will. They know not that a wayward will is a curse, and that a will that masters itself to obedience is the truly strong will. No wonder that the children later on should be disobedient or unruly. And then with others the neglect of the duty comes from simple weakness and sloth.

They admit that it is their duty, but it is so hard; it takes so much time and thought. It is so trying to their love to punish or to thwart the child, and, under cover of the name of tenderheartedness, the authority with which they have been entrusted of God is neglected and abused. Let parents take time and thought to realize: to rule a child is as distinctly God's command as to love it or to care for it. The interests of parent and child demand it; the time and labor spent in cultivating this grace will be richly rewarded.

But still there are parents in whom neither of the causes of failure mentioned hold good. They do rule themselves, and they do seek to rule their children, and yet have failed. The cause must be sought deeper: the want of the Divine blessing must be sought in the want of true faith and consecration. There are some children easily ruled; there are others of nervous temperament or wayward disposition who appear to defy control. "The things that are impossible with men are possible with God." Education is a work in which the parents are meant to be God's servants, his fellow workers; but to work really with God means to walk closely with him. It is to the soul that is wholly given up to him, and seeks undividedly to do his will, that the power of faith will be given to hold fast the covenant, and to live in the assurance that God himself will do the work. Let there be but simple, childlike heart-searching, to see if there has not been in our aim with our children desire for worldly honor or position; the spirit of the world is the most secret but most certain hindrance to true faith. Let the surrender of ourselves and our children—not only to God's mercy to save, but to God's will to rule and use—be complete and unreserved; we shall find God to be our ally, our covenant-helper in training the children; and with him on our side we must prevail. To have had power with him in prayer is the sure guarantee of victory with the child.

Parents! The work entrusted to us is holier than we know. The precious instrument, so delicate, so wonderfully made, so marred by sin already, and so exposed to its power, is of such inconceivable worth. To take charge of an immortal soul, to train a will for God and eternity, surely we ought to shrink from it. But we cannot. If we are parents, the duty is laid upon us. But, thank God, sufficient grace is prepared and promised also. If we do but give up our home and our life to God for him to come in and rule, he will himself take possession, and by the gentle influence of his Holy Spirit bow their will to himself. And the discipline which our thus ruling the children brings will be the best preparation for our ruling in God's house, with that rule of which Jesus speaks: "He that is chief among you, let him be servant of all." If, for the sake of serving God in our homes, we deny ourselves to acquire real influence and power to rule with our children, he will count us worthy of influence and power with our fellow men and in his Church. Faithfulness in the home rule will give power to take care of the Church of God—will be, as it was with Abraham, the secret of admission to the counsel of him who rules the world, to the power that prevails with God and men.

Adorable Lord God! We worship you as the Ruler of the universe. Righteousness and judgment are the foundation of your throne. You are gracious and full of compassion; slow to anger, and of great mercy. Your kingdom rules over all; and your rule is everywhere the fountain of all blessing and good.

O Lord, it has pleased you to ordain that in each home on earth your heavenly rule should have its reflection. You have given to parents power and authority over their children to rule in your name. You have promised to give them all needful wisdom and strength for maintaining that authority and ruling their children well.

We have to confess with shame how often this holy trust of ruling in your name has been neglected and abused. We beseech you to forgive us. We beseech you to deliver us from all that hinders that rule. We desire to take it up as a life-work in your strength. May a holy self-rule fit us for a happy home rule. We desire to make the work you give us a study and a pleasure; to fit ourselves carefully for doing it well. Be yourself our Teacher and our Help.

Lord Jesus, we do indeed yield our homes and our children, our lives and all our powers, to be wholly yours. You are able to keep that which we commit to you. Keep our homes as your sacred dwelling-place, where we and our children serve you in righteousness and love, in peace and in great joy. Amen.

Children and Scripture

"Having been reminded of the unfeigned faith that is in you, which dwelt first in your grandmother Lois, and your mother Eunice."—*2 Timothy 1:5*

"Abide in the things which you have learned, and been assured of; knowing that from a babe you have known the sacred writings, which are able to make you wise unto salvation through faith which is in Christ Jesus."—*2 Timothy 3:14–15*

If we connect these two passages, we find in them the true relation in which children and Scripture ought to stand to each other. Between the unfeigned faith of the mother and grandmother, and the faith of Timothy, Scripture had been the connecting link. Scripture needs the believing parent as its messenger. The believing parent needs Scripture as the vehicle for the communication of his faith. A parent's faith teaching the word of faith may count upon the child's faith as the fruit of his labors.

God has so ordered it that it is mostly through the Holy Spirit dwelling in his saints that the Word is brought to sinners in the power of the Spirit. It is one Spirit dwelling in the Word and in the child of God; in the combined action of the two the Word is made a blessing to others. It is one of the highest honors God has for the believing parent, that he has made him the minister of his holy Word to his children. It is the unfeigned faith of father or mother, a faith which lives on and according to the Word, and speaks of it in the power of personal testimony and experience, that will be used of God to awaken a child's faith. In real living faith there is something contagious; the life of the Spirit breathes in it, and makes its words a blessing. This truth suggests some very precious lessons a parent should seek to learn.

Teach your child to *believe* the Word of God. Of old God sought above everything to train his saints to be men of faith. There is nothing more pleasing to him than faith. Faith is the soul's surrender to God, to hear what he says, to take what he gives, to receive what he works, to be entirely at his disposal. Faith in God begins with faith in his Word, and there is no habit a parent can cultivate in a child of deeper importance than that of a trustful acceptance of all that God has said. In an age of doubt and questioning, teach it to accept what it cannot understand, even what appears mysterious and contrary to reason, because God who is wise and great has said it. Teach it to believe in his love, in the gift of his Son, and in the life through him, as realities which come true to us as our faith simply trusts the Word and is assured of what it says. Teach it day by day to look upon every promise, every truth in the Word, as the food of faith, meant to make our faith, and through it our life, stronger. Parents! A child is naturally trustful; guide its young trust to that Word which never fails. The child wants to trust; the Word wants to be trusted; let your unfeigned faith bring them into contact.

To the end teach your child to *know* the Word of God. Faith depends upon knowledge. Timothy had known the sacred writings as able to make him wise unto salvation. If the grace of God is to save us, it must teach us; it is a wisdom from above; we must love God with the mind as well as the heart. Let the parent seek to give the child a clear and intelligent apprehension of the great truths of salvation God has revealed. He may not entrust this work to school or church; it is astonishing how vague the knowledge thus obtained often is. Let family worship be so ordered as to be really helpful in the knowledge of God's Word. Try always to make it clear at what stage in the history of the kingdom and in the progress of revelation it was that the word you read was given. Take trouble to lodge in the mind not only the truths and the history of the Bible, but especially to store the memory with some of God's own words. Be not content with the child's learning and saying his text at fixed times; it is often forgotten as soon as said. But seek to have some of these words, by frequent repetition, so rooted in the mind that nothing can efface them. Teach the child to know the book itself, too; to be at home in it, to feel at home and more at ease in it; to be taught by unfeigned faith thus to know the sacred writings is an inestimable blessing.

Teach your child to *love* God's Word. This is more difficult than to teach it to believe and to know it. There is often the assent of faith, and an interest in the knowledge of Scripture, with very little of real love to it. To teach this is no easy task. Its first requisite is, of course, that we love it ourselves. "Oh, how love I your law," is an expression of piety which many an earnest believer will be afraid to utter. Love and joy ever go together: what I love, I rejoice to possess. Reverence and respect for God's Word, the earnest study of it, and the desire to be guided by it—these are good—but they do not necessarily breathe that bright spirit of delight which says to God, "Oh, how love I your law." And yet it is love of which a child's heart is especially susceptible. Childhood is the age of feeling and impression; the child can be won before it can give a reason of its hope. And a parent's holy, tender love to the Word of God will be the surest means of inspiring the child's love. Let this be a distinct matter of desire and prayer, and of careful study, too, so to guide the child in his dealing with the Bible, that he may not only not dislike it, not only like it for its stories and its study, but truly and heartily love it as the Father's Word. This will indeed be the token of Divine grace, and the preparation for all blessing.

And then, teach your child to *obey* the Word of God. God connects all believing, knowing, loving, with doing; obedience is God's test of uprightness and reality. Teach the child to make what the Father has said the standard of conduct. Let him see and hear that you do so. In our ordinary Christianity, children are educated into the belief that God's commandments are grievous; the idea of obedience to him, whole-hearted and unceasing obedience, being simply happiness, is never thought of. And yet this is the only religion that really will be mighty to plant itself in the hearts of our children. The Bible must not be as a law continually holding us in check, keeping us from what we would like, and demanding what is difficult. No! With our children we must take up an entirely different position. As the Father's redeemed ones, the children of his covenant and kingdom, we must say, with the only-begotten Son, "I delight to do your will, O God; yes, your law is within my heart." It is his covenant promise to work this in us and our children. If in Christ Jesus we enter into the blessed life of the liberty of God's children, our children will learn from us how impossible it is to us to read the Father's Word and not do it.

Our study of it with them will all have this as its one purpose: we want to know and do the will of God.

The custom of family worship is to be found in almost every Christian family. Every day a portion of God's holy Word is read there. But, alas, in that reading there is often little power or blessing. Many an earnest Christian parent looks more to his private reading for profit and nourishment. And yet the daily gathering of the family round the Word of God might become such a season of spiritual refreshment and nourishment! If the same care we take to have a properly prepared meal placed on the breakfast table, and each child served with just what he needs, were only taken to see that the children really receive and enjoy the feeding with the Divine Word. Let parents make a study of it to have their family worship so ordered, as indeed to lead the children into the holy place, to be presented before the Lord, to be fed with the bread each one requires, and to receive the Father's blessing for the day. Let them prepare for reading the Word with the family. Let the reading be as of God's Word, in his presence, and waiting on his Spirit. Beware of the hurry which just gives time enough for the hasty reading of a chapter. Family worship becomes a dead and deadening form, hardening children into a habit of careless dealing with the Word and with God himself. A few moments devoted to a quiet, loving, calling of the attention to what God says, and to making the personal application, encouraging the children to take and keep the word, may be the beginning of great blessing.

Parents! God's Word is your child's heritage from the Father in heaven. And you are commissioned to lead him into the knowledge and the love and the possession of its treasures. Make it a matter of earnest prayer that you may wisely and rightly do it. Let that word dwell richly in you in all wisdom. In giving his promises, Jesus said, "If you abide in my word; if my words abide in you." Let your life be one of unfeigned faith, that lives and delights in doing God's Word; such faith will pass on into your children. The quiet confidence that comes from God's Word is a power that makes itself felt with our children. And if you often feel that you know not how to bring the Word aright to them, or see in them what hinders its reception, be still of good cheer, you have God to do the work, to make the Word effectual. Pray and believe for the Holy Spirit's working; he will make the Word, which you speak and live in unfeigned faith, the seed of faith to your children also.

* * *

Gracious God! We ask you to give us a very deep sense of the blessedness of this part of our work as parents, to bring your holy Word to them. May the privilege Timothy had be that of our children: from earliest youth to have the unfeigned faith of a loving parent as the interpreter of holy Scripture. May a deep, full, and very joyous faith in your blessed Word be the power in which all our Scripture teaching comes to them. Give us to see clearly how their hearts are claimed by you, to be filled with your words, that these may be in them the seeds of all holy thoughts and dispositions.

We ask of you the grace of wisdom, and faith, and patient faithfulness, to bring your Word day by day to our children. May our family worship every day be a holy season of communion with you, the Unseen One, in which we lead our children into your presence to hear your voice speak, and to receive your teaching. O our God, we yield ourselves to the supremacy and the power of your Holy Word; let it so abide in us, that our life may be the shining forth of its holy light. Let us be so full of faith and love and obedience to the word, that our dear children learn from their youth to love and believe and obey it too.

Father, forgive us that this has been too little so. Will you not by your mighty power make it so now? Amen.

FIFTY-FIRST DAY

Believing Children

"Ordain elders, if any be blameless, the husband of one wife, having children that believe, not unruly."—*Titus 1:6*

GOD EXPECTS that the children of believers should be believers too. There is nothing so honoring or pleasing to God as that we believe him; nothing that so opens the way for his blessing and love to flow in and take possession of us, as that we believe him. And the very object and purpose of God in the institution of the parental covenant is that believing parents should educate believing children. They are the children of the promise; God and his grace are theirs in promise; a promise has no value but as it is believed; parents who truly believe will understand that it is their privilege and their duty to train "children that believe."

We have seen how, on the day of Pentecost with the outpouring of the Holy Spirit, Peter announced that the foundation-principle of God's covenant with Abraham was in the New Testament to remain unchanged, and children were still to be regarded as the heirs of the promise. Family life, as ordained by God in Paradise—the household—was still to be the channel for the transmission of the blessing of the Spirit. Faith was not to be an individual thing, but to embrace the household, and then from the parent out to pervade it. It is in harmony with this that we so often find in the Acts—that book of the Acts of the Holy Spirit—mention made of the household. "Cornelius feared God with all his house." "Lydia was baptized, and her household." To the jailor of Philippi Paul said, "Believe, and you shall be saved, and your house," and "He was baptized, and all his, immediately," and "He rejoiced greatly with all his house, having believed in God." "Crispus, the ruler of the synagogue at Corinth, believed in the Lord with all his house." In the Epistles of Paul we find that he four times uses the expression "the church in your house." He does not say the church *assembling* in your house, but the church which is *in* your house, referring evidently to the circle of believers constituting the family. Though in these cases no express mention is made of children, the principle of the organic unity of the family, on which the idea of a household rests, assures us that the children were comprehended in it, too. And it is so clear to Paul that believing parents ought to have believing children; that, when such is not the case, he regards it as a matter of blame, as a sure index that there has been something wrong on the part of the parents, that their own faith and life has not been what it should be; they are at once debarred from holding any place of honor or influence in the Church of Christ. When the father, as the ruler of the church in the home, has not trained children that believe, he is unfit for taking care of the house of God. Children that believe are to be looked for from parents whose life is truly that of faith. Let us try and once again take home the lesson God would teach us.

Even children can be believers. Trustfulness, the power of simply believing what is told, of resting on what love has promised, is one of the most beautiful traits of true childlikeness. It is this wonderful power of a child's heart, of which the parent avails himself every day, and which often fills him with such gladness, that must be guided heavenward, and led to cling to God and his Word, to Jesus and his love. There is nothing more natural to children than to believe; it is through a parent's faith that the Holy Spirit loves to take possession of the child's, and makes it the living link to a living Savior. As the child grows, the faith may grow; a deep and hidden root of life that even amid temporary coldness or declension still holds on to the blessed Savior.

God expects our children to grow up believers. We ought to expect it, too. It is of the very nature of faith in God that it ever seeks to think as he thinks, to count upon him for what with man and nature is impossible, to make his promise and his power the measure of its hope. Let us take time to realize that God's wonderful promise to our children is meant so to take possession of us that it shall fill us with the sense of his holy power waiting to fulfill it, and draw us to live in his presence and in presence of our children as the channels of that power and that blessing. The confidence that our children will grow up true believers—something much higher than the confidence that they will eventually be saved—will exercise its influence on us and on them. On us as a daily call to a life of pure holiness and consecration; on our children in the creation of an atmosphere of faith around them in which they breathe and live. In our homes God expects that there shall be children that believe.

The proof that our children are believers will be their conduct. Paul writes, "Elders having children that believe, not unruly." Faith is ever perfected by works; like every other function of life, it can grow and become strong only by action. A life of faith is always a life of obedience. And a child's faith must prove itself in a child's obedience—that is, obedience to the parents. Children that are allowed to be unruly and disobedient and self-willed will speedily lose their childlike faith. What is said of men, that, having thrust from them a good conscience, they have made shipwreck of the faith, holds good of children, too. Faith is surrender. I yield myself entirely to the influence of the news I hear, of the promise I receive, of the person I trust. Faith in Jesus is entire surrender to him, by him to be ruled and influenced and mastered. Faith in Jesus is the surrender to him and his will. Faith in Jesus, to be saved by him, is the surrender for him, to let him save us in the way he has opened up, the way of trusting, loving, holy obedience. Let parents seek to lead the little one's simple faith in Jesus to this surrender. Let them claim the child's obedience to themselves as obedience to Jesus. Let them educate the child to obey conscience in Jesus' name; their home will be the happy proof that believing children are not unruly.

If ours are not children that believe, let us seek the cause with none but ourselves. God's promise is sure, and his provision is perfect. There is something wrong in our consecration. It may be—alas, how frequently it is so—that the spirit of the world so prevails in heart and home that while the Sunday talks teach the children faith in Jesus, the weekday life trains them to faith in the world, to a surrender to its spirit and rule. Or it may be that, while we are earnestly engaged in religion and religious work, there is but little of true spirituality, of the joy and the love and the power of holiness which alone make religion a reality. Religion has been an occupation like any other; but the holy presence of Jesus has not been felt by our children. Or even when there has been a striving after this, there may have been failure in our not devoting ourselves to the holy task of training children; we have entrusted the work to others, and neglected the self-denial and the study needed to fit ourselves for the work of ruling them well and of guiding them in the ways of the Lord. Let us seek very honestly and very earnestly to discover the reason of failure, to solve the sad enigma: we are believers, we have a faithful God, and yet we have not what he claims, "children that believe, not unruly."

God calls us to heart-searching and confession and return. And even if we have children that believe, but of whom we cannot but confess that their faith is not in such power and devotion as we could wish, let us turn to God with humbling and a new surrender. Our home life needs the power of a true consecration. The warm light of a Savior's love and the joy of his near presence shining from us: it is this our homes need as the secret of a successful education. Each new step in the path of entire separation to God, and of larger faith in his abiding and keeping presence, must make itself felt in the family. If there are circumstances and influences that appear to make it impossible, let us remember what faith can do: it can bring Almighty God and his power into the scene. It may not obtain at once what it asks. But it can live the life God wants his child to live; it can keep the soul in peace and rest; it can in secret exert its slow but sure influence. It is the faith of an entire surrender that our homes need, and that will transform them into what God would have, the nurseries of believing, obedient children. Both with God and with our children, let us study and remember this well: there is no power so mighty as that of a quiet, restful faith that knows that God has given what we have asked, that he has taken charge of what we have entrusted to him, and that in his own hidden, silent ways he is already working out what he has undertaken. Parents who are believers, who believe with their whole heart and strength and life, will have "children that believe, not unruly."

Blessed Lord God, the God of the families of Israel! We thank you for each message that reminds us of what you would have our children be, as the proof of the reality of our faith in your Word and our life in your love. We pray to you, blessed Lord, to imprint it deep in our hearts that in every believing home you do expect and do seek for believing children. Lord, as trees of your planting, we would yield you the fruit you seek.

When you do not find it, we beseech you to work a deep conviction of the sin that is the cause of the shortcoming. Whether it be unbelief or worldliness, the want of ruling well or the want of living well, reveal, we pray, the sin, that it may be confessed and cast out. Reveal especially how it is chiefly the lack of our undivided consecration to your will, with its consequent want of a full assurance and experience of your presence, that is the secret cause of all our failure.

Blessed Lord Jesus, it was your presence, the tidings of your being so near and so loving and so mighty to bless, that drew so many parents to trust you when you were on earth. O our Lord, it is your presence with us which will strengthen our faith and give us children that believe. We do set our homes open to you. Come in and reign. Be our joy and gladness every day. We have yielded ourselves to live each moment under your rule; we have believed in your acceptance of our sacrifice to keep us abiding in you; oh, give us the wisdom and sweetness, the faith and the power to be a blessing to our home. Oh, give us children that believe, children whom in the power of faith you can use for your glory. Amen.

FIFTY-SECOND DAY

I and the Children

"Behold, I and the children which God has given me,"—*Hebrews 2:13*

THESE WORDS were originally used by the prophet Isaiah: "Behold, I and the children whom the Lord has given me are for signs and for wonders in Israel." The prophet and his family were to be God's witnesses to certain great truths which God wanted his people not to forget. In the Epistle to the Hebrews, these words of the Holy Spirit are put into the mouth of Christ as his confession of his relation to those whom he is not ashamed to call his brethren. They are words which the Holy Spirit still uses as the language of the believing parent who presents himself with his children before the Lord, in the consciousness of that wonderful unity of the Spirit in which the family is one before God. As we draw our meditations to a close, these words invite us to gather up all that the Word has taught us of the Purpose and the Promise of our God, of the work of Love committed to us, and the abounding Hope in which we may look to the fulfillment of what God has led us to expect.

"Behold, I and the children which God has given me!" Let this be the language of a deep and living faith, as we think of the wonderful ground of our unity. I am one with my children in virtue of God's eternal purpose, when he created man and instituted the family. He meant the parent to beget children in his own likeness, to impart his own life and spirit to them, to have one life with them. When sin entered, the promise and the covenant were given to restore the blessing that had been lost; again, the parent was in faith to receive for the child, and communicate to him, the grace God had bestowed. In virtue of that promise I am one with my children, and my children are one with me, in the enjoyment of the love and the life that comes in Jesus. In that faith I present myself before the Father with that same "Behold!" with which Jesus called the Father to look upon him and his, and I say also: "Father! Behold, I and the children you have given me." You have given them me, with a Divine giving, to be inseparably and eternally one with me. God has given them me, in the power of the complete redemption of his Son, with the sure and full promise of your Holy Spirit for them as for me. God has given them me to keep and train for him, and then present before him as mine and his, too. In this faith I want day by day to look upon my little God-given flock, to believe that they are one with me in the possession of all the promises and blessings of the covenant, of all that the love of my God can give. As often as the thought of the corruption of their evil nature or the sight of its out-bursting comes up, when for a time it may appear as if they are not growing up as one with me in Christ, my faith will still say, "Behold, I and the children you have given me." And even when the thought of past sin and neglect in my training makes me fear lest my guilt is the cause of their being unconverted, I will still say, looking to the blood sprinkled on the door-posts of my home, the precious all-availing blood, that cleanses all my sin too: "Behold, I and the children you have given me. We are one; we must be one through your grace; we shall be one to all eternity."

In Jesus Christ nothing avails but faith working by love. "Behold, I and the children God has given me." When spoken in loving faith, the words become the inspiration of love for the work God has committed to it. The bond between a parent and child is a double one—there is the unity of life and of love. What has apparently become two lives love voluntarily and joyfully links together and makes to be still one. This love in nature cares for and rears and nurtures the child. It is this love that God takes possession of and sanctifies for his service. It is this love that becomes the strength for the difficult and yet delightful work the parent has to do.

Love is always self-surrender and self-sacrifice. It gives itself away to the beloved object; it seeks to enter into it, and become one with it; true, full love has no rest apart from perfect union with the beloved; all it has must be shared together. God calls his redeemed ones thus as parents to love their children, to identify themselves with them, to seek and claim their salvation as much as their own. And as the Spirit of Christ takes possession of the heart, the parent accepts the call; and in the unity of a love that cannot think of itself without the children, that is ready to sacrifice everything to make them partakers of its own blessedness, the parent learns to say with a new meaning, "Behold, I and the children which God has given me."

I and the children! I, the author of their life, the framer of their character, the keeper of their souls, the trustee of their eternal destiny. I, first blessed that I may bless them, first taught how my Jesus loved me and gave himself for me, that I may know how to love and how to give myself for them. I, having experienced how patient and gentle and tender he is with my ignorance and slowness and willfulness, now set apart not to think of my ease or comfort, but in the meekness and gentleness and long-suffering of Christ to watch over and to bear with their weakness. I, made one with these children, that in the power of love I may be willing to study what they need, and how I may best influence them; to train myself for the work of ruling well, and training them to self-rule. I, walking in the obedience and the liberty of a loving child of God, and guiding them in the happy art of an obedience to authority that is always free, and a freedom that is always submissive to law. Yes, I and the children! The consciousness grows upon me that in the unity of love, what I am the children may and will be. And the more tenderly my love to them is stirred up, the more I feel that I but need first myself to be wholly and only the Lord's, entirely given up to the Love that loves and makes itself one with me; this will fill me with a love from which selfishness shall be banished, and which gives itself in a Divine strength to live for the children that God has given me.

When faith and love thus have spoken, hope will have courage to take up the song, and in full assurance to say, "Behold, I and the children which the Lord has given me!" We are inseparably and eternally one. Hope is the child of faith and love. Faith is its strength for waiting and watching, love its strength for willing and working. Hope ever looks forward. It sees even in this life, when things are dark, the Unseen God coming through the clouds to fulfill his word. It sings the song of victory, when others see nought but defeat. Amid all the struggles through which it may see a loved child passing, amid all trials of faith and patience it speaks: "In his word do I hope: I will hope continually, and will praise you yet more and more." Through its own buoyant tone it inspires with hopefulness the children when discouraged in the fight with evil; it seeks to be the morning-star of the home. It looks forward to each one of the circle being not only a saved one, but a sanctified one, fit for the Master's service here on earth. And as often as it looks for the blessed hope, the appearing of our Lord Jesus, and the glory that is to follow, it rejoices in the full assurance of an unbroken family circle in heaven. It even now trembles with joy as it thinks of the privilege that awaits it, when the Son has presented himself with his brethren in his "Behold, I and the children God has given me," of also coming forward to fall down and worship and say likewise: "Father, behold! Here am I, too, and the children which you have given me." May God teach us to rejoice in this hope! "Now the God of hope fill your hearts with joy and peace in believing, that you may abound in hope in the power of the Holy Spirit."

Behold, I and the children which God has given me." Beloved fellow believers, whom God has honored to be parents, shall we not seek to have the spirit of these words breathe through our whole home life? It is God who has given us the children; it is he who regards them as one with us in his covenant and blessing, and teaches us to regard them so too. It is his love which calls and fits for a life of self-sacrifice and unselfishness; it is his grace which will accept and give success to our efforts to be one, perfectly one with our children in the power of faith and love and hope. In God's sight and promise we are one; in our life and love and labor let us be one with them, too; we shall be one through the glory of eternity.

Our gracious Father! We thank you for all the blessed teaching of your Holy Word concerning our children. We thank you that it has set them before us in your own light, as created by you, ruined by sin, redeemed in Christ, and now entrusted to us to keep and care for, while the Holy Spirit renews them to your eternal life and glory. We thank you that you yourself have come as our Teacher to fit us for teaching them. We pray to you for your blessing on each word of yours, that we may indeed become such parents as you would have us be.

O Lord, we pray to you to establish in our thoughts and hearts and lives all the wonderful truths that gather round the home life. We would count your covenant and its promises as exceeding precious to us. Our faith would see the names you give to our children, children of the covenant, of the promise, of the kingdom, as written on their foreheads. We would treasure all the promises of your Spirit and your blessing as their sacred heritage. We would read of all your dealings with your saints in the birth of their children, and their upbringing for your service, as the revelation of your will with ours. We accept all your warnings and all your instructions concerning children as the law of our home. O Lord, open our eyes, that we may ever have before us the picture of a believing home as you will it, and will to make it for us.

Above all, blessed Lord Jesus, let your presence and your love and your joy, filling the parents' hearts, be the power to fulfill the Father's will, and to win our children's love. It is in you all the promises are "Yes" and "Amen"; come yourself, and accept our consecration to be wholly yours; come yourself, and let our home be the abode where you love to tarry. Then shall it be blessed indeed, and each of us say with never-ceasing gladness of hope, "Behold, I and the child God has given me."

Even so, Lord Jesus. Amen.

The Church's Duty to Parents

A short account of the origin of this book may not be without its interest, and may be the best explanation of its object.

When first I entered the ministry, thirty-six years ago, I was placed in charge of the whole of what is now the Orange Free State. As the neighboring territory of the Transvaal was at that time also without a minister, I had to supply its wants, too. With a large population, so widely scattered, each of the separate congregations could only be visited at distant intervals. When services were held there always was a large gathering, with very large numbers of children to be baptized; in the Transvaal I repeatedly baptized a hundred and upward on each of several consecutive Sabbaths.

In some of the congregations of our Church, the custom existed of meeting the parents, when they applied for the baptism of their children, to explain the meaning of the ordinance, and to insist upon earnest preparation for a believing reception of it, as well as for the duties undertaken in it. In the course of these conversations I became deeply impressed with the ignorance prevailing as to the object of the ordinance, and the large extent to which it had become a mere religious ceremony. And I was almost involuntarily led, in connection with every baptism service, to make parental duty the subject of the sermon. I began to realize very painfully of how little value infant baptism could be apart from the parent's believing apprehension of God's promise, and his faithful fulfillment of parental duty.

In the course of my further ministerial labors in my own congregation, these convictions were deepened. In the effort to encourage parents to seek religious instruction for their children, it became manifest how much labor in this direction was lost because the foundation which God had meant should be laid, in parental instruction, was wanting. I saw that God would not allow even a faithful minister to usurp the place or do the work destined by him for the parent. It became plain that, in the threefold cord of home, school, and Church instruction, the home had the first and in some respects the most important place. If the Church would do her work successfully, she must direct to the training of parents her first and best efforts. Through these she would reach the children far more effectually than by any other methods.

I looked around to see how the Christian Church elsewhere was combating the evil. I heard some voices crying in great earnestness that the children are the Church of the future, and that they ought to have a larger place in her care than hitherto. I saw that Sunday schools, and, later on, children's services, were wakening large interest; that faith in children's conversion and in revival work among them was gaining ground. And yet there appeared to me to be something lacking. I listened to hear whether I could hear a clear and distinct witness in the Church in regard to the parents' place, their inalienable right, their incomparable influence as the ministers of God's grace to the children. I fancied I did not. The truth was acknowledged by all, but little insisted on. In but few cases could I hear of systematic attempts, on the part of the Church, to instruct and encourage parents by the full exposition of their duties and God's promises.

A little thought will convince us that this is a fatal mistake. One of the marks of men who have succeeded in influencing and ruling their fellow men, and one of the secrets of their success, has ever been the gift of enlisting and inspiring the service of others. This is what the Church must study to do, not only with regard to those who are ordinarily called Christian workers, but specially with that band of God's own workers, the parents there are in every congregation, to whom its children are entrusted. Teach, train, stir up, encourage these to their work, and there is hope—there is more than hope—there is assurance for the future. Let the minister, instead of preaching almost solely to individuals, whether it be conversion or sanctification, for a season or at stated intervals, make it his special object to guide the parents of his congregation; he will stir and strengthen one of the mightiest agencies in the service of God's kingdom. The work of a parent is one of extreme solemnity and difficulty. It needs great wisdom and patience, much self-control and prayer and faith. As we do not expect a believer to advance in the Christian life without the teaching of the Word, much less must we look for a parent to be able to do his work aright without instruction and encouragement.

It was under the impression of thoughts such as these that I was led, when other ministers took part of the work from me and I could devote myself to my own congregation, to appoint one Sunday in every mouth for the celebration of baptism, and to arrange that the whole service — singing, reading, prayer, and preaching — should have reference to the one thing: God's purpose with the family and the way in which parents had to fulfill it. It cannot but strike any but the most thoughtless observer what a difference is ordinarily made between the two sacraments instituted by our Savior. With the Lord's Supper, how much solemnity, what earnest preparation, how much of teaching and preaching and praying to make it profitable. With baptism, on the contrary, what haste, what absence of teaching, what irreverence often where it is performed at the close of a service or in the house. With the Lord's Supper, how much definite promise and expectation of blessing; with baptism, how little. And yet the two sacraments are equally sacred; they equally represent the precious blood and the new covenant of which it is the seal; they equally claim the faith and the surrender of the heart. The attempt on the part of the Church to connect baptism more definitely with the faith and the duty of parents, to let them feel more deeply how it was to their faith that the promise of the covenant for their child was given, and to their faithfulness that its training was committed, would most assuredly bring a blessing.

I soon found that baptism-Sunday was looked forward to with special interest. One might have thought that for ordinary hearers the subject would be less attractive; on the contrary, no sermons were listened to with greater attention. Brethren in the ministry have asked whether the supply of texts was not speedily exhausted: experience has taught here, as in other matters, that when once God's Word is searched with a special object in view, words and histories which were never noticed before become luminous with a new meaning. In illustrating the lives and characters of the parents and children of the Bible, in setting forth all God's teachings and dealings with reference to them, abundance of the richest matter was found. In dealing with the special sins of children, or inculcating children's virtues, in setting forth the wondrous nature of the being entrusted to them, and some of the laws by which his conduct is actuated, it was found that often the teaching given for the control of children was the most profitable that could be found for those who wanted help in their own moral self-culture.

It is now more than twenty years since the original of the present volume was published in Dutch, in meditations for a month, each containing a short summary of some sermon that had been preached on such occasions. Since that time many a new subject has been treated, and I have been led now to prepare a series of fifty-two—one for each week. I have done this in the hope that some Christian parents, who feel the need of such help, perhaps young parents, may be led once a week, on the Sunday afternoon or evening, or at some other time, to read and meditate and pray together over some of the precious words of God with regard to their calling. In these God has revealed his loving purpose toward our children, and abundantly promises us the grace we need to make us truly and surely a blessing to them. Such a use of it need not hinder the perusal day by day for those who prefer this. I hope very specially that to more than one young mother, in that sacred period, when, as she bides her time and waits to receive her little one from the Lord, and then after its birth is kept in weakness and solitude to think of the precious little life that has been entrusted to her, and prays for grace to do it aright, this little book may be God's messenger to encourage and guide to that entire consecration to God in which alone a godly education can find its strength.

But it is not only to parents that I would offer this work, but very specially to my brethren in the ministry, in the hope that where they have not already done it, they may make their duty, and the duty of the pulpit, toward parents matter of earnest prayer and study. They may be sure that the time, and energy, and preaching devoted to parents will bring a double reward. It may be doubted whether God teaches and blesses children more through their parents, or parents through their children. Spiritual efforts for the parents are a blessing to parents and children both. Let us carefully notice how much of the Bible, and of God's dealings with believers, has reference not to individuals, but to parents for the sake of their children. Let us try and realize how deep, in God's people, the foundations of the kingdom were laid in parental instruction and family religion. With Israel at the Passover, in the laws of Moses, in the Psalms, how much more mention is made of the teaching of the parents than of the priests. To elevate the standard of thought, and faith, and duty among the parents, is one of the highest tasks a Church can have.

And a Church that believes in infant baptism has in this ordinance the most wonderful opportunity of coming into contact with parents. With each child baptized publicly, not only its own parents, but the whole assembly of parents are reminded of God's covenant engagement with them and theirs with God. What an opportunity (especially if a fixed Sabbath could every month be devoted to it) to let the light of God's Word shine into the home and the family life, to discover shortcomings and unfaithfulness, to teach and to help, and to stir up to faith and prayer.

If there is one subject on which systematic Bible teaching is needed, it is this. The training of children is one of the most important and difficult tasks that can be undertaken. The welfare of society and the Church depend upon it. God's Word gives abundant teaching on the subject; but the Church has hardly yet given herself to the systematic effort of teaching and training parents for their holy work. One of our modern philosophers has expressed so well the utter folly of thinking that parents can perform their duties without preparation, and the need of providing for instruction in parental duties, that I give the passages at length:[5]

> We now come to the third great division of human activities—those which have for their end the rearing and discipline of offspring—a division for which no preparation whatever is made. If, by some strange chance, not a vestige of our literature descended to the remote future save a pile of our schoolbooks, we may imagine how puzzled the antiquary would be on finding in them no sign that the learners were ever to be parents. "This must have been the curriculum for their celibates: I find no reference whatever to the bringing up of children. They could not have been so absurd as to omit all training for the gravest of responsibilities." Seriously, is it not an astonishing fact that though on the treatment of offspring depend their lives or deaths, and their moral welfare or ruin, yet not one word on the instruction of offspring is ever given to those who will by and by be parents ? If a merchant commences business without any knowledge of arithmetic, we should exclaim at his folly and look for disastrous consequences. But that parents

5. *Education: Intellectual, Moral, and Physical* by Herbert Spencer.

should begin the difficult task of rearing children, without having ever given a thought to the principles which ought to guide them, excites neither surprise at the action, nor pity for their victims. . . . We find the facts to be such as might have been inferred *a priori*: the training of children —physical, intellectual, moral—is dreadfully defective. And in great measure it is so because parents are devoid of that knowledge by which their training alone can rightly be guided. What is to be expected when one of the most intricate of problems is undertaken by those who have scarcely given a thought to the principles on which its solution depends? For shoemaking or housebuilding a long apprenticeship is needful. Is it, then, that the unfolding of a human being in body and mind is so comparatively simple a process that anyone may superintend and regulate it with no preparation whatever? If not—if the process is, with one exception, more complex than any in Nature, and the task of ministering to it one of surpassing difficulty—is it not madness to make no provision for such a task? . . .

The greatest defect in our program of education is entirely overlooked. While much is being done in the detailed improvement of our system, the most pressing *desideratum* has not yet been even recognized as a *desideratum*. To prepare the young for the duties of life is tacitly admitted to be the end which parents and schoolmasters have in view; yet no care whatever is taken to fit them for the position of parents. While it is seen that for the purpose of gaining a livelihood, an elaborate preparation is needed, it appears to be thought that for the bringing up of children no preparation whatever is needed. While years are spent by a boy in gaining knowledge, of which the chief value is that it constitutes the education of a "gentleman," not an hour is spent in preparation for that gravest of all responsibilities, the management of a family. Is it that this responsibility is but a remote contingency? On the contrary, it is sure to devolve on nine out of ten. Is it that the discharge of it is so easy? Certainly not; of all functions which the adult has to fulfill, this is the most difficult. Is it that by self-instruction each may be trusted to fit himself for the office of parent? No; not only is the need for such self-instruction unrecognized, but the complexity of the subject renders it the one of all others in which self-instruction is least likely to succeed. Whether as bearing on the happiness of

> parents themselves, or whether as affecting the character and lives of their remote descendants, we must admit that a knowledge of the right methods of juvenile culture—physical, intellectual, and moral—is a knowledge of extreme importance. The topic should be the final one in the course of instruction passed through by each man and woman. As physical maturity is marked by ability to produce offspring, so mental maturity is marked by the ability to train their offspring. The subject which involves all other subjects, and therefore the subject in which education should culminate, is the Theory and Practice of Education.

Many will doubt the wisdom or the possibility of the proposal to make the art of educating children part of ordinary education. Education requires practice—exercise in the art that is being taught. When people are parents they can no longer go to school again. There is but one way out of the difficulty. The Church has the solution of the problem in her hands. In God's Word, with its wonderful lessons as to parents and her children, she has a Divine class-book. In the Church gathered at the sacrament of baptism, she has her class. In the feeling of parental responsibility and affection, in the experience of the difficulty of training the children aright on the consciousness of failure, there is a stimulus to learn which no class in the mere art of educating children ever can have. Could the Church, with her views of the power of sin and the power of grace, with her faith in God's Word and God's Spirit, but realize the absolute need, the infinite importance, the rich blessing of training her parents for their work, how speedily ways and means for having it done could be found. I am persuaded that a monthly baptismal service would, in course of time, be welcomed by many parents as a boon of unspeakable value.

Where this is not possible, other arrangements might be made. Mothers' meetings already exist in many places: these might be utilized for giving more distinct instruction. And is there not as much need of fathers' meetings? We have Bible classes for the young: a parents' class, with the pastor leading and teaching, could in some cases be organized, even were it but for a short course. Parents would gradually become conscious of their high calling and themselves seek the help they need. If the Church is content, let us not wonder that parents are content, too. The misapprehension by which parents expect from the public teaching of the Church more than from their own training is a very fatal one, and no effort ought to be spared to dispel it. A writer on this subject has well said:[6]

> What can be more strangely wide of all just apprehension than the immense efficacy imputed by most parents to the Christian ministry, compared with what they take to be the almost insignificant power conferred on them in their parental charge and duties? Why, if all preachers could have their hearers for whole months and years in their own will, so as to move them by a look, a smile, a frown, and act their own emotions and sentiments over in them at pleasure; if, also, a little further on, they had them in authority to command, direct, regulate their pleasures, their company, and call them to prayer every morning and evening—who could think it impossible, in the use of such a power, to produce almost any result ? Should not such a ministry be expected to fashion all who come under it to newness of life? Let no parent, shifting off his duty to his children, think to have his defects made up, and the consequent damages mended afterwards, when they have come to maturity, by the comparatively slender, always doubtful, efficacy of preaching.

The Church does much of her work through the press: a parent's *Manual of Education* would supply a real want. We have a great number of handbooks of education and school management, in which a summary of what a teacher requires to know of is presented; in these parents would find much that is suggestive in some of the chapters. Various religious works exist, with valuable hints on parts of a parent's work. But what is required is a work in the spirit of Christian science, in which what the science of psychology teaches of the wonderful nature of the being that has to be trained, and what the science of education of the laws under which its powers can best be developed, and what the science of ethics of the principles by which the child's powers can be ruled and guided aright, and what Scripture of the wondrous work that grace will do in sanctifying all this, is presented in popular and practical form.

6. *Christian Nurture* by Horace Buslinell, a most suggestive volume. Though he may find thoughts or expressions he may not agree with, every minister who wishes to realize his duty to the parents of his flock will find himself well rewarded for the study of this work.

But, in whatever way the work is to be done, only let it be done. Let the Church, the teacher of the nations, the messenger of God to his people, lift up her voice and secure the aid of the hundreds of thousands of parents that belong to her to train the coming generations for God. Let the ministry hold forth God's Word to dispel the ignorance, to shame the indifference, to banish the unbelief that hinders, and to make the family again what God meant it to be—his first and mightiest means of grace for the maintenance of his kingdom among his people.

Meantime, I trust the present work may be accepted of the Lord and of his people, and be blessed to bring to some parents words of guidance and encouragement. All the teaching clusters round the four great central thoughts of God with regard to the family: God, as its Creator, its Redeemer, its Sanctifier, its Covenant God; faith, as the one condition for bringing parent and child into relation with God, and making both partakers of its covenant-promise and blessing; parental faithfulness in life and training as the path in which the blessing apprehended by faith is appropriated and brought down upon the home and the child; the children, God's property, to be trained for his glory and service.

Baptism: Adult or Infant

IN THE BAPTIST CONTROVERSY, the opponents of infant baptism consider that Scripture is so clearly on their side, and are so sure that it is only the influence of human custom and authority that holds its supporters in their fetters, that they feel justified in saying that the only reason believers in infant baptism cannot see God's will in Scripture on this point to be what Baptists practice is their unwillingness to make the sacrifice which would follow their acceptance of the truth. Even men who are large-hearted and loving men find it difficult to explain the hold which infant baptism maintains on the Church of Christ on any other ground.

It would indeed be a terrible thing if the charge were true. Tens of thousands of Christians, professing with intensest longing to know the will of God in Scripture, and yet maintaining that to them it teaches that the baptism of the children is his will, not able to see what their brethren assure them is clear as day, only because they are not willing to do his will! Hardly less terrible is the charge if it is not true; because such judgments, however for a time they may be covered by Christian love, yet at times cannot but spring up and bring forth the bitter fruits of division and estrangement, to the weakening of the body of Christ.

And what answer has infant baptism to give to its opponents? Our book, though not written for the purpose, may be taken in answer. There are truths we believe, and duties we consider binding, for which one clear single chapter-and-verse proof cannot be given. Take our keeping holy the first day of the week, instead of the seventh, as the fourth commandment requires. Because there is no distinct command for the change, we have men who insist that they alone truly obey God's commandment who keep the seventh day. And such servants of the letter utterly refuse to listen to or understand the teaching of the Spirit in Scripture, on which the Church, without any literal command, grounds its keeping holy the Lord's day. It is just so with the question between infant and adult baptism. Though there is no literal command to baptize the little ones, the study of God's Word as a whole makes so clear both the ground on which it rests, and the reasons why no literal command on the subject was needed, that the Holy Spirit leads men, wholly given up to follow him in teachableness and obedience, to find in God's Word the confident assurance that infant baptism is according to his will.

And their judgment, then, on adult baptism? "Who are you that judges another man's servant? To his own master he stands or falls." In the very remarkable chapter from which these words are taken, God has for all time given his Church the principle that ought to guide her in matters in which those who seek to follow the leading of the Word and Spirit differ as to duty. It is a most significant fact that while Paul knew that it was lawful to eat the meat by which some were offended, or to esteem every day alike, he did not interpose his authority, much less the authority of God, to tell the weak brother to give up his ignorant prejudice. Such a decision might have settled that question, but it would have left the Church a great loser; it could ill miss the teaching the chapter conveys, by which, as it is, she has profited all too little. That natural character and other circumstances may give rise to differences of view; that such diversities may at all times exist, which it is not the will of God to settle by any absolute rule; that, therefore, the judgment of the brother is not ours, but the Lord's; and that the exercise of humility and forbearance, for which the diversity calls, may be a far greater blessing than the uniformity which we think so desirable: these are lessons of the utmost importance, which have their applicability here, too.

Our place on the earth is such that we can only see one-half of the starry heavens at a time. And so in the great sphere of Divine truth no mind is large enough to grasp the whole. Every truth in man's hands becomes one-sided. God's way of remedying this defect and its danger is to entrust one aspect of truth to one portion of His Church, while another holds the abuse of it in check by testifying for some different aspect. In this way the dependence of all on each other is to be maintained, and the triumph of love in the midst of difference to be made manifest. So with baptism. Infant baptism, with its discipling and baptizing the nations, has its danger. When the Church becomes lax, and the ministry is not faithful in teaching the word of faith, through which alone a sacrament is effective, infant baptism, may come to be a form without power. And then adult baptism comes in as a needful protest, to plead for the spiritual character of the rite, and the absolute necessity of a living faith to make it acceptable with God.

But adult baptism—that is, man's teaching concerning it—has its danger, too. In the individualism which cannot understand God's dealing with the family, on the groundwork of the covenant of grace, nor the power of a parent's faith, as according to God's will it embraces the child, nor the free mercy which when it takes a child into the covenant for the parent's sake can give it the seal of the covenant before it has believed, it would utterly fail of gathering in the nations. And while it holds that it alone witnesses aright for the faith through which the sacrament can have its value, and a spiritual blessing be received, infant baptism claims that it is a still bolder witness for the power of faith, as it teaches, in accordance with all God's revelation, how a parent's faith can accept and keep the blessing for the child, too.

I sincerely trust that the study of God's words and thoughts concerning parents and children will lead those who hold infant baptism to see the Divine ground on which it rests, its deep spiritual significance for them and their seed, and the need of a living faith, as that without which it may become but a lifeless form.

Notes

Note A: Twenty-Second Day

It may be helpful to parents, to young mothers especially, to give a short summary of the principles on which all training rests. Let them meditate carefully and prayerfully on what it implies: they will find that it is a work that cannot be performed without careful thought and earnest purpose. It is only as reflection opens up to them the infinite significance of the holy work of moulding, of really forming and giving shape to, an immortal spirit, that they will feel urged with due fervor and faith to plead the promise, "If any man lack wisdom, let him ask of God, who gives to all liberally; and it shall be given him."

1. Training is more than teaching. Teaching makes a child know and understand what he is to do; training influences him, and sees that he does it. Teaching deals with his mind; training, with his will.

2. Prevention is better than cure. Not to watch and correct mistakes, but to watch and prevent mistakes, is true training. To lead the child to know that he can obey and do right, that he can do it easily and successfully, and to delight in doing it, is the highest aim of true training.

3. Habits must precede principles. The body is formed and grows for the first years of life while the mind is to a great extent dormant. Habits influence the person by giving a certain bent and direction, by making the performance of certain acts easy and natural, and thus preparing the way for obedience from principle.

4. The cultivation of the feelings precedes that of the judgment. The early years of childhood are marked by the liveliness of the feelings and the susceptibility of impressions. The parent seeks to create a feeling favorable to the good, to make it attractive and desirable. Without this,

habits will have little value; with it, they have a connecting link by which they enter and grow into the will.

5. Example is better than precept. Not in what we say and teach, but in what we are and do, lies the power of training. Not as we think an ideal to train our children for, but as we live do we train them. Not our wishes or our theory, but our will and our practice, really train. It is by living a thing that we prove that we love it, that we have it, and that we influence the young mind to love it and to have it, too.

6. Love that draws is more than law that demands. To train needs a life of self-sacrifice, of love that seeks not its own, but lives and gives itself for its object. For this God has given the wonderful mother-love: it needs but to be directed into the right channel as the handmaid of God's redeeming love. Law alone always works sin and wrath. It is love that gives itself with its thought and strength to live for and in the other, and breathes its own stronger and better life into the weaker one. Love inspires, and it is inspiration is the secret of training.

Note B: Thirtieth Day

Among the first traits of the heavenly spirit in the child is restfulness. The following remarks on cultivating this, even during the two first years of a child's life, are well worthy of a thoughtful perusal.[7]

> We may even from the earliest infancy cultivate those dispositions which are unfavorable to the growth of dangerous inclinations. Certain habits, which exercise a salutary influence on the moral feelings, may be given to the infant, even before his character distinctly shows itself. Inward tranquility will calm the restlessness of his wishes, and the kindness bestowed upon him will direct his attention out of himself, and make him feel kindly toward others.
>
> I have often thought that we are too much accustomed to keep infants constantly in motion. We ought certainly not to allow them to grow weary—*ennui* is the lethargy of the soul; but nothing is more likely to produce this evil than an excess of variety in our methods of amusing them. The more tranquility a child has enjoyed in infancy,

7. From *Progressive Education* from the French of Madame Necker de Saussure.

the more he will possess hereafter; and a calm cheerfulness of disposition may be permanent, which gaiety and mirth seldom are. It is for this reason that it is so much more desirable for children to be occupied with things than with people; things are tranquil objects which do not interest them too eagerly. With people their feelings of sympathy or dislike are continually excited.

Note C: Fortieth Day

The following extract, from *Life in Jesus: A Memoir of Mrs. Mary Winslow by Her Son*, gives a very touching and instructive illustration of a widowed mother claiming God's covenant on behalf of her children. And in later years, after her death, her son, Dr. B. Winslow, loved to tell how wondrously God had proved himself faithful in fulfilling his promise to all her children:

> She was now a widow with a large family of sons, dependent upon her for their training and settlement in life. "She that is a widow indeed, and desolate, trusts in God." Such was her present condition. The surges of grief now yielded to a calm, intelligent survey of her position. She threw herself upon God. The covenant she made with him when a wife, she now and more solemnly renewed as a widow—that the Lord should be her God. It was at this important crisis of her history that the following touching incident in her experience occurred.
>
> "I had sent one of my sons, a youth of ten years old, accompanied by a servant, across the river on a matter of business. The appointed hour for his return arrived, but he did not appear. Hour after hour passed away, and nightfall drew on, but he came not. The last steamboat touched the pier, but he was not on board. I walked my room for hours in prayer, and in great agitation of mind. Keenly did I feel my lonely, helpless widowhood. Again and again I sought the Lord. After passing hours in this state of mental anxiety, I sent a brother in search, and soon after, all made their appearance. He had missed his way. The Lord heard a mother's prayer, and brought him in safety to me. After all had retired for the night, I was left

alone with God. My mind and heart had been greatly exercised throughout the day. I felt deeply my helplessness and responsible situation. I thought, 'How can I, a helpless woman, care for and train up these children to manhood?' I felt I should sink beneath the overwhelming conviction of my weakness and insufficiency. I paced my room in prayer, tried to take hold of a promise; but all was dark, the present and the future, as midnight. It was late before I retired to rest. In vain I endeavored to console myself; sleep had forsaken me. Again I lifted up my heart in prayer. I tried to cease from thinking, and to close my eyelids, but in vain. All night I continued in prayer, until just before the dawn of day these words were spoken to my ear and heart, as if an audible voice had uttered them: 'I will be a Father to thy fatherless children.' I knew this voice, and could make no mistake. So powerful was it, I instantly replied aloud, 'O Lord, be the Father of my fatherless, and my God!' Oh, the solemnity of that hour! I felt God was with me, and my soul was filled with joy and holy reverence. He had condescended to visit my lone room, and fill it with His presence. He had come to comfort His widowed child, and I was comforted. My soul poured out its grateful acknowledgments. I could adore, and praise, and bless his holy name. A solemn, sacred influence pervaded the place. God was with me of a truth. Fatigued with the anxieties of the day, and exhausted with the mental exercises through which I had passed the night, I composed myself to rest. The Lord withdrew, and my weary eyes were closed in refreshing sleep. Years have passed since then, and the Lord has not for one moment forgotten his promise. But I take the promise to extend beyond this poor dying world. Had the Lord given each of my children a world, and they should lose their souls, what would it profit them? I believe he designs to be their Father to all eternity, and then I shall meet all my children in heaven. How often have I gone and pleaded this promise before him, and have always found my faith increased. And still my faith holds out: 'For he is faithful that has promised.'"

From the moment God sealed upon her heart this special and remarkable promise, causing her to rest on his own veracity as the pledge of its fulfillment, she became animated as by a new and mighty impulse. Her natural spirits, unstrung by grief, and her mental powers, paralyzed by anxiety, now acquired fresh tone and energy. An overwhelming pressure of despondency and care seemed suddenly and entirely to be lifted from off her mind. Strengthened with might in the inner man, she cast her care on God; and, girding herself afresh for the arduous duties to which he now summoned her, with a calmness of judgment, a firmness of resolution, and a reliance of faith, equal to the dignity of her position, she cheerfully met and vigorously discharged all its claims. The promise thus given proved a sheet-anchor to her soul in many a subsequent hour of storm and cloud. And when at times—for such there were—the sentence of death seemed written upon it, her faith in God never faltered; giving to that promise, as she herself tells us, its widest range of meaning, she rose above the temporal blessing it involved, and claimed, as the only limit of its fulfillment, a Divine inheritance, a spiritual birthright, an eternal home for her orphan ones. She knew that she had to do with a Being, all whose resources of power, wisdom, and love were as boundless as his own infinity; who was not only a prayer-hearing and a prayer-answering, but also a prayer-exceeding God; and who in the bestowment of his blessings upon his people never gave less, but always more, than he had promised or than they had asked. She reasoned—and it was the logical reasoning of true faith—that if God, in the lone hours of that night of weeping and of prayer, had engaged to be a father to her fatherless children, that engagement bound him to them as their heavenly Father. To this broad interpretation of the pledge she held him, with a grasp which never for an instant relaxed. And when she died, it was in the firm, unfaltering faith of that promise. Not having received its complete fulfillment, but viewing it afar off, she was persuaded of it, embraced it, and closed her eyes with an undimmed, unshaken assurance that it would be even as God had said, and that she would meet again all the children he had given her—AN UNDIVIDED FAMILY IN HEAVEN.

CPSIA information can be obtained at www.ICGtesting.com
Printed in the USA
LVOW111550240212

270297LV00002B/117/P

9 781926 777177